CHURCH:
CHARISM AND POWER

CHURCH: CHARISM AND POWER

Liberation Theology and the Institutional Church

LEONARDO BOFF

Translated by John W. Diercksmeier

CROSSROAD | NEW YORK

1985
The Crossroad Publishing Company
370 Lexington Avenue, New York, N.Y. 10017

Originally published under the title *Igreja: Carisma
e poder* © Editora Vozes, Petrópolis, RJ, Brazil, 1981

English translation copyright © 1985 by The Crossroad
Publishing Company.
Printed in the United States of America

Library of Congress Cataloging in Publication Data
Boff, Leonardo.
   Church, charism and power.
   Translation of: Igreja, carisma e poder
   1. Church.   2. Catholic Church—Doctrines.
3. Liberation theology.   I. Title.
BX1746.B52513   1984   262   84-21431
ISBN 0-8245-0590-5

CONTENTS

Editor's Note   vii

Preface   ix

1. Models and Pastoral Practices of the Church   1

2. Theological Tendencies and Pastoral Practices   12

3. The Church and the Struggle for Justice
   and the Rights of the Poor   22

4. The Violation of Human Rights in the Church   32

5. The Power of the Institutional Church:
   Can It Be Converted?   47

6. Roman Catholicism: Structure, Health, Pathologies   65

7. In Favor of Syncretism: The Catholicity of Catholism   89

8. Characteristics of the Church in a Class Society   108

9. The Base Ecclesial Community: A Brief Sketch   125

10. Underlying Ecclesiologies of the
    Base Ecclesial Communities   131

11. *Ecclesia Docens* versus *Ecclesia Discens*   138

12. An Alternative View: The Church as Sacrament
    of the Holy Spirit   144

13. An Alternative Structure: Charism as
    the Organizing Principle   154

Notes   165

EDITOR'S NOTE

Few who read *Church: Charism and Power* will be unaware of the controversy surrounding it. For that very reason it may be useful to recall the principal events and to alert the reader to the relevant documents. On May 15, 1984, Leonardo Boff received a letter from Joseph Cardinal Ratzinger, prefect of the Sacred Congregation for the Doctrine of the Faith, summoning him to Rome for an interview regarding his book *Church: Charism and Power*, which had originally appeared in Portuguese in 1981. Then, on September 3, Cardinal Ratzinger released to the press a thirty-six-page "Instruction on Certain Aspects of 'Liberation Theology,'" whose purpose was "to draw attention . . . to deviations, and risks of deviations, damaging to the faith and to Christian living, that are brought about by certain forms of liberation theology which use, in an insufficiently critical manner, concepts borrowed from various currents of Marxist thought." While severely critical of "certain aspects" of liberation theology (rightly or wrongly perceived), the document, whose opening words in Latin are "Libertatis nuntio," or "The proclamation of freedom," is widely regarded as one of the most outspoken condemnations of social injustice in Latin America ever to appear in a Vatican statement. In the words of one knowledgeable observer, "in critiquing liberation theology, the document affirms its deepest premises." Furthermore, as if anticipating criticism, the instruction admitted its "limited and precise purpose" and announced the doctrinal congregation's intention of dealing "with the vast theme of Christian freedom and liberation . . . in a subsequent document." The true import of the instruction will only emerge in time; for the moment it is sufficient to note that on September 7, four days after the instruction's publication, Father Boff met with Cardinal Ratzinger as scheduled, in a four-hour session in which he presented a fifty-page reply to the "observations" and "questions" contained in Cardinal Ratzinger's letter of May 15. Also attending the meeting, at least in its later stages, were two Brazilian cardinals, Aloisio Lorscheider of Fortaleza and Paolo Evaristo Arns of São Paulo, who, in an unprecedented demonstration of solidarity and support, accompanied Father Boff to Rome.

PREFACE

We are living in privileged times. There is an upsurge of life in the Church that is revitalizing the entire body from head to toe. The Church has been placed on the road to renewal, which will surely result in a new manifestation of the Church as institution. There are powerful and living forces, particularly at the grassroots, that are not sufficiently recognized by the traditional channels of the Church's present organization. The grassroots are asking for a new structure, a new ecclesial division of labor and of religious power. For this, a new vision of the Church is necessary. This vision has not yet been developed systematically in a way that responds to the demands of our global reality, but it is necessary given what is happening in Latin America and elsewhere in the world.

The present book does not pretend to fill this need. It does, however, take on certain challenges, raise criticisms, make suggestions for a new model of the Church, and reflect on them in a radical way. This book will most certainly be understood by those who love the Church warts and all. In fact, it will be understood by them precisely inasmuch as they have overcome the triumphalist mentality. Others will judge this work as superfluous and even inopportune. This will not trouble me in the least. What readily comes to mind is the thought of St. Augustine, echoed by the philosopher Ludwig Wittgenstein:

Et multi ante nos vitam istam agentes, praestruxerunt aerumnosas vias, per quas transire cogebamur multiplicato labore et dolore filiis Adam.

And many before us, leading this life, trod tortuous paths which we were obliged to follow with the weariness and suffering imposed on the sons of Adam.

Petrópolis, Rio de Janeiro

ix

Chapter 1

MODELS AND PASTORAL PRACTICES OF THE CHURCH

More and more the Church in Latin America occupies the attention of religious analysts, owing primarily to its numerical importance, to the ecclesiological studies being developed there, to the new positions of the episcopacy on various social problems, and to the emergence of a Church that is being born out of the grassroots, the *base*. What are the tendencies that describe this Church today, and what kind of future is projected by each of them?[1] True ecclesiology is not the result of textbook analysis or theological hypotheses; it comes about as a result of ecclesial practices at work within the institution. Thus, if we want to identify the principal tendencies emerging in the Latin American Church, we must analyze the various practices in effect and from there arrive at the theoretical premises and formulations behind these practices. This will enable us clearly to outline those aspects that apply not only to the Church in Latin America but also to a new ecclesiology of the universal Church. This is what we hope to do in the following pages.

Kingdom-World-Church

In order to go beyond mere phenomenological analysis, we must identify the theological poles that enter into our understanding of what it is to be Church. The Church cannot be understood in and of itself because it is affected by those realities that transcend it, namely, the Kingdom and the world. World and Kingdom are the two pillars that support the entire edifice of the Church. The reality of the Kingdom is that which defines both the world and the Church. *Kingdom*—the category used by Jesus to express his own unique intention (*ipsissima intentio*)—is the utopia that is realized in the world, the final good of the whole of creation in God, completely liberated from all imperfection and penetrated by the Divine. The Kingdom carries salvation to its completion. The *world* is the arena for the historical realization of the Kingdom. Presently the world is decadent and stained by sin; because of this, the Kingdom of God is raised up against the powers of

1

the anti-Kingdom, engaged in the onerous process of liberation so that the world might accept the Kingdom itself and thus achieve its joyous goal.

The *Church* is that part of the world that, in the strength of the Spirit, has accepted the Kingdom made explicit in the person of Jesus Christ, the Son of God incarnated in oppression. It preserves the constant memory and consciousness of the Kingdom, celebrating its presence in the world, shaping the way it is proclaimed, and at the service of the world. The Church is not the Kingdom but rather its sign (explicit symbol) and its instrument (mediation) in the world.

These three elements—Kingdom, world, and Church—must be spelled out in their proper order. First is the Kingdom as the primary reality that gives rise to the others. Second is the world as the place where the Kingdom is concretized and the Church is realized. Finally, the Church is the anticipatory and sacramental realization of the Kingdom in the world, as well as the means whereby the Kingdom is anticipated most concretely in the world.

There is the danger of too close an approximation, or even identification, of the Church and the Kingdom that creates an abstract and idealistic image of the Church that is spiritualized and wholly indifferent to the traumas of history. On the other hand, an identification of the Church and the world leads to an ecclesial image that is secular and mundane, one in which the Church's power is in conflict with the other powers of the world. And there is the danger of a Church centered in on itself, out of touch both with the Kingdom and the world, such that it becomes a self-sufficient, triumphal, and perfect society, many times duplicating the services normally found in civil society, failing to recognize the relative autonomy of the secular realm.

These dangers are theological "pathologies" that cry out for treatment; ecclesiological health depends on the right relationship between Kingdom-world-Church, in such a way that the Church is always seen as a concrete and historical sign (of the Kingdom and of salvation) and as its instrument (mediation) in salvific service to the world.

Models of the Church from the Past

Having presented these brief clarifications, we want to explore four ecclesial practices and ecclesiologies that exist (latently or explicitly) in Latin America and elsewhere in the world. Three of these are inherited from the past. The fourth we present as a "new model."

The Church as City of God

There still exists, albeit to a lesser extent than previously, a practice of the Church that is almost exclusively turned in on itself. In this understanding, the Church is the exclusive bearer of humanity's salvation; it makes real the redemptive acts of Jesus by means of the sacraments, the liturgy, study of the Bible, and by organizing parish activities around the religious-sacred in a strict sense. The Pope, the bishops, and the general hierarchical structure constitute the organizational axis for this understanding of Church. It is an essentially clerical Church, for without the clergy nothing decisive can happen within the community. Tradition, official and orthodox formulas, and a fixation on juridical-canonical aspects of the liturgy are fostered among the faithful. The world has no theological value for this Church; it must be converted because only through the mediation of the Church can it arrive at the state of grace (*ordo gratiae*). Because its field of activity is strictly bound to the sacred, the Church is found to be insensitive to human problems that arise beyond its borders, in the world and in society. The political realm is "tarnished" and is to be avoided at all costs. More than neutral, the Church is indifferent to "worldly" realities.

Behind these practices lies an ecclesiology of the Church as a perfect society, parallel to that other society, the state. This is nothing more than a theological expedient for the affirmation of the Church's power, though it is seen as religious power. Religious power, here, is not understood by the Church as a way of understanding reality or as a "spirit" in which to embrace all things; rather, religious power is concerned with a narrow aspect of reality controlled by the hierarchy.

In this view, there is no connection between the Church and the Kingdom or the world. The Church is practically identified with the Kingdom because it is only within the Church that one finds fulfillment. The Church is removed from the world because it believes itself to be apart from it while, at the same time, serving the world. This does not mean that the Church is not organized in the world. Because it is only through the Church that salvation and the supernatural are made explicit, the Church undertakes projects that have the explicit title of "Catholic" such as Catholic schools, the Catholic press, Catholic colleges and universities, Catholic credit unions, and so forth. This is how the presence of God in the world is guaranteed. The Church thus maintains itself apart from the world while duplicating many of the world's services.

What is the future of this model of the Church? Theologically, it has been widely eclipsed by Vatican II. However, traditional practices are not easily changed simply by the introduction of a new theology. As new ecclesial practices gain ground, the model of the Church as *civitas Dei* is left behind and becomes more openly reactionary rather than traditional. The future is linked to those bishops who allow history to assert its rightful place in the Church. As such, this model of the Church appears to have not much hope for survival.

The Church as Mater et Magistra

Much of the world was missionized from within a definite model of the Church, namely, that of colonialism. According to this model, the Church is present in the world by virtue of a pact or treaty with the state that provides for all of the Church's needs and guarantees its existence. There is, therefore, a relationship between two hierarchies, one civil and one religious. Church, in this sense, is synonymous with hierarchy. With the eventual end of colonial rule and the birth of various republics around the globe, the Church adjusted this model. Taking on a slightly different cast, the Church allies itself with the dominant classes that control the state, organizing its projects around these classes, giving rise to colleges, universities, Christian political parties, and the like. The Church now gives the following interpretation to its pact with the state: it wants to serve the people, the majority of whom are poor; they are in need and have no livelihood, education, or political strength. In order to help these people, the Church approaches those who have the means to help them, that is, the upper classes. The Church then educates the children of these upper classes so that, imbued with the Christian spirit, they may liberate the poor. Following this, a vast network of assistance programs are established, leading the Church to become a Church *for* the poor rather than a Church *with* or *of* the poor.

On a doctrinal level, this Church is conservative and orthodox. It is suspicious of any innovation. Dogma is rigid; and vision, legalistic, confined to those in positions of power within the Church, the hierarchy. There is the ever present appeal to authority, especially to that of the Pope; preaching is priestly and devoid of prophetic witness. The deposit of faith is presented as complete and perfect; nothing can be added to it and nothing can be taken away from it. All social practices must be derived from it. The Church emerges, fundamentally, as *mater et magistra*, mother and teacher: it has an answer to every question taken from the deposit of faith, formed by Scripture, tradition, the magisterial teachings, and a specific understanding of natural law.

In terms of Kingdom-world-Church, a definite relationship with the world is apparent. A bond is created between the established powers, and not formed between the emerging movements such as those of reformers, innovators, or revolutionaries; the Church understands itself in terms of power and law (the *potestas sacra* transmitted through the sacrament of orders). This model also continues to see the Kingdom as exclusively within the Church, and in the world only by way of the Church's presence there.

What future does this model have? It will most likely be around for a long time, for it enjoys a very powerful historical foundation. Furthermore, the concentration of its power in the hierarchy facilitates the Church's relationship with other worldly powers. Agreement is never very difficult between the "powerful" who make decisions for the rest of the people who are both religious and oppressed. This type of Church, founded upon priestly and magisterial power as well as the sacred authority of the hierarchy, conforms to the centralist policies of Rome. The Church suffers crisis only when the state becomes authoritarian and totalitarian, oppressing the people beyond acceptable limits. When this happens the gospel character of the Church prevails; the hierarchy pleads for neutrality. Then one hears discourses on the apolitical and irreducibly religious character of the Church. In every other case the Church appears to be comfortable with authoritarian regimes; it never questions their legitimacy, only their abuses. In Latin America, where this model of Church tends to predominate, it is not surprising that in those dioceses that follow this model there is a lack of the prophetic spirit. The struggle for human rights is not fought openly but through secret contacts made between the leaders of the hierarchy and the military. Any other path is taken to be political, considered to be within the strict competence of the state or the laity acting alone.

This model appeals greatly to dominant political powers in that it reduces the Church's field of activity to the sacristy. It presupposes a functionalist sociology wherein each body is defined by its practices and does not interfere with other segments of society. Therefore, the Church is not to interfere in the political arena. Although it is true that the Church is not a political institution, it does have a relationship to the political inasmuch as it is an objective dimension of the Kingdom, thereby possessing an ethical character. Therefore, the Church must speak out on the ethical or religious character of political actions by virtue of its evangelizing mission. However, the above model of the Church is often too committed to secular powers to assume a critical stance toward the oppression that embitters the life of the poor.

The Church as Sacrament of Salvation

From the beginning of the present century, modern society has been marked by the rise of dynamic, nationalistic, and industrial middle classes that have had to overcome the technical backwardness in which they often found themselves—especially in Latin America. There followed a rapid modernization of the entire structure of material production; the demon that had to be exorcized was "underdevelopment." Every effort was made in the name of progress and development. Together with this modernization of the means of production, new forms of social involvement were created: popularly based democracies and unions.

The Church took part in this program of development. The Church opened itself to the world. The principal problems were not doctrinal (i.e., the struggle against Protestantism and secularism) or liturgical; they were linked to society: justice, social participation, and integral development for everyone. In this way the Church accelerated a process that it could not stop. It came to value science and the relative worth of earthly realities, developing an ethics of progress and thereby committing itself to social transformation, participating in all of the great debates concerning education, economic development, unions, and agrarian reform. Thus the secular came to be of theological value.

The Second Vatican Council developed a theology proper to such practices as these, legitimating them on the one hand and critically enlightening them on the other. It made clear the fact that we must think of all reality in terms of the mystery of salvation and the universal offer of salvation. It is important to understand that fundamentally salvation (as offering) is universal and impregnates all history. The Church is the focus and the celebration of this universal salvation. The Church, in turn, becomes universal in the measure that it points out the salvific love of the Father for all people through his Son and and in the power of the Holy Spirit. Because this is the case, so-called worldly realities are also possible means of salvation and grace. They deserve to be sought out in themselves and not only insofar as they have a part in the work of the Church. This theological perspective colors the commitment of Christians in their struggle for the building of a more just and fraternal world.

In light of this theology, the Church took its place among the modern sectors of society, especially among those involved in the transformation of the world. The Church did not immediately seek out the state but rather the groups that held scientific, technological, and political power in civil society. The Church itself modernized its structures, adapting them to the functional mentality of the day. It secularized many of its symbols, simplified the liturgy, and adapted itself to the spirit of the times. The Church's word became more prophetic in the sense that it denounced the abuses of the capitalist system and the marginalization of the poor. However, it did not present an alternative perspective but a reformist one, acceptable to the dominant sectors of society. Basically, it did not demand another type of society but rather sought greater participation for all in the modern liberal system of advanced technological capitalism.

In terms of Kingdom-world-Church, theological reflection was very astute: the Kingdom was seen as the great rainbow beneath which are the world and the Church. The world is understood as the place of God's activity, of the building of his Kingdom here and now, open to the eschatology that has yet to be realized in its fullness. The Church, then, is seen as sacrament, the sign and instrument through which Christ and his Spirit act for the realization of the Kingdom within the world in an explicit and concrete way within the Church. The world is understood as the product of modernity, the product of a great scientific-technological process. The Church sought a partnership, a reconciliation, with this "world" and so offered its collaboration.

What is the future of this model? We must recognize that this model has the greatest number of adherents throughout the world. The vast majority have assimilated and accepted the teachings of Vatican II and have made the change that was needed in terms of theology (theory) and presence in the world (praxis). The Church has been liberated from a traditional burden that made it unsympathetic to the modern world. In this way it was able to develop a new understanding of faith that could respond to the critical spirit of the cities, one that arose from within the capitalistic system. Intellectuals, who previously were quite anticlerical, now had an ally in the Church. The Church had more confidence in those power groups that tried to commit themselves to ecclesial tasks, and it imbued them with a new spirit, born of Vatican II. Various movements like Cursillo, the Christian family movement, charismatic renewal, and others draw most of their members from those who have a comfortable place in society and not from the working poor. The future of this type of the Church's presence, united with the modern sectors of society, is dependent upon the future of that society. The Church will try to evangelize this society in accord with modernity's own values and vision. The relationship with the poor will thus be defined from the perspective of the rich; the rich will be called upon to aid in the cause of the poor but without necessarily requiring a change in social class practices.

A New Model: A Church from the Poor

In the 1970s arose a growing consciousness of the true causes of underdevelopment as a problem that is not simply technical or political. It is the consequence of a type of capitalistic development in the countries of the North Atlantic which, in order to maintain current levels of growth and accumulation, need to establish unbalanced relationships with those countries that are technologically backward, though rich in raw materials. These latter countries are *kept* in underdevelopment, that is, the other side of development. This dependency creates oppression on economic, political, and cultural levels. In view of this, the long-range Christian strategy is to achieve a liberation that guarantees a self-sustained development that meets the real needs of the people, and not the consumerist needs of rich countries and groups associated with those countries.

A Political and Religious Liberation

The historical subjects of this liberation are the oppressed who must develop a consciousness of their oppressed situation, organize themselves,

and take steps that will lead to a society that is less dependent and less subject to injustices. Other classes may, and should, join this project of the
oppressed, but without trying to control it. In this way, beginning in the
early seventies, countless young people, intellectuals, and a whole range of
movements arose to make such a liberation viable. They made an option
for the people: they began to enter the world of the poor, embracing their
culture, giving expression to their claims, and organizing activities that
were considered subversive by the forces of the status quo. More than a few
took on the violence of urban guerillas and *campesinos*, and were violently
repressed.

Countless Christians and organizations took part in this process. They
were generally individuals and groups of middle-class extraction, full of
idealism but lacking political sense in terms of the concrete viability of
such a popular liberation.

Later, after years of harsh repression, the bases of the Church took on
exceptional importance both ecclesiologically and politically. The people
themselves took responsibility for their destiny. This generally began with
reading the Bible and proceeded to the creation of small base or basic ecclesial communities (*comunidades eclesiales de base*). Initially, such a
community serves to deepen the faith of its members, to prepare the liturgy,
the sacraments, and the life of prayer. At a more advanced stage these
members begin to help each other. As they become better organized and
reflect more deeply, they come to the realization that the problems they
encounter have a structural character. Their marginalization is seen as a
consequence of elitist organization, private ownership, that is, of the very
socioeconomic structure of the capitalist system. Thus, the question of
politics arises and the desire for liberation is set in a concrete and historical
context. The community sees this not only as liberation from sin (from
which we must always liberate ourselves) but also a liberation that has
economic, political, and cultural dimensions. Christian faith directly seeks
the ultimate liberation and freedom of the children of God in the Kingdom,
but it also includes historical liberation as an anticipation and concretization of that ultimate liberation.

A Church Born of the People's Faith

How do individuals move from the religious to the political? In general
the two realities come together as one. To begin, the religious points up the
injustices that God does not desire. Later the people proceed to an understanding of the true structures that produce such injustices, realizing that
it is imperative to change those structures in order to keep them from generating such social sin.

Political commitment is born of the reflection of faith that demands change. Faith is never absent from an analysis of the mechanisms of oppression; faith provides a means of understanding, a powerful spirituality for action, and a focal point for human activity. The base ecclesial community does not become a political entity. It remains what it is: a place for the reflection and celebration of faith. But, at the same time, it is the place where human situations are judged ethically in the light of God. The Christian community and the political community are two open spheres where what is properly Christian circulates. The community celebrates and is nourished by its faith; it hears the word of God that engenders a commitment to one's brothers and sisters. In the political community one works and acts side by side with others, concretely realizing faith and salvation, listening to God's voice which is fully expressed in the Christian community. Both spheres are clothed in the reality of the Kingdom of God which is being realized (under different signs) in both the political and religious community.

Primarily, the base ecclesial community is more than an instrument by which the Church reaches the people and evangelizes them; it is a new and original way of living Christian faith, of organizing the community around the Word, around the sacraments (when possible), and around new ministries exercised by lay people (both men and women). There is a new distribution of power in the community; it is much more participatory and avoids all centralization and domination. The unity of faith and life, of Gospel and liberation, is given concrete form without the artificiality of institutional structures. It makes possible the rise of a rich ecclesial sacramentality (the entire Church as sacrament), with much creativity in its celebrations and a deep sense of the sacred—all belonging to the people. A true "ecclesiogenesis" is in progress throughout the world, a Church being born from the faith of the poor.

The base ecclesial community is also the place where a true democracy of the people is practiced, where everything is discussed and decided together, where critical thought is encouraged. For a people who have been oppressed for centuries, whose "say" has always been denied, the simple fact of *having a say* is the first stage in taking control and shaping their own destiny. The *comunidad eclesial de base* thus transcends its religious meaning and takes on a highly political one.

The formation of these small communities is based on an ecclesiology that is grounded in the categories of People of God, *koinonia* (communion), prophecy, and *diakonia* (service). This type of Church presupposes what was crystallized at the Latin American bishops' meeting at Puebla in 1979: a preferential option for the poor. The exact meaning of this option is to recognize the privileged status of the poor as the new and emerging historical subject which will carry on the Christian project in the world. The poor, here, are not understood simply as those in need; they are in need but they are also the group with a historical strength, a capacity for change, and a potential for evangelization. The Church reaches out to them directly, not through the state or the ruling classes. Thus, we are no longer speaking of a Church *for* the poor but rather a Church *of* and *with* the poor. From this option for and insertion among the poor the Church begins to define its relationship with all other social classes. It does not lose its catholicity; its catholicity becomes real and not merely a matter of rhetoric. The Church is directed toward all, but begins from the poor, from their desires and struggles. Thus arise the essential themes of the Church: social change creating a more just society; human rights, interpreted as the rights of the poor majority; social justice and integral liberation, achieved primarily through sociohistorical freedom and concrete service in behalf of the disinherited of this world, and so on.

A Church Rising to Human Challenges

The categories People of God and church-communion call for a better distribution of *potestas sacra* (sacred power) within the Church and so demand a redefinition of the roles of bishop and priest while allowing for new ministries and a new style of religious life incarnated in the life of the people. The hierarchy is functional and is not an ontological establishment of classes of Christians. (This is not the place to develop the ecclesiology present in the practices of this type of Church; it is already found in an advanced stage in the theology being done in Latin America.)

This type of Church allows for a proper dialectic of the relationship of Kingdom-world-Church. The Kingdom is certainly the Christian utopia that lies at the culminaton of history. But it must be repeated that this Kingdom is found in the process of history wherever justice and fraternity are fostered and wherever the poor are respected and recognized as shapers of their own destiny. All individuals, institutions, and activities directed toward those ideals favored by the historical Jesus are bearers of that Kingdom. The Church is an official and distinctive bearer, but not an exclusive one. The category of world takes on a historical meaning: the world of the poor, the "subworld" that must be transformed into the world of mutual human sharing; the Kingdom and the anti-Kingdom (the "subworld" of misery) that exist together in the world. The Kingdom is built above and against the anti-Kingdom, whose agents must be denounced. The Church proposes, in this mode, to enter into the subworld of the "nonhuman" to aid in the process of integral liberation, carrying with it its special character: its reference to the religious and its reading of the Kingdom of God already in process.

It seems that through the Church's pact with the poor (the greatest symbol of which was Pope John Paul II's gift of the pontifical ring to the *favelados* of Rio de Janeiro in July 1980) a new path for the Church has opened up. Ever since Theodosius founded the Christian state in A.D. 380 the Church has been a Church *for* the poor but it never became a Church *of* the poor. Today the poor are not looked upon simply from a charitable perspective but from a political one. This new historical subject, the poor, will decide the shape of future society. They are growing in their level of consciousness, organizing their activities, and demanding a more participatory and less elitist society. The Church in its reflection and praxis (at least in Latin America) is meeting these demands. It has let go of inadequate models and is rising to the challenge of the present. It would seem that future society will be structurally marked by Christian and gospel elements, owing to a Church that is giving birth to that future. This fact is so overwhelming that in Latin America some analysts state that any society that does not possess a high level of Christian participation will be antipopular and elitist. The model followed by the people is a Christian one; this model is being expressed in a structure that responds to the demands of history. Now is the time to demonstrate its strength and truth. It is in this light that the most promising future of the Church will be defined.

A Call to the Universal Church

In conclusion, we can say that there are distinct pastoral practices in the Church, each with its latent image of what it is to be Church. Some prolong the tradition of colonial Christianity, others adapt themselves to new historical realities, especially to the need to explore the capitalist system more deeply and critically, advocating changes that are contrary to dominant social trends but that are nevertheless linked to a deep current of desire for the liberation of the poor. This multiplicity of images makes up the vitality of the Church of Christ, living and suffering its paschal mystery on the periphery of the powerful societies and the venerable churches of Europe. But the voice of this new Church speaks out more and more loudly and can be heard in the heart of the centers of power. This is a call to the whole Church to be more evangelical, more at service, and more of a sign of that salvation that penetrates the human condition. The various pastoral practices outlined above incarnate what they are called to incarnate, and this has invincible historical power.

Chapter 2

THEOLOGICAL TENDENCIES
AND PASTORAL PRACTICES

From One Theology to Many Tendencies

Theology as regulated knowledge has its own mode of considering all things, that is, in the light of God. Thus, all things possess a theological dimension in that everything can be seen in reference to God or contemplated as coming from God. In this sense, as a perspective and a vision (the scholastic *ratio formalis*), theology is one.

However, there are various ways of carrying out the theological task. If one focuses on the wisdom character of theology, we find ourselves with patristic theology. Other ages were interested in the scientific, rational, and systematic character of faith, and so there appeared the theological *summas* of medieval theology. Other times felt the need to underscore the *existential* element of faith or its *liberational* and *social* character, and so we find ourselves with contemporary theology. In this way one can speak of various theological tendencies. Each tendency strives to hear the entire apostolic truth and remain faithful to the Gospel, orderly arranging all facts around a specific need or concern. History and society normally give rise to the basic perspectives taken up by a specific theological tendency.

Scope and Limitations

No tendency can monopolize theology and present itself as *the* theology. With all that is stated there are always those things left unstated. Reason (including theological reason) is finite and limited. Consequently, no Christian generation can raise and resolve all the questions presented by faith. Therefore, every theological tendency must recognize its scope and, above all, its limitations. Knowing this, it can proceed to present the truth from within its own fragment of historical time. It must be open to the other possible ways of systematizing faith while, at the same time, conscious of the fact that theology must always phrase its questions in view of the concrete demands and challenges facing the historical Church.

"Enemies" or Counter-trends

Each theological tendency has a truth to propose and corresponding errors to counter. From its situation in the Church it defines itself with respect to other practices and ways of thinking. Many times the true intentions of a theological tendency are revealed in the identification of its attacks, condemnations, or criticisms.

Function in Relation to Church and Society

A theologian does not live in a vacuum but participates in the daily life of the Church and of society, both of which are marked by tendencies, interests, and conflicts. The theologian has a well-defined place, and the work of the theologian serves a definite function for various groups within the Church or society, be it support, criticism, condemnation, or justification. This function is apart from and independent of the individual's personal desires. It is epistemologically impossible for the theologian to be totally neutral, uncommitted, and purely theological, due precisely to the theologian's place in the daily life of the Church and society. No one has the power fully to control the effects of the theologian's words or actions on those for whom they are meant. But the aware theologian is able to control and direct the functionality of his or her position.

The Most Useful and Necessary Theology for Church and Society Today

In a truly open Church, theological ideas circulate and affect its pastoral practices, helping to nourish the *intellectus fidei* (understanding of faith). However, one cannot avoid the truly decisive question: Which is the most useful and necessary theology for the Church and society here and now? The Church occupies a place within society; it has made its decisions and presents itself in terms of certain actions and reflections. Society, in turn, confronts faith with deep challenges that must be taken seriously by theologians in order to aid the Church to see clearly and make decisions proper to those challenges. Because of this *diakonia* (service) that every true theology must offer the Church, no single theological tendency is enough. A Church may only consider itself to be mature if it makes use of its experts to develop a theory of faith that takes into account the challenges of sociohistorical reality, thereby utilizing serious reflection in the formation of its pastoral practices.

With this said, what is the most proper and necessary theology for a Church that must walk alongside the people, the majority of whom are poor as well as Christian?

Theology as Explanation of the Depositum Fidei

The *depositum fidei* (deposit of faith) contains the truths necessary for our salvation. According to this theology, this deposit was entrusted to the magisterium which guards it faithfully, defends it zealously, and interprets it authentically. Theology has the task of explaining the truths of this sacred deposit, separating the core from its various mysteries, and explaining them in terms of human reason.

How does theology accomplish this task? It attempts to present the truths systematically, beginning with apologetics (*de vera religione, de revelatione, de Ecclesia*) and resulting in new truths.[1] Truths are presented as proposed and defined by the Church; the ancient enemies are identified (Arianism, Pelagianism, etc.) as well as more recent ones (those from the Reformation, the Enlightenment, and existentialism); proofs from Scripture, tradition, and theological reasoning are then derived. Scripture, as used here, is considered to be a repertory of statements (*dicta probantia*) that prove, inspire, and reveal. Phrases and quotations are also taken from tradition, without recognizing the theologies internal to the sources of their historical development. What is most important is the clarity of the truths of faith, qualified by theological notes according to their degree of certainty (*de fide, fidei proxima, opinio theologica*, etc.) or, if erroneous, their degree of censure (*haeresis, haeresi proxima, piis auribus offensiva*, etc.).

The importance that this theology has for pastoral practice is minimal because it does almost nothing to highlight ecclesial problems that are often mixed with social, political, and ideological questions. Its greatest influence lies in the area of catechesis due to its doctrinal methodology, though it lacks better pedagogical resources. It is rigid in the area of morals, and in terms of sacraments it strictly follows canonical prescriptions. Its "enemies" are heretics and any innovation in theology and pastoral ministry.

The importance of this theology for society also appears to be minimal. It does not avail itself of theoretical, analytical, or theological tools to judge a particular social system or to speak out on secular topics. It is a theology of consequences, arguing, for example, that more discipline and more catechesis in the family and in school would have prevented the current rise in crime. In other words, this theology is geared for the internal use of the Church.

The scope and limitations of this theology are that it is strong in terms of its content of faith, formulated with utmost care and precision; the faithful are given the impression that they know what is true as opposed to what is erroneous. Its principal limitations are that it is not existential, has no historical basis, runs the risk of rigidity, and creates bounty hunters for heretics and for those who criticize doctrinal statements.

Theology as Initiation into the Christian Experience

Knowledge of faith is not only intellectual but existential. There is the recognition of the Christian mystery of the Divine becoming human. This theological tendency is the same as the first in that it takes the Church as its primary axis, but it understands the Church as the People of God or the mystical body of Christ.[2] Faith is the faith of the entire Church and not only that of the hierarchy. The work of theology, according to this tendency, is the rational explication of the Christian mystery, touching upon dimensions beyond those of "revealed truths," such as its cultic or liturgical aspects as well as community life.

Because of this, there is the demand to assimilate many of the contributions of modern reflection on existence, history, the process of conversion, and interpersonal relationships. The basic arguments follow the same pattern as the previous tendency but with more concrete limits, such as a use of Scripture that respects and makes use of exegetical studies and an argument from tradition that is preceded by a study of patrology and the history of dogma; also the *sensus fidelium* (sense of the faithful) carries more weight.

This theology has an ecumenical appeal. While the first tendency is centered solely upon the Catholic Church (the hierarchy), this one touches upon the entire Christian phenomenon; its opponents are isolated humanists and totalitarian systems—anyone who denies the transcendence of God or that of the individual person.

The importance of this tendency for pastoral activity is substantial in that the codification of faith is presented in a language that speaks to the meaning of life and encourages faith as an experience of the encounter with God. Catechesis here includes human experiences as mediators of Christian mysteries; moral theology does a better job of pointing out the concrete conditions necessary for ethical decisions; and the liturgy takes on a greater celebrational character.

Its importance for society is found not in structures but in human relations. The richness of modern personalism becomes the optimal value when viewed in its communitarian aspect. Conversion affects the heart, individual as well as that of groups, allowing faith to reveal the humanizing and magnifying dimensions of human dignity.

This tendency recovers the wealth of the great biblical and patristic traditions, which emphasized a more sapiential and mystagogical theology. Truth is lived as a transforming encounter (*metanoia*) rather than being the mere presentation of facts, thus helping to ground the Church as a community of faith. Yet this tendency has the following limitations: it may dilute the content of faith through countless anthropological, existential, and personalistic interpretations, incapable of arriving at the structural and institutional character of the wider ecclesial and social phenomenon due to its insistence on the dynamic of purely personal conversion.

Theology as Reflection upon the Mysterium Salutis

Whereas the theological center of the previous tendencies is the Church, either as hierarchy or as People of God, the present tendency sees the mystery of salvation as the primary focus.[3] *Mysterium salutis* is a key concept both in ancient tradition and in the theology of Vatican II. God offers himself as salvation to all persons, universally, in such a way that there is a single history of salvation *ab Abel usque ad ultimum electum* (from Abel to the last of the elect) encompassing the entire history of the human race. The history of the Old Testament and that of the New emerge as one sacramental history (sign and instrument), the conscious reflection of salvation offered to all peoples. This unique consciousness, born of a specific revelation by God to the people of Israel, has its own history as codified in the sacred Scriptures.

This theology is conscious of the universal phenomenon of religion, of human response to the divine offer, of God's grace and forgiveness despite human sin and rejection. This theology understands the sources of faith (Scripture and tradition) within a broader context of the history of universal salvation/perdition. The great testimonies of other religions play a part in its argumentation. Ecumenical dialogue is not restricted to Christian churches only but is open to the religions of the world.

The "enemies" of this tendency are theoretical atheists who are blind to the innate openness of each individual to Mystery, as well as secularists following the ideology that considers earthly realities as self-contained and without reference to a greater Other.

The importance of this tendency for pastoral practice is its appearance as a breath of fresh air in the dogmatic edifice of the Church. Pastoral sensitivity is greater due to a faith that is open to other manifestations of God in the world, valuing the signs of the times that possibly manifest the Spirit's true will. There is also the wider understanding of the sacraments as visible signs of a grace that is offered constantly and present to humanity, rather than as the instruments of a preexisting grace.

Its importance for society is its demonstration of an open Church able to learn from modern science, discerning the moments of salvation/perdition in various social situations. It has an interest in everything that leads to human growth because these things prepare for the Kingdom of God that is begun here and now.

The scope of this theology lies in it demonstration of the true catholicity of the Church derived from the universality of the offer of salvation. It gives rise to the contemplative perspective on life and history where they are seen as "shadows of Christ and the Mystery," thus overcoming a dualism of sacred and profane, natural and supernatural, as juxtaposed realities.

The principal limitation of this theology is that it often emphasizes the history of grace to the exclusion of the history of sin. It is frequently too optimistic, praising work, science, and technology, ignoring the fact that often these have been used as instruments of domination by individuals and nations over those that were technologically backward.

Theology as Transcendental Anthropology

Every individual who comes into the world is the recipient of God's offer of salvation. This tendency makes the typically modern turn from the object to the subject.[4] Human beings, listening to God, give rise to all theological themes. The focus of this tendency is not mere human acceptance or the empirical individual as presented by anthropology. It is the image of the individual as presented in the Scriptures: as hearer of the word in continual dialogue with the Ultimate who is present in the human consciousness, in living transcendence and so never fully categorizable. Therefore, this tendency is not immanentism; rather, it rescues transcendence and presents the individual as mystery and infinite openness for whom God is the only adequate and fulfilling object.

This tendency attempts to show the *quoad nos* (reference to the individual) in every mystery, the extent to which it enters the encounter of the human search for fulfillment. This stems from the ontological presupposition that the human person was "made" by God, that one is only fully human when in contact with divine revelation. Only in Jesus Christ, God made human, is the anthropological mystery deciphered. The human cry in every age is the echo of the eternal and infinite voice that beckons the individual. Thus, the mystery of the incarnation does not refer only to Jesus of Nazareth but to every individual, because every individual's vocation is achieved through the incarnation.

The "enemies" of this tendency are those who attempt to separate Christianity from those movements in search of the Absolute, those who see no evidence for human realization in God's revelation, that is, the immanentism of modern science that hides more than explains the transcendent element present in each individual.

The pastoral importance of this tendency is evident. It seeks to give value to the truly human elements in culture because behind them is the Spirit of God. The community is seen as the place where salvation, achieved in history, is celebrated, where the exegesis of the signs of the times is undertaken. Besides being a representative of the Church, the priest as the vicar of Jesus, the *novissimus Adam* in whom the divine in the human is totally revealed, should also be a representative of every individual as touched by God.

The importance of this theological tendency for society is also worth noting in that it places Christians together with all other human beings rather than separating them. It values every instance that illustrates human openness and transcendence as well as all responses to the divine call heard by all people, however unconsciously. This tendency struggles for an open, antiauthoritarian society because only in such a society can there be the conditions for the realization of true human transcendence.

The scope of this theology lies in its giving value not only to Judeo-Christian history (sacramental history) but to the whole of human history. It develops the idea of the human person as sacred, thereby transcending the "profanity" and naturalism present in classical theology. It aids in the understanding of the human-divine reality formerly expressed by natural and supernatural categories, that is, God's constant openness and call to every individual.

The limitation of this tendency is that it runs the risk of historical close-mindedness, of not seeing the history of evil with its structures and leaders. In trying to underscore the transcendental character of the human person and the Christian mysteries, it loses sight of worldly categories; it is not sufficiently dialectical and so does not sufficiently consider the conflictive character of history.

Theology of the Signs of the Times

In *Gaudium et Spes*, the Second Vatican Council insisted that the Church is in the world, sharing its hopes and fears. This consciousness allowed theology to discover new avenues and aims for its reflection. The great theological tradition, with tools taken from philosophy and the historical and linguistic sciences, had already systematized the definitively theological subjects: God, Jesus Christ, revelation, the saving acts of the Son and the Holy Spirit, the Church, the sacraments, eschatology, and so on. The challenge for theology today is in approaching those realities that in and of themselves are not definitively theological, such as the political arena, ruling social systems, economic realities, liberation movements, and the scientific-technological enterprise.

Before one can speak theologically about these topics, it is necessary to have a proficient knowledge of them. So the theologian must begin with a reading of the analytical texts of the various positive and sociohistorical sciences. Theology thus finds a new partner in dialogue: the sciences of the individual and of society. Theological and ethical interpretation is therefore built upon scientific and critical knowledge.

In this way, in the first few years of the postconciliar Church, there arose a number of theologies that came under the heading of "theologies of the signs of the times."[5] The phenomena mentioned above were presented as signs that challenge us to see in them either the presence or the denial of the will of God. We found ourselves with political theology, the theology of secularization, the theology of hope, and process theology. All of them have this in common: they deal with collective, public phenomena that in turn demand a public and political expression of faith. These theologies do not add anything to the content of faith but rather bring to the fore those dimensions of faith that were previously hidden by a personalistic, individualistic, and self-centered living out of that faith. Secularization becomes the consequence of a faith that has freed the world from magical characteristics and has returned it to the individual as a place for responsible creativity. Hope, more than being a virtue, is considered as an ontological dynamic within every person and society, preventing stagnation and promoting change and even revolution. Theology rediscovers "the subversive and dangerous memory of Jesus of Nazareth" who, while among us, did not say "I am tradition" but rather "I am the truth," and thereby began a process of change that goes beyond the heart and involves society and the whole of creation.

The polemic that opposes this tendency is the one that reduces Christianity to its personal and familial dimensions, excluding any mention of the political and social, ignoring the problems of the modern world, of political and religious conservativism and thereby delaying the coming of the Kingdom.

The importance for pastoral activity is clear: new forms of presence and witness become available to the Christian community amid social structures in need of change based on faith.

The social importance of this tendency likewise does not need to be spelled out because it is based on a reflection of the social and historical elements in life. If the Church spent the last millennium in the legitimation of the established order, it is now gathering its forces in order to be an agent of change and a historical force for the humanization of the world.

The principal scope of this theology lies in its having opened up other areas for pastoral activity and theological reflection. Its primary limitation is that its analysis of the world has yet to be well articulated within theological circles, leading to an apparent juxtaposition or contradiction that is as dangerous for theology as it is for a true understanding of reality.

Theology of Captivity and Liberation

In the postconciliar years, theology was not only confronted by the problems of an open, industrial, and secularized society but also by the need to respond to the question of how to be Christian in a critical, mature, and work-oriented world. An even greater challenge presented itself: the poor of the third-world countries were emerging as a social phenomenon. They unveiled the reality that they were marginalized from the benefits of a society that values technical and social solutions to its problems. The question for theology became: How to be Christian in a world of poor and impoverished peoples? Today there is the need not for reform but for a process of liberation by which the poor regain their dignity and help give birth to a society that is not necessarily richer but rather more just and fraternal.

The methodological steps of this theological tendency have already been developed and taught throughout Latin America.[6] It begins with indignation at the poverty experienced by God's children, a poverty that God surely does not will. At the same time, this poverty is seen as a religious experience for the poor in whom the Suffering Servant is present. The second step is the investigation of the ways that produce such wanton misery on one side and scandalous wealth on the other. Here, the historical, social, political, and economic analyses are brought into play. Third, this reality of misery, already deciphered with socioanalytical tools, is read with the eyes of faith and theology, discerning the paths of sin and the avenues of grace. Finally, pastoral activity is developed that enables the Church and all Christians to help in the process of complete liberation. Christian faith lends its specific contribution to this global process of liberation by pointing out nonviolent means, the strength of love, the inexhaustible capacity for dialogue and persuasion as well as by helping to understand the sometimes unavoidable violence toward those who block any change whatsoever.

The enemies of this tendency are those who are unable to see the liberating dimension present in the life of Jesus Christ and in Christian faith and those who reduce the expression of faith to prayer and liturgy, insensitive to the cries rising to the heavens of the modern Job.

The importance of this tendency for the pastoral activity of the Church can be seen in the various practices of many "peripheral" churches of Latin America in their efforts in defense of human rights, especially those of the poor, in their denunciation of capitalist and neocapitalist systems, and in their formation of *comunidades eclesiales de base* where the people's faith is expressed, nourished, and strengthened in the face of the realities that are oppressing them.

Its importance for social life is no less crucial. For theological reasons the Church becomes a partner with those who struggle for an alternative and more participatory society; the theological and pastoral solidarity of the episcopacy in many parts of the world with those who are oppressed has made the Church an important social force in those societies.

The scope of this theology is measured by its acceptance among both intellectuals and the masses. Thanks to this theology, interest in theological reflection has reached the streets. It is a theology that is powerfully prophetic and missionary. Many people, after contact with this theology, are returning to the Church to commit themselves together with other Christians to work for necessary change.

The limitations of this tendency are due to its strong insistence on the structural character of social sin and on the need for an equally social and institutional grace. It runs the risk of ignoring the need for personal conversion and the search for perfection in Christian life. There is also the risk that its politics may completely hide the horizon of faith. Faith does have a political dimension and it would seem that this is the Spirit's challenge to the Church today. However, the political dimension does not cover the entire wealth of faith that must also find other expressions such as the mystical, the liturgical, and the personal within the process of integral liberation.

Theology Appropriate for the Church Today

All of the above theological tendencies are useful because each one highlights dimensions that remain hidden or obscure in other tendencies. However, we must still ask the question: Which of the theologies arise from the pastoral, religious, and mystical practices of the Church today? Which of them is an example of enlightenment and encouragement for such practices? I believe with Puebla (368) that the theme of liberation is one of the original creations of Christians today and that it is a positive contribution to all churches who stumble along with different sets of challenges and problems. However, other tendencies should not be disregarded because everything that helps us to be more faithful to the Gospel, to tradition, to the People of God, and especially to the desire of the poor for liberation must be assimilated.

The theologian, having done everything within his or her reach, can do nothing but listen to the word of the Lord: "We are poor servants; we have done all that we had to do."

Chapter 3

THE CHURCH AND THE
STRUGGLE FOR JUSTICE AND
THE RIGHTS OF THE POOR

Urgency of the Struggle for Justice Today

"From the depths of the countries that make up Latin America a cry is rising to heaven, growing louder and more alarming all the time. It is the cry of a suffering people who demand justice, freedom, and respect for the basic rights of human beings and peoples. . . . The cry is increasing in volume and intensity, and at times is full of menace. . . . The situation is one of *injustice*" (Puebla, 87, 89, 90, cf. 28). The cry of the Latin American bishops gathered at Puebla is one for justice that, at the same time, denounces social and structural injustices.

Behind this cry lies the true drama. For example, in Brazil, 75 percent of the people live in relative economic marginalization; 43 percent are condemned to a minimum salary in order to survive. A worker from São Paulo, Manuel Paulo, says it best: "What I earn is so little that it only proves that I am still alive." And his wife, Helena, adds: "This is no life for anybody."[1]

Once one of the most promising countries in the world, Brazil serves as an appropriate example: 40 percent of all Brazilians live, work, and sleep with chronic hunger; there are 10 million who are mentally retarded due to malnutrition; 6 million suffer from malaria; 650,000 have tuberculosis and 25,000 suffer from leprosy.[2]

Although the statistics may scandalize some of us, others of us have grown callously used to them. But this dire situation does eat at the conscience of many Christians, giving them no relief. This is the ferment that is giving rise to the growing commitment of more and more churches to the struggle for justice.

Theological Foundation for the Commitment to Justice

There is some basis for the *duty* of every Christian to enter into the struggle for justice. One needs only to look at the recent official documents of the

Church. In so doing, one has the security of a doctrine that is obliging upon all Christians. These documents are the various pontifical and episcopal statements that developed the social doctrine of the Church during the 1970s. We will refer here to the 1971 Synod of Bishops' *Justice in the World*, Paul VI's *Octogesima Adveniens* (1971) and *Evangelii Nuntiandi* (1975), John Paul II's *Redemptor Hominis* (1979), and the Latin American bishops' statement at Puebla, *Evangelization in the Present and Future of Latin America* (1979).

Fundamental Affirmation and Central Thesis

In *Justice in the World* the Synod of Bishops said: "Action on behalf of justice and participation in the transformation of the world fully appear as a constitutive dimension of the preaching of the Gospel, or, in other words, of the Church's mission for the redemption of the human race and its liberation from every oppressive situation" (6). "The Gospel message contains . . . *a demand for justice in the world*. This is why the Church has the right, indeed the duty, to proclaim justice on the social, national, and international level and to denounce instances of injustice" (36).

We should note that the bishops do not say that justice is an integral or even central theme but rather a *constitutive* element. Without the preaching of justice there is no Gospel of Jesus Christ. This is not to politicize the Church; it is to be faithful. And if we are not faithful, we mutilate the heart of Jesus' message and we pervert the very mission of the Church. Thus, we understand why the document speaks of "duty." A duty must be fulfilled; unfulfillment of a duty is a sin, even when one who acts is a bishop. For this same reason it is easy to understand the words of Pope Paul VI in *Evangelii Nuntiandi* and often repeated at Puebla: "The Church has the duty of proclaiming the liberation of millions of human beings, many of whom are its spiritual children, the duty of aiding this liberation at its start, of giving witness in its favor, and of accompanying its efforts that it may be achieved. This is not apart from evangelization" (30). Note that duty is mentioned twice, and that the Pope was not speaking only of a spiritual liberation. The sentence immediately preceding this speaks of human oppression: "needs, chronic illnesses, illiteracy, pauperism, injustice in international relations, neocolonialism, etc." (30).

Three Principal Arguments

On what is this duty based? *Justice in the World* adduces two arguments, one from the Old Testament and one from the New. "In the Old Testament God reveals himself to us as the liberator of the oppressed and the defender of the poor, who demands faith in him and justice toward one's neighbor from all. Only in the observance of the duties of justice is God recognized in truth as the liberator of the oppressed" (30). *God is only encountered on the path of justice.* The living God is not a God of prayers, incense, and asceticism. In Isaiah 1:11–18 we learn that what pleases God are not sacrifices and prayers but to "seek what is just, to help the downtrodden, and to do justice to the orphan." Jesus, in the same way, establishes a hierarchy of values: justice, mercy, and faithfulness are more important than religious observance. Love is the core of the biblical message, but in order for it to be true love, justice is presupposed. Thus, the bishops taught that "love implies in fact the absolute demand of justice that consists in the recognition of the dignity and rights of one's neighbor. Justice itself reaches its inner fulness only in love" (34). As such, "love of neighbor and justice cannot be separated" (34). Justice is the minimum requirement without which interpersonal relations cease to be human and become violent.

Because the true God is the God of justice and love, we must denounce the use that is often made by many social systems of the Christian God and Christian tradition. These systems call themselves theistic; in reality, they worship the idols of money, power, and material goods. The true God cannot be found in these realities when they exclude others. Pedro Casaldáliga, the poet-bishop, points out this error in this short poem:

> When you say law, I say God.
> When you say peace, justice, love, I say God.
> When you say God, I say liberty, justice, peace.[3]

God abides in the realities of justice, love, and freedom. He is not automatically present in pious words. If we do not include the realities of freedom, justice, and love when we speak of God, then we are speaking of some idol and not of the living God.

The other argument that underlies the duty to struggle for justice is derived from the New Testament. Summarizing the argument, the bishops say that, due to the incarnation of God in Jesus Christ, "the attitude of man toward other men is integrated in his [or her] attitude toward God" (34). In other words, the truth of our relationship with God is measured by the truth of our relationships with others.

Justice is thus placed at the very heart of religion itself. This is how we understand the eschatological criterion of our final judgment: our relationship to the economic "nobodies" and the human "nobodies" in our daily life (Matt 25:31–46).

Furthermore, the bishops emphasize that Jesus revealed the Father and, at the same time, brought God's *intervention of justice* on behalf of the poor and oppressed (Luke 6:20–23: blessed are the poor, the hungry, the sad, the accursed . . .). John Paul II reminded the bishops in Puebla that

"Jesus' option was for the most needy." When Luke says, "Blessed are the poor for theirs is the kingdom of God" (6:20), he means, according to the most exacting exegesis, happy are you who are impoverished, you who suffer injustice and violence, because yours is the Kingdom of God, which is the Kingdom of justice, love, and peace.[4] Faced with the injustice that is made concrete in poverty, God himself is indignant. He is being challenged and decides to intervene. Jesus historizes this intervention: God comes and restores justice to the oppressed not because the oppressed person is pious and good but because he or she is a victim of the oppression that has caused his or her situation of poverty.

In a word, justice is so crucial that without its advent there is no coming of the Kingdom of God. The sign that the Kingdom of God approaches and begins to abide in our cities is that the poor have justice done to them, that they participate and share in the goods of life as well as in the life of the community, and that they are raised in terms of their dignity and defended against the violence they suffer at the hands of the current economic and political system.

Another decisive argument that is developed at great length in *Evangelii Nuntiandi* and repeated in many ways by Puebla is the inclusion of justice in the basic content of evangelization (all of part III of *EN* and part II of the Puebla document, chaps. 1 and 2).

The core of evangelization is "salvation in Jesus Christ . . . that had its beginning in this life and will come to total completion in eternity" (*EN* 27). The definition of evangelization developed here contains an explicit message about common life in society, international life, peace, justice, and development—an overwhelmingly powerful message for our day about liberation (*EN* 29). Although the current situation of the oppressed in the world adds nothing to the gospel message, the Pope emphasizes that liberation is part of the essential content of evangelization (*EN* 30, Puebla, 351): from sin and injustice and liberation for the grace of justice and fraternity.

Avoiding Reductionism

In *Evangelii Nuntiandi* Paul VI warns against two types of reductionism in the commitment to justice and liberation, one religious and the other political. Religious reductionism encloses the Church in the sacristy and in sacred gestures: "The Church does not circumscribe its activity to the religious realm as if it were disinterested in the temporal problems of humanity" (34). Therefore, the Church must include the world with its pluses and minuses, in its basic evangelization. The other reductionism is political, trimming the Church's mission by reducing its dimension to a simply temporal concern (32). The Church relates the religious to the political, making public statements of solidarity based on the gospel imperative. The Church does not speak politically about politics but rather speaks evangelically, understanding that politics and the struggle for justice anticipate and make real the Kingdom of God; it transcends politics but at the same time penetrates and assumes it.

Politics and the Struggle for Justice

When one speaks of social justice and liberation, one has already placed oneself in the heart of a situation of political domination. But there is no more ambiguous word than "politics." Reactionary forces within the Church and society take advantage of this ambiguity to free themselves from the struggle for justice. We read headlines such as "The Church must not be involved in politics," "Pope prohibits priests and bishops from involvement in politics," "No politics in the Mass," "No politics in the churches." But what exactly is meant by "politics"?

The Various Meanings of "Politics"

In *Octogesima Adveniens* Paul VI stated: "Under the term 'politics' there are many confusions that must be clarified" (46). The bishops at Puebla have helped us to clarify some of these confusions (521–30).

For more than a few people, politics is something dirty, a lie, demagoguery, a prejudice that results from bad political experiences involving corruption, manipulation, and the struggle of special interest groups. However, this is but a pathology of politics which in itself is a highly positive concept such that Aristotle claims that human beings, like it or not, are essentially political animals.

The bishops at Puebla give politics the highest acclaim that it has received in the recent history of the Church: "The necessity for the Church's presence in the political arena flows from the very core of Christian faith" (516). Politics is understood in the context of the lordship of Jesus Christ. He is not only the Lord of small places like the heart, the soul, the Church; he is the cosmic Lord, of large spaces like that of politics. Politics has to do with the Kingdom of God because it has to do with justice, a messianic good. Primitive Christians professing "Jesus is Lord" were making a political statement. The second statement of the bishops is to be understood in this context: "[The Church's interest in politics] is a way of worshipping the one God, desanctifying and at the same time sanctifying the world to him" (521: cf. *Lumen Gentium*, 34). To practice politics is to struggle for the justice of all. To struggle for and achieve justice is to give glory to God, the worship that is demanded by Paul in Romans 12:2. *Octogesima Adveniens* teaches: "Politics is the best way—if not the only way—of living out one's Christian commitment, in service to others" (46). Political commitment expresses the love that has found its social dimension of solidarity.

The two meanings of "politics" presented by Puebla are:

1. Politics with a capital *P*: the common search for the common good, the promotion of justice and rights, the denunciation of corruption and violence to human dignity. Politics with a capital *P* "spells out the fundamental values of the entire community—internal harmony and external security—reconciling equality with freedom, public authority with legitimate autonomy, and the participation of all persons and groups.... It also defines the means and ethics of social relations. In this wider sense, Politics is of interest to the Church and, as such, to its pastors, ministers of unity" (521). Politics contains all the ideologies (Marxism, capitalism, the social teaching of the Church) that present the utopic images of humanity and society. The Church has its vision of the world, of the person, of social life, of the distribution of goods, and so on. By proclaiming the Gospel it proclaims the Politics of the Gospel; the Church has an interest in Politics and always has had such an interest.

The Church cannot cease to be involved with Politics; that is, it cannot be indifferent to the justice or injustice of a cause nor can it be silent in the face of the obvious exploitation of any people. There is no neutrality in Politics: one is either for change in the direction of greater social participation or one is in favor of the status quo, which in many countries marginalizes a vast majority of the people.

Apoliticism, lack of interest in the common good and social justice, is formally criticized by Puebla: "The Church must criticize those who would restrict the scope of faith to personal or family life, those who would exclude the professional, economic, social and political orders as if sin, love, prayer, and pardon had no relevance for them"(515). There is an even harsher text:

> There is a manipulation of the Church that may derive from Christians themselves, and even from priests and religious, when they proclaim a Gospel devoid of economic, social, cultural, and political implications. In practice, this mutilation comes down to a kind of complicity with the established order, however unwitting [558].

Neutrality is impossible. We all take stances; it happens that some people have not been conscious of their position. Generally, these people assume the position of the dominant class, of the established order, which in many cases is manifestly antipopular, unequal, and unjust. Attempted apoliticism results in the manipulation and mutilation of the Gospel. We need to become more conscious of the political dimension of the Gospel and our faith.

This dimension is the core of evangelization: "Christianity must evangelize the totality of human life, including the political dimension" (515). It has a place in the pulpit and in the Mass. If our homilies do not touch upon justice, fraternity and participation, if they do not denounce violence, they are mutilating the Gospel and emasculating the message of the prophets and, above all, the good news of Jesus Christ.

2. Politics with a small *p* is all the activity corresponding to the administration or transformation of society through the conquest and exercise of the power of the state. It is the exercise of "political power to resolve economic, political, and social questions according to the criteria or ideology of citizen groups" (523). It is in this sense that one speaks of "party politics" (523). It has to do not with the whole but with a part; it is a faction and fraction of the whole. This does not involve the whole Church but only a part of it, namely, the laity.

Party politics is properly the realm of lay people. Their lay status entitles them to establish and organize political parties, "using an ideology and strategy that is suited to achieving their legitimate aims" (524). However, lay people must observe the minimum requirements for participating in and creating political parties in their role as lay Christians: that of being yeast and salt within the dough of party politics.

Politics and Clarity: Authentic Politicization

Social reality today is extremely sophisticated and unclear, tinted by every type of ideology. There is an especially dangerous ideology, fostered by the ruling classes who control the mass media, that hides the conflicts, slants the news, and thereby paints a rosy picture of a truly tragic reality. The Christian involved in the struggle for justice must be able to avoid such chicanery. For this reason, the Puebla document recommends the use of rational tools to help us see clearly (86, 719, 1046, 1160, 1307, esp. 826). In order to see clearly and act efficaciously we must utilize two primary instruments:

—*Analytical tools.* One must study the mechanisms that generate poverty and violence against human rights; the problem is generally not personal but structural. One must read very technical literature to discover how our society functions, what each person has, how prices and salaries are set and distributed, the importance of multinational corporations, and the nature of existing labor or union legislation.

—*Practical tools.* No desire is efficacious without organization. Thus, there is the importance of organizing centers and offices such as those for legal defense, human rights, justice and peace, and so forth. The Christian must join in the work of these centers as well as participate in unions and neighborhood organizations, thereby joining others in the struggle for justice.

Education is necessary for participation in both Politics and politics. Pope Paul VI speaks of "the importance of an education for life in society" (*Octogesima Adveniens*, 24). Puebla speaks of an education for justice (1029), of liberating education (1026), even though "certain governments have come to consider certain elements of Christian education as subversive" (1017). "Catholic education must produce the agents who will effect the permanent organic change that society needs. This is to be done through a civic and political formation that takes its inspiration from the Church's social teaching" (1033).

This activity is called politicization, which must not be confused with political chicanery. Politicization is a positive concept that signifies an educational activity aimed at social and political coresponsibility. Political chicanery is the utilization of social organizations, created for all, for the sole benefit of a few individuals or the interference of the hierarchy in questions of party politics.

The Distribution of Responsibility within the Church

The Church, fundamentally, is organized into three large bodies: the hierarchy, from the Pope to the deacon; the laity, who are baptized but who do not share in the leadership of the Christian community; and the religious, who are somewhere between the hierarchy and the laity, with elements of both. When it comes to responsibility, religious are considered to be among the hierarchy.

Responsibilities of the Hierarchy

A close reading of the texts of Puebla and *Justice in the World* reveals that it is the responsibility of the hierarchy to *announce* ("a word capable of changing society" [Puebla, 518]) and to *denounce, promote,* and *defend* human rights and dignity. It is their responsibility to be *in solidarity* with lay people and to *encourage* their creativity. They must *interpret* the aspirations of the people of each nation, especially the longings of those whom society tends to marginalize.

The hierarchy does not have a technical responsibility; they do not say *what* to do. They have an ethical responsibility; in the light of the Gospel they may say whether something is just or unjust, whether it favors participation or hinders it. "The service of peace and justice is an essential ministry of the Church" (Puebla, 1304).

Responsibilities of Religious

In *Evangelica Testificatio* Paul VI confronts religious with the "cry of the poor." He states that this cry "must prevent you from committing yourselves to any form of social injustice. It obligates you to awaken your conscience to the drama of misery and the demands of justice found in the Gospel and in the Church" (18). He ends by inviting religious to move closer to the poor in their condition of poverty. Puebla teaches that religious "must also cooperate in the evangelization of the political" (528) but without yielding to the temptation of a commitment to party politics (520).

Responsibilities of the Laity

According to *Lumen Gentium* (33) we must first recognize that the activity of the laity is not an extension of the hierarchy. Lay people have their own place in the Church and they must act within this sphere. The lay person is not a secular person. He or she is a member of the Church in the secular world and has a direct mandate from Jesus Christ.

According to Puebla the place of lay activity is the world (789). Political activity deserves special emphasis (791). In a world scarred by injustices, lay people "may not excuse themselves from a serious commitment to promote justice and the common good" (793). They must become involved in party leadership (791), including "founding and organizing political parties" (524) with sufficient ideology and strategy (524). They are to do this not only under the direction of the bishops but with their own leadership. The texts of both *Justice in the World* and Puebla are clear on this point: "under the direction of the Gospel spirit and the doctrine of the Church" (*Justice in the World*, 38), "always illuminated by faith and guided by the Gospel and by the social doctrine of the Church, and at the same time by intelligence and ability toward appropriate activity" (Puebla, 793). The bishops emphasize the fact that the Gospel is not enough; clarity is required.

We thus arrive at the conclusion that the laity are exercising a right and a duty when they unite, mobilize, march, and initiate movements for action, peace, and justice. According to the official teaching of the bishops themselves, the laity do not need the backing of their bishop or pastor for their movement to have a "Christian character." These movements have a Christian character because the laity are true members of the Church, and with their dignity as lay people they act in their own milieu, the world and the field of politics, including party politics. According to Puebla the bishops should "demonstrate their *solidarity*, contributing to their formation and their spiritual life and stimulating their creativity that they may seek options ever more in line with the common good and the *needs of the weakest*" (525). "And by developing these activities, they [the laity] act on their own initiative, without involving the ecclesiastical hierarchy in their decisions; in some way, however, this implies the responsibility of the Church, given that they are its members" (*Justice in the World*, 38). Here, the clear distinction is made between Church as hierarchy and Church as the totality of its members.

Two Criteria for the Laity's Commitment to a Political Party

The political party is within the competence of the lay person. However, in the light of faith and the Gospel, not just any political party can be recommended. The Gospel does not point out any particular party, but there are negative criteria that exclude the Christian's participation in some political parties. Criteria have varied throughout history; the bishops in Latin America, given their situation of social injustice and the growing consciousness of the Church there, have offered us two particular criteria for our age.

The entire Church must make a *preferential option for the poor* (Puebla, part IV, chap. 2, 1166–1205), as an expression of its fidelity to the Gospel and to the cry of the oppressed. In close connection with this option, the Church must also make another option for *integral liberation* that seeks the transformation of the present situation toward one that is more fraternal and just (470–506).

These two criteria orient the conscious Christian who wishes to walk with the Church: Which political party best favors the poor? Which one contributes most to integral liberation? These are not simply questions having to do with being *for* the people; the Church must march alongside and *with* the people as they move toward their own complete humanization.

Conclusion: Understanding, Support, Participation

Commissions for peace and justice are springing up all over, linked to the Church's pastoral activity on diocesan, parish, and community levels. The Church must reinforce this way of living the Christian faith toward a fuller humanization of life. Three points deserve mention:

1. Understanding the commitment to justice as a response to the official teachings of the Church and as an expression of the maturity of the laity, incarnating their faith in a reality of conflict.

2. Supporting the movement. To fight for justice is not a bed of roses. It is to enter into a conflict situation and denounce every instance of injustice. It is to live amid tension and to nourish a spirit of peace without being carried away by the instinct of revenge or self-righteousness.

3. Participation in the movement. There is a place for everyone given various levels of commitment and different needs, be it participation on a legal board, research of case studies, doctrine and conscientization, and so on.

"For us today the love of God must become first and foremost a labor of justice on behalf of the oppressed, an effort of liberation for those who are most in need of it" (Puebla, 327). The bishops have given us a powerful mandate.

Chapter 4

THE VIOLATION OF HUMAN RIGHTS
IN THE CHURCH

There is no institution today that has upheld human dignity more than the Christian community. The Church considers the human person to be an image and likeness of God, believing the individual to be a child of that absolute Mystery, a brother or sister of Jesus Christ, God incarnate, bearer of a nature hypostatically assumed by God himself, and so the Church affirms that human destiny is irreversibly linked to the eternal destiny of the most Holy Trinity. The Church has developed an understanding of the human person that highlights his or her inviolable dignity and sacredness. This anthropological reality forms the basis for inalienable rights that establish unquestionable duties of respect that are so radical that human causes become God's causes.

The theme of basic human rights and privileges has only recently arisen in the consciousness of Christians, but it has always been present in the theoretical understanding of what it is to be human: "The ferment of the gospel, too, has aroused and continues to arouse in man's heart the irresistible requirements of his dignity" (*Gaudium et Spes*, 26). Given this view of humanity, the Second Vatican Council states the following principle in *Dignitatis Humanae*: "The freedom of man [should] be respected as far as possible, and curtailed only when and in so far as necessary" (7). Thus, *Gaudium et Spes* warns citizens to "be on guard against granting government too much authority" (75).

However, the Church is also conscious that freedom, in practice, is limited by personal and social responsibilities shaped by the rights of others, duties toward others, and the common good (*DH* 7). Even so, all forms of discrimination are unjustified: "With respect to the fundamental rights of the person, every type of discrimination, whether social or cultural, whether based on sex, race, color, social condition, language, or religion, is to be overcome and eradicated as contrary to God's intent" (*GS* 29).[1]

32

Human Rights in the Church: Theory versus Practice

Given the consciousness of human rights within the Church, one might expect that there be a practice commensurate with that theory. However, it is never easy to go from the pristine clarity and internal cohesiveness of theory to practice, with its necessary translations and ambiguities. Nor is every theory reversed by its consequent practice. Theory serves as an imperative and utopic model. The Church is not above this dialectical difficulty; in the Church, as elsewhere, theory is one thing and practice often quite another.

In spite of the inevitable gap between proclamation and implementation, there is today another gap that results from power structures, institutional deficiencies, and distortions—both practical and theoretical—inherited from models that no longer reflect reality. There are violations of human rights within the Church itself. These are not those abuses that are the result of individual abuses of power which are temporal in nature; we refer to those that are the result of a certain way of understanding and organizing the reality of the ecclesial structure—a somewhat permanent state of affairs. In pointing out these abuses, we will confine ourselves to those instances in which there has been a stated commitment to human rights without the resulting practice within the Church itself; we will attempt to explain and understand them, with a view toward improving those practices.

I do not intend to denigrate the Church; this book presupposes an explicit adherence to the sacramental worth of the Church that must not only desire to affirm itself but also to foster self-criticism because "the Church . . . is at the same time holy and always in need of being purified" (*LG* 8). The credibility of its proclamation of human rights and its denunciation of their violations depends upon the respect that the Church itself practices. *Justice in the World* emphasizes this very fact: "While the Church is bound to give witness to justice, she recognizes that anyone who ventures to speak about justice must first be just in their eyes. Hence we must undertake an examination of the modes of acting, of the possessions and lifestyle found within the Church herself" (40).

The purpose of this reflection is to foster a greater and more effective authenticity in the commitment of the local churches to human rights; the contradiction in terms of theory and practice is not found within these churches themselves but in their collision with authority. The prophetic power of these churches must not be weakened.

Practices of the Church

At this point our interest is not so much in the theories of the Church as in its practices, some of which violate human rights as our understanding of them has developed.[2] The principal issues concerning the Church and human rights were brought to the fore and frankly expressed at the Synod of Bishops in 1971 when the document *Justice in the World* was being ironed out.[3] The synod fathers made the attempt to present not only injustices in the world at large but also those within the Church itself.

The Institutional Level

The centralization of decision-making within the Church is well known, the fruit of a long historical process, crystallized in various forms that were perhaps valid at one time but which today conflict with our consciousness of the rights and dignity of the human person.

For example, election to administrative posts within the Church, from the papacy to the priesthood, is not preceded by grassroots consultation of the People of God. When, by accident, such a consultation does take place, it is often disregarded. Leaders are chosen within the strict confines of those who hold ecclesial power; they are imposed on local communities, thrusting to the margins the vast majority of the laity who often possess greater professional, intellectual, and even theological qualifications. The centralization of decision-making inevitably leads to marginalization; this has an effect on basic rights to information and participation in those decisions that affect the responsibility of both the individual and the community. In view of this, *Justice in the World* proposed the correction of the injustice of excluding the laity from ecclesial decisions: "The members of the Church should have some share in the drawing up of decisions, in accordance with the rules given by the Second Vatican Council and the Holy See, for instance with regard to the setting up of councils at all levels" (46).

Even priests are often considered to be incapable of reflection, of being able to organize and make decisions about matters affecting the unity of the Church. It is the bishops who think, act, and speak for the priests in councils, synods, and other ecclesial gatherings. Juridically, priests are auxiliaries to the bishop. Groups of priests have often organized but many times they have been immediately choked by suspicion, gossip, and pressure on the part of their superiors. *Justice in the World* insists on the creation of such groups: "Within the Church rights must be preserved. No one should be deprived of his rights because he is associated with the Church in one way or another" (41).

Another conflict with regard to the basic rights of the human person has to do with the return of priests to the lay state.[4] The desire to leave the ministry is treated practically as a sin, because the encyclical *Sacerdotalis Coelibatus* (written as an open letter) considers these priests as "sadly unfaithful to the vowed obligations of their consecration" (83).[5] Their decision of conscience is not granted moral legitimacy. They are punished with a series of prohibitions, reducing them to a sub-lay status. Among other things, the laicized priest cannot share in the liturgy of any community where his status is known; he may not preach; he is not permitted to exercise any pastoral office; he is prohibited from teaching in seminaries, on theological faculties or any such institution (SEDOC 1971, 308). In a later document, restrictions were outlined that affect the ability to earn a living, not to mention the dangers to the individual's faith and relationship with the visible Church. Those who leave the priesthood are not allowed access to faculties, institutes, schools of religious or ecclesiastical science (e.g., faculties of canon law, missiology, church history, philosophy, pastoral ministry, religious education, catechetics, etc.); nor are they allowed access to any other center of higher studies in which theological or religious disciplines are taught—whether or not the center is directly under ecclesiastical authority. No laicized priest may be trusted with the teaching of theological material or anything closely connected with it such as religious education and catechetics (SEDOC 1973, 1049).

It is not hard to see that such discrimination affects not only the priests themselves but the entire community, deprived of their exceptional training in leadership and the explanation of faith.

Discrimination against women in the Church is one of the most clear examples of the violation of human rights. Women make up at least half of the faithful and women religious are ten times the number of their male counterparts. However, they are juridically considered to be incapable of almost any leadership function, rarely present in secretariats, commissions, and sacred congregations. Due to cultural tradition as well as the historical expression of the word of God, they are excluded from ministerial duties associated with the sacrament of orders. This tradition was institutionalized as normative doctrine and recently reaffirmed[6] without taking into consideration both exegetical and dogmatic arguments formulated by some of the leading contemporary theologians.[7] The basic argument presented by the statement of the Sacred Congregation for the Doctrine of the Faith stems not from the tradition against the priestly ordination of women, nor from the attitude of Christ, nor from the practice of the apostles, but rather from biology: the biological fact that Jesus was male. The text states:

> It must not be forgotten that Christ is a man. And as such, in spite of wanting to ignore the importance of such symbolism for the economy of Revelation, one must admit that in those actions that demand the character of ordination and in which Christ himself is represented, as author of the covenant and spouse and head of the Church, in the exercise of his ministry of salvation—as takes place to the highest degree in the Eucharist—the role must be fulfilled . . . by a man [p. 7].

Because there is no such being as a man-male in the abstract but only males who are radically determined, linguistically characterized, geo-graphically situated, we ask ourselves if it would not be equally legitimate and consistent with the logic of the above official argument to demand that not just any male may receive the sacrament of orders but, like Jesus, that he be Jewish, born in Galilee, that he speak Aramaic, that he be cir-cumcised. Does the Church not recognize that Jesus chose eleven married apostles and only one bachelor? Does this not carry any weight in the deci-sions of the Church? The text cited above reserves the word *person* for males, leading one to conclude that women, being unfit for the sacrament of orders, are not persons.

The former archbishop of St. Paul-Minneapolis, during the 1971 synod forcefully declared: "There is no argument that can serve to exclude women from any ecclesial service, especially when it is based solely on masculine prejudice and blind dependency on mere human tradition that reduce the place of women in society to anachronistic representations and Sacred Scripture to fragile interpretation."[8] Paulo Evaristo Arns, cardinal arch-bishop of São Paulo, affirmed: "How can we not think of the situation of women in society and the Church? It would be very myopic to limit our-selves to the ways and customs of the past without opening new horizons to such a decisive force in the development of humanity."[9]

Freedom of Information and Opinion

Participation is linked to the circulation of information. How can mem-bers of the Church help in making decisions if they lack the information necessary to form intelligent opinions? The hierarchy speaks out strongly against censorship practiced by the state and yet the Church exerts almost inquisitorial control of the Catholic means of communication. Any article in theological, scientific, or spiritual journals not in line with a particular ecclesial interpretation, any theological hypothesis that is advanced in view of new problems raised by society, provokes an often violent reaction with threats of submitting the author to a doctrinal trial held by hierarchial superiors.

There are dioceses where a theologian may only speak to women religious or to groups of priests after having survived an interrogation that, by its tenor, is almost equivalent to a cross-examination in court. In other places, the simple fact that a person may be a theologian makes him or her suspect of heresy, of defending heretical propositions, of being in opposition to established authority. Many bishops substitute authoritarianism for their own ignorance, an authority based on an unreflected knowledge, mo-notonously repeating the pronouncements published in *L'Osservatore Romano*.

The servility and silence that characterize Catholic culture is not to be admired. Dom Helder Camara coined an expression that summarizes an entire discourse: a large part of the Catholic press has succumbed to the marriage that introduced the devil to the Church, that of mediocrity wedded to bad taste. Such a spurious wedding results in excessive ideological control over intelligence. *Justice in the World* proclaims: "The Church recognizes everyone's right to suitable freedom of expression and thought. This includes the right of everyone to be heard in a spirit of dialogue which preserves legitimate diversity within the Church" (44).

Doctrine and Discipline

In terms of doctrine the practice of the Church is laden with a long, persistent, and obvious curtailment of basic human rights, to such an extent tht a well-known canon lawyer concluded a detailed study on the subject with the following statement: "There is no tradition in the Church that has been helpful for procedures either for the verification of errors of faith or in defense against them. In the western Church, especially, orthodoxy has always enjoyed primacy over orthopraxis."[10]

The Church today lacks the political means for punishing those accused of heresy but the fundamental mentality and proceedings of the past have changed little. Physical torture has been abolished but psychological torture continues: the juridical insecurity of the doctrinal processes; the anonymity of the denunciations; the lack of knowledge as to the reasons behind the charges; the judgments apart from the process; no acknowledgment of offered explanations; repeated accusations to known questions; long intervals between correspondence; the insecurity and uncertainty as to whether the process is being continued or discontinued or whether the procedures have been further refined. All of this, accented even more by the marginalization one suffers in the local church due to the scrutiny of the Sacred Congregation for the Doctrine of the Faith, leads some theologians to the dark night of lonely suffering, psychological worry, and even physical death.

The rules for the examination of doctrine, drawn up by the Sacred Congregation for the Doctrine of the Faith (till 1908 the Congregation of the Inquisition or Holy Office), were published on 15 January 1971. That document curtails a series of sacred human rights that are acknowledged even in manifestly atheistic societies.[11] The process begins without notifying the accused. Later, after those within the Congregation have already taken positions, the accused is informed and requested to respond to the various interrogators. Often, sentences or phrases are taken out of context, truncated, and many times poorly translated from the original into Latin.[12] The accused has no access to the concrete accusations, to the proceedings, or to the various viewpoints of the Sacred Congregation. A *relator pro auctore* is appointed, but the accused is not given his name nor may he choose his own *relator*. This is a Kafkaesque process wherein the accuser, the defender, the lawyer, and the judge are one and the same. There is no right to counsel or any other recourse. Everything is done in secret which, in the absence of any assured rights, gives rise to rumors that are prejudical against the person and activity of the accused.

The accused's only right is to respond to the solicitation from the Sacred Congregation; he cannot count on any response to questions he may ask or expect to be informed about the course of the proceedings. The incriminating letter has already been written, in condemnatory phrases; the propositions of the accused are labeled "theologically uncertain, dangerous, erroneous, irreconcilable with Catholic doctrine and the rule of faith." Even before he responds to the Congregation, the accused is punished: he may not speak or write about the subject under scrutiny. According to Hans Küng there is no alternative but to sign one's own condemnation.[13] The meeting in Rome to which the theologian is summoned, as his last chance for defense, is held without the juridical assurances evident in civil law: there is no access to the minutes, one may not be assisted by a lawyer. "It appears that a Catholic theologian must travel to Rome like the Czechs for a 'meeting' in Moscow with the Soviet Politburo. . . . A meeting makes sense when there is true dialogue, mutual give and take, and not the dictate by one party that demands the unconditional capitulation of the other."[14]

The ecclesiastical magisterium must present Christian doctrine in a positive way and defend it against possible errors. It is a task and a duty that aids the community of faith and it must include—as *ultima ratio*— eventual doctrinal procedures. The principal of subsidiarity is crucial to such proceedings. First, there should be competent organizations within the episcopal conferences to test the developing theological doctrines that may clash with common doctrine and create conflict among believers. The Sacred Congregation would remain as the final judge, its function linked to that of the national conferences. Second, investigations should be carried out in formal and open fashion in which those bringing charges are distinct from those rendering judgment. The rights of the accused must be guaranteed. Third, from the start, the accused should have the right to present his doctrine and defend it. This presupposes complete access to records and the choice of a competent theological advocate, who can help spell out the doctrine and translate into other words and language understandable to those who must decide the case. There are many scientific, historical, dogmatic, and exegetical problems (the frequent motive for accusations) that could be clarified in this way.[15]

Regula fidei and *doctrina Catholica* (the rule of faith and Catholic doctrine), which it is the function of the Sacred Congregation to uphold, are at the service of faith, faith in the salvation embraced in Jesus Christ. The purpose of theology is to present the essence of faith in such a way that it can be existentially lived by the faithful as well as being plausible to human reason in each age. The rule of faith must preserve the essence of faith but without maintaining it in immutable formulas. What is extraordinary about the Christian faith is that it always maintains its identity throughout its various historical changes and distinct formulations. This was the case with the gospels and will continue throughout history. As our experience of the world changes so do our problems and questions. If theology does not consider these historical factors and does not include them in its presentation of Christian faith, then the rule of faith becomes a caricature of empty, fictional realities.

Great theologians like St. John the Evangelist, St. Paul, Origen, St. Augustine, St. Thomas Aquinas, Johann Adam Möhler, Karl Rahner, and others had the courage to accept the questions of their times and seek answers from the arsenal of faith. This cannot be accomplished with the simple recitation of formulas; there must be the attempt to create new grammar and syntax for faith in each age.[16] Because of possible deviations in this task there is the responsibility for defending the correct understanding of faith by means of the investigation of theological teaching. However, one must proceed in such a way that neither the basic rights nor the dignity of the individual are violated. Thus, *Justice in the World* proclaimed: "The form of judicial procedure should give the accused the right to know his accusers and also the right to a proper defense. To be complete, justice should also include speed in its procedure" (45).

These are only some of the problems that call into question the credibility of the Church in its proclamation of human rights and its struggle for them.

A Possible Explanation

The gap between ecclesial theory and praxis in terms of human rights is a challenge to all who try to interpret it. A shortsighted interpretation would attribute such a contradiction to human deficiencies of those in authority in the Church and of those who are simply cast as victims of a doctrinal understanding of faith or of the primary instincts for power and self-affirmation. This is possible in individual cases because where there is power there may be abuses of that authority. But we must remember that the majority of those in authority in the Church are men of good faith, clear conscience, impeccable personal character.

The problem lies on a deeper level, on the structure that to a great degree is independent of persons. We will approach this problem from various points of view in order to better understand the causes of the contradiction.

Sociohistorical Collision

One explanation is, without a doubt, the power structure in the Church. In terms of decision-making, the pole runs from the Pope to the bishop, to the priests—excluding religious and laity. From a sociological perspective, the Church operates out of an authoritarian system.[17] A system is authoritarian when those in power exclude the free and spontaneous acknowledgment by their subordinates of that authority. The free and spontaneous submission of a group of people to one individual or institution distinguishes authority from power and domination.[18] Without these natural conditions for relationship, authority becomes authoritarian. The system of power within the Church believes itself to come directly from God, and believers must accept it in faith. Socialization through catechesis, theology, and the accepted exercise of its power guarantees the preservation of the structure from generation to generation.[19]

Underlying every true human authority there is divine authority, above all in the case of the Church of Christ. The problem is whether the present *structure* can directly claim divine origin or whether it stems from the insertion of divine authority and the Church in history. Good theology, with help from the New Testament, may be able to uphold the idea that the authority of Christ is present in the entire Church, the body of Christ, in a primary and fundamental manner, and then organically differentiated in the various members of that Church (Pope-bishops-priest-laity). The concrete forms are taken to be the contribution of diverse cultural situations.

The primitive Christian communities felt the powerful need to organize. They inevitably took social and political models from the surrounding world in which to incarnate their authority from God and Christ. The power structure in the Church today is indebted to centuries-old patterns, and two patterns are worth noting in particular: the experience with Roman power and the feudal structure. The Church assumed customs, titles, expressions, and symbols from them. Hierarchy, as a term and as a concept, is a result of this process. This assuming of societal characteristics by the Church was necessary for its continuation in the world and, in the theological sense of incarnation, desired by God. The Roman and feudal style of power in the Church today, however, constitutes one of the principal sources of conflict with the rising consciousness of human rights.

The Roman and feudal style of authority is characterized, first, by a hierarchy with distinct "orders" (Tertullian); second, this hierarchy is personal in nature. The one in power is such for life; his will is law (*lex animata*) within his own "order" but always linked by obedience to the superior "order." Third, it is a sacred and cosmic hierarchy. In other words, its legitimacy comes not from below but from above, from the will of God.

The higher someone is in this hierarchy the closer one is to God and so has a greater share in God's divine power. To obey one's superior is to obey God, making obedience a religious act. Fourth, this style of authority is untouchable and not subject to any internal criticism. Criticism from within any of the orders is only possible from a higher authority. A questioning from below would be equal to a revolution in the universe. Thus, any thought of transformation is the same as an attack on God who is author of both the order and structure of sacred power.[20]

This understanding of authority gave meaning to personal and social life. The Church's experience with this structure was so successful that it has continued almost without change, even in the face of the great modern revolutions (French, industrial, socialist, and others) that gave rise to new power structures. With the social transformations of the last centuries, the Church has had to defend itself politically and doctrinally. What the Church defends is not so much its divine authority but the historical form that this authority has assumed. Previously, society recognized the power and authority of the Church; today it has become a ghetto. Society at large does not pay any attention to what happens in the Church, in terms of power, because the Church's presence is no longer decisive in the events that shape the history of a nation.

As we will see later, the Second Vatican Council recognized the historicity of the forms of power within the Church and elaborated a theological understanding of authority that was less monarchical and more congenial, in itself paving the way for new structures of participation in ecclesial life. The Council did this especially through the documents *Lumen Gentium* (on the Church), *Christus Dominus* (on the bishops), *Apostolicam Actuositatem* (on the laity), and *Gaudium et Spes* (on the Church in the modern world).

Analytical Collision

Another explanation of the human rights contradiction arises through an analysis of the Church's consciousness of its own authority. Emile Durkheim asserted: "A society is not simply the mass of indivduals that comprises it, nor the territory it occupies, nor the things it uses, nor the movements it carries out, but *above all it is the idea that it has of itself*."[21] The self-awareness that a group develops about itself is one of the most important factors for explaining its behavior. What self-concept forms ecclesiastical authority? It considers itself to be the principal if not exclusive bearer of God's revelation to the world, with the mission of proclaiming it, explaining it, and defending it.[22] This revelation is found in the sacred Scriptures and interpretation is given by the magisterium of the Church. As such, revelation is doctrinally understood as the collection of truths necessary for salvation.

This is the crux of the problem: the doctrinal understanding of revelation. God reveals necessary truths, some unattainable by reason, to facilitate the road to salvation. The magisterium possesses a collection of absolute, infallible, and divine truths. The magisterium presents an absolute doctrine, free from any doubt. Any inquiry that is born of life and that calls into question a given doctrine is mistaken. Doctrine substitutes for life, experience, and everything from below.[23]

This understanding has grave consequences for the problem of human rights: intolerance and dogmatism. The bearer of an absolute truth cannot tolerate any other truth. As Rubem Alves has noted, "Those who pretend to possess the truth are destined for intolerance." In this understanding, salvation depends on the knowledge of orthodox truth. Having and being coincide: whoever has the truth is saved. Truth is more decisive than goodness. The Inquisition was not bothered by moral crimes but by those related to orthodox truth.[24] One who commits a moral transgression sins but he or she does not jeopardize the understanding and system of truths and power. The sinner contradicts the truth but repents because the truth is recognized. The heretic, on the other hand, denies the validity of the system of truths and proclaims another truth. With a doctrinal understanding of revelation, the heretic is a criminal not only against the unity of the Church but against the very reality of the Church-as-bearer-of-divine-truths. He is like the atheist and is characterized as such by the edict of Constantine (Eusebius, *Vita Constantini* 3, 64). The rigor of the Inquisition was necessitated by the harsh logic of the system itself and even today governs the doctrinal mentality of the Sacred Congregation for the Doctrine of the Faith.

As long as this type of dogmatic and doctrinaire understanding of revelation and salvation continues, there inevitably will be repression of the freedom of thought within the Church. This repression will be carried out with the clean conscience of one fulfilling a sacred duty of preserving the divine right of revelation to which every human right must give way.

Structural Collision

The two previous aspects are not sufficient explanation for the gap between the consciousness of human rights and the fact that they are unrealized historically within the Church. Those aspects are on the level of ideas and models. There is a deeper and more structural level of the concrete practice of those in certain positions of power. Ideas are the products of a concrete life and they serve that life. In other words, in order to understand any phenomenon structurally one must begin not with what is thought and stated but rather with what actions have marked daily life.[25]

Using the model inherited from the Industrial Revolution—one that characterizes modern society—we may speak of the means of production versus the goods and services of that production. In terms of the Church, those who hold the means of religious production, the realm of the symbolic, also hold power and so create and control official discussions. From a sociological point of view there is an undeniable division and inequality in the Church: one group produces the symbolic goods and another consumes them. There are the ordained who can produce, celebrate, and decide and the nonordained who associate with and assist the ordained. The capacity for production and participation in decision-making, although latent in the nonordained, remains untapped. The group that holds the means of symbolic production develops a corresponding theology that justifies, reinforces, and socializes its power by attributing divine origin to its historical exercise of that power. Theology aside, the underlying conflict is one of the power of some over others, a power that will not abdicate its privileges and rights, at odds with the inviolable rights of human persons (participation, symbolic production, free expression, etc.). The Christian lay person is made to believe that, due to being a simple Christian, he or she is faced with divine givens that exclude or subordinate the lay person to a group whose power comes from above. There is nothing left but the acceptance of the fact that although the hierarchy recognizes certain rights they cannot be exercised because they do not fit into the ecclesial organization. The rights of the individual lose their inalienable character and are thus violated.

There is no argument as to the legitimacy of the authority of the Church; it exists and is willed by God. The historical form that it has taken, the ideologically justified imbalance of power among the members of the Church, is called into question.

Paths toward Improvement

How does one overcome or bridge the gap between the Church's theory and praxis? Because of the officially created doctrinal burden that reinforces the interests of those holding sacred power, what will open the path of renewal that will affect the structure itself? There is a reasonable hope that such is possible because of the internal contradiction within the ecclesial consciousness itself. There are practices that limit basic human rights, justified by their corresponding theological theories; there is also another authority, of the Gospel, upon which the Church stands, that constantly criticizes and denounces every abuse of power and calls for respect and service. Jesus' message does not favor the domination of some over others or the curtailment of their rights; the same holds true for the Church that exists because of that message and that incarnates him in the world. On the contrary, these two realities presuppose, guarantee, and promote freedom, fraternity, and mutual and disinterested service. We live under the "law of freedom" (Jas 1:25; 2:12). "That we might be free

Christ has freed us" (Gal 5:1). These are the imperatives that foster our hope and lead us to shape practices that strive toward those ideals.

We must first do away with the idealist temptation that is satisfied with raising people's consciousness in order to change the structure of the Church. It is not new ideas but new and different practices (supported by theory) that will modify ecclesial reality. These modifications in turn open the way for a corresponding theory, leading to a new reading of the Gospel and tradition.

We must recognize that in the past few years, especially after Vatican II, extremely important steps have been taken. Just as the Church previously took on Roman and feudal structures, it is now taking on structures found in today's civil societies that are more compatible with our growing sense of human rights. This is the often argued "democratization of the Church." This term does not refer so much to concrete practices and organizations as it does to the intentions and structures of a different type of Church. In this view, the fundamental nature of the Church remains unchanged, with its revelation of Jesus Christ, with the basic doctrines about his life and work, the ethical imperatives implied in his message, and the sacramentality of the Church, but at the same time it favors a free and fraternal community with the participation of the greatest number of people.[26] Those in the hierarchy who favor a centralist feudal model are few; the model for bishops and priests is more that of true shepherds, leaders among their people, in service devoid of all titles, and according to a style that reveals the gospel model of the diaconate. It would take too long and this is not the place to detail the various transformations that are taking place on all levels of church power.[27] Not only is established power being modified (and humanized) but new ways of being Church are springing forth, especially in Latin America among the *comunidades eclesiales de base*, such that today we are experiencing a true ecclesiogenesis.

Second, these new church practices, better able to meet the demands of human rights, lead us to a gospel understanding of authority. We are made conscious of the concepts latent in the present conception of ecclesial authority: a metaphysics of creation, the absolute power of the Creator, cosmic harmony—elements that have little to do with the New Testament understanding of service. The authority of the Church stems from the authority of Jesus:

> "Jesus was, or became, authoritative by what he said and did and this is because his words and actions were felt by men to be helpful, liberating, good and beneficial. In other words, Jesus' authority can be defined as *full saving* power." Jesus did not resort constantly to this full saving power, not did he try to justify it or least of all boast of it in an authoritarian manner. On the contrary, he looked for and tried to provoke human freedom.

His methods were those of convincing clarity and insight, rational argument and non-casuistical openness and directness. He had authority because all that he said and did arose from the authority of freedom and love and he gave men the power to create, to love and to be free.[28]

Ecclesial authority that is based on this tradition must be founded upon the equality of brother and sister (Gal 3:26–29: you are one in Christ; Matt 23:8: you are all brothers; Jas 2:2–4: there must be no distinction between you), in a fraternity that is opposed to qualifications such as teacher, father, and so forth (Matt 23:8–9), and in service that is devoid of all domination and pretension to having the final word (Mark 10:42–45; Luke 22:25–27; John 13:14).

Authority was incarnated in many different ways in the primitive Church. In the Pauline communities (Corinth) there was a charismatic structure; in the community at Jesusalem, a synogogal (council of priests) structure. The communities of the pastoral letters had structures centered around the apostolic delegates with their presbyterate, thereby reducing the participation of all baptized Christians who, for Paul, were each bearers of the Spirit. The form mattered little; authority meant service.

However, the historical form of the pastoral letters predominated: the minister with powers that were received through the laying on of hands, giving rise to various *orders* in the Church. This is the root—especially in those cases where the spirituality of service was lacking—for the focus that would one day result in discrimination among the faith community, to such an extent that the ordained kept all power in the Church for themselves. This is certainly against the basic intention of fraternity present in Jesus' message. The centralized form of power is but *one* form that, for historical reasons (in this case, the threat of gnosticism) may be justified but which cannot claim exclusivity through the centuries. The diversity of forms of authority in the New Testament suggests another direction. Authority was congenial before it was monarchical.[29]

The Second Vatican Council, influenced by new styles and practices of authority in the Church, accepted the idea of collegiality not only on the episcopal level but throughout the entire Church. While preconciliar theology excluded the laity from any office because they were not ordained, Vatican II teaches that because of their baptism lay people "are in their own way made sharers in the priestly, prophetic, and kingly functions [*munus*] of Christ. They carry out their own part in the mission of the whole Christian people with respect to the Church and the world" (*Lumen Gentium*, 31). While Pius XII's encyclical *Humani Generis* taught that the hierarchy is solely responsible for the administration of the word of God (18), Vatican II affirms that "lay people announce Christ, explain and spread His teaching according to their situation and ability" (*Apostolicam Actuositatem*, 16).

Finally, an improvement in the doctrinal understanding of revelation and faith is taking place in theology. God, in the first place, did not reveal true propositions *about* himself, man, and salvation. He revealed himself, in his mystery, life and will. Divine life invaded human life. What saves us are not truths formulated in neat sentences but rather God himself who is given as salvation. Faith primarily means the total adherence to the living God, not simply the acceptance of a creed of propositions.

The Church is not only the bearer of revelation and salvation; it also, and rightly, is responsible for doctrine because there may be doctrines and ways of articulating faith that give rise to false representations of God and his love. Doctrines and theologies must always reflect faith. This is the criterion for the correctness of any theology that is presented to the ecclesial community. But the Church must be on guard against dogmatic rigidity and doctrinal fixation, as if doctrine were the ultimate judge. Doctrine is always the historico-cultural translation of God's revelation. We have salvation not through our doctrines but through our practices that follow our encounter with the living and true God.

This existential and biblical understanding of revelation and faith opens the door to various approaches to absolute Truth. This is an eschatological gift; within history our formulations express the absolute Truth but cannot express everything absolutely about the Truth. In everything said there is something left unsaid; every point of view is the view of a point. Therefore, there will always be different ways of articulating faith through doctrines expressed in the words of another culture and even another social class.

Conclusion

The Church recognizes the unfathomable dignity of the human person and so can be the conscience of the world with respect to human rights. But proclamation alone is not enough. The Church will only be heard if it gives witness by its practices, if it is the first to respect and promote human rights within its own reality. Otherwise, one would be right to criticize a Church that sees the speck in the eye of another while ignoring the beam in its own: "Hypocrite, remove the beam from your own eye and then try to remove the speck from your neighbor's eye" (see Matt 7:3–5).

There is a quote from Cardinal Arns, of Brazil, who has become a spokesman in the Church for the defense of human rights, especially those of the nameless, and who because of this knows a great deal about the onerous path of the prophet: "The modern Job has great poems to write. And these poems will not be read except by the heart of God. Do the churches have the courage to be the heart of God in this moment of history?"[30]

Chapter 5

THE POWER OF
THE INSTITUTIONAL CHURCH:
CAN IT BE CONVERTED?

Frustrated but Living Hopes

There are two distinct stances evident in the Church: one that is turned outward toward the world and society, and the other turned inward toward the various structures of the Church. In the first instance, the Church emerges as a homogeneous and strongly coherent totality. In the past few decades it has gained a respectability and moral authority rarely seen before in the history of the West. It has come to represent what is highest and most holy in the mystery of humanity and God. It embodies humanity's hope that not everything has come under the domination of self-interested power structures. The Church inspires confidence and the Gospel, joy of life and hope.[1]

The other stance is focused on intrasystemic relationships; Christians are steeped in venerable traditions, liturgical prescriptions, well-defined moral codes, ecclesiastical structures, and forms of power—all powerfully controlled and centralized by a body of experts, the hierarchy. Tensions, conflicts, and instances of authoritarianism arise on this internal level,[2] often unrecognized because of similar domination within civil society. A bishop may decide to halt a project that affects priests, religious, pastoral leaders, and dozens of communities. Without any previous discussion, he may literally expel religious from his diocese and dismiss the lay leaders, leaving the faith community confused. There is no one to whom they can appeal because they are dealing with the final judge. In cases like this, many are often led into crises of faith provoked by the actions of their cardinals, bishops, and pastors.

Does this have anything to do with power as service described in the Gospel? Is the Church as institution able to be a liberator among the poor and oppressed? Is conversion possible given the spirituality of the sacredness of power held only by pastors and bishops? Is it possible to trust the stated preferential option for the poor, to hope that the Church may break

47

its historical pact with temporal rulers and be converted to gospel poverty, in solidarity with those who are denied their rights, converted to prophetic courage, fearless in the face of persecution, torture, and death, and so follow the Suffering Servant, Jesus Christ?

Committed by faith in this Church, we will attempt to analyze the reasons behind these hopes, frustrated as they may be. Through this analysis we hope to nourish faith in the strength of the Spirit that is capable of awakening the dormant heart of the institutional Church, encouraging the living presence and the dangerous yet powerful memory of the life, death, and resurrection of Jesus Christ.

When we speak of the Church as institution, we do not mean the community of believers who give witness in the world to the presence of the risen Christ. We refer to the organization of this community with its hierarchy, sacred powers, dogmas, rites, canons, and traditions.[3] By means of its institutional organization the community responds to the needs for stability, for identity, the spreading of the Gospel, internal assistance, government, and so on. No community can exist without some institutionalization that lends it unity, coherency, and identity. The institution does not exist for itself but is in service to the community of faith. As such, it evolves, following the same path as the historical transformation of the community itself that faces crises and discovers institutional responses to them. What we call ongoing or permanent conversion belongs to this historical process of fidelity and service to the community and the Lord. This presupposes an interior attitude of detachment and poverty that allows the institution to abandon its search for glory in order to better serve the community and the Lord present within it. It is only by means of this ongoing conversion that the community with its institutions will be of salvific service to the world. Otherwise it will become an empty ghetto, thereby betraying its vocation of universality.

The Church as institution is characterized by endurance, stability, and by the rules of the game followed by its members.[4] It runs the risk of losing the beat of history, of stagnating, of forgetting its primary function of service, of fostering passivity, monotony, mechanization, and alienation. It begins to understand itself ideologically, as the epiphany of the promises it safeguards. It imposes itself on the community it is meant to serve. Truth is substituted by internal certainty and factions are created by cutting short those movements that will not be constrained by the institution. Every institution runs these risks and has the tendency to become autocratic, that is, to become a system of power and repression over creativity and criticism. Institutions mean power. And, as Lord Acton rightly observed "power tends to corrupt and absolute power corrupts absolutely."

The institution of the Church has suffered from this; power became a powerful temptation for domination and a substitution for God and Jesus Christ. This institutional sclerosis has kept the Church from responding properly to the challenges of the modern world. It has become conservative and has created a deep chasm between the Church-People of God and the Church-hierarchy in terms of ecclesial praxis, between the Church that thinks, speaks, and yet does not act and that Church which does not dare to think, cannot speak, and yet acts. This breach in practice is so serious that the proclamations of the Second Vatican Council on the place of the laity in the Church as People of God are only now reaching the level of general theological discussion.

What chance is there of the institutional Church actualizing the Gospel and, in its light, responding to the great challenges of the world today, a world that for almost four centuries has been beside, outside, opposed to, and everywhere but together with the Church? What challenges and criticisms can we formulate in the freedom given all of us by the Gospel of Jesus Christ, a Gospel that predates the institution? What type of conversion is needed?

The Challenge of Power

In order to be realistic in our examination it is necessary to consider the historical activity of the institutional Church in view of the social upheavals that have taken place throughout western society. The Church's reaction to these upheavals, whether in Europe or in Latin America, has been uniform given the centralization of ecclesial power.[5]

The first thing that must be recognized is the fact that Christianity is the fruit of an upheaval. For Judaism, even today, it is a heresy. The first two generations of Christians intensely lived the good news of Jesus that was not a mere prolongation of Judaism as practiced at the time of the apostles. It was the new covenant, the new eon, the new man, fulfilled promises, the freedom of the children of God, the gift of the Spirit, the Kingdom already anticipated by the glorification and ascension of the Lord. All of these themes, as José Comblin has observed in detail, are undeniably revolutionary and call the Church out from its structures where these seeds of transformation have been compromised so as to be offensive to no one.[6]

The early Church, particularly St. Paul, was still preoccupied with the interpretation of this new Christian life, with giving it a global theological perspective through sophisticated discussions with the intertestamentary and rabbinic traditions. The irruption of Christianity was not easily tamed; it was the work of the evangelists and Pauline theology to develop powerful and impressive syntheses. The communities of the third generation thus found themselves in a more tranquil setting. They were already established and had their theological syntheses; their problems were not those of building but rather of preservation, of proper order within the community and the safeguarding of pure doctrine. This situation would be decisive for the later Church as institution.[7]

The important thing about the Church of the first three generations was not its institutional character.[8] Unity was guaranteed by the commonality of faith and by the courage of public martyrs, and not by institutional structures. It is true that the threat of heresy forced the community to define the canon of the New Testament and the line of apostolic succession: the two pillars of the ecclesial institution. But this Church is free of power. It is poor and for the poor, yet it still has its defenders of the faith. Statements of St. Ignatius such as these—"nothing without the bishop, everything with the bishop" (*Phld* 7:1) or "the bishops are Christ-figures and God-figures" (*Magn* 3:1; *Smyrn* 8:1) and "deacons should be venerated as messengers of God and as Christ himself" (*Trall* 3:1; *Smyrn* 8:1)—are far from any later clericalism. What was championed was not a juridical and power-hungry vision but a mystical one that saw the risen Christ present through the charismatic individuals who exercised offices of service and unity for the community. Their authority came from their exemplary living of the mystery of Christ and not from the sacred power with which they were invested.

This situation changed radically with the conversion of Constantine. From a *religio illicita* (illicit religion), Christianity became both the official religion and the sacred ideology of the empire. This was the opportunity for the Church to cease being a ghetto church and become a true *ecclesia universalis*. The Church thus embarked upon its great cultural and political adventure. It took on great power, with all of the risks that such power implies. Would it be able to use the historical *kairos* in order to exercise power in the gospel sense, as opposed to the power of the pagans, giving rise to another form of human sharing, another humanism, another meaning for political activity?

Everything happened too fast. The Church, in spite of persecutions, was not prepared to face the challenges of power from an evangelical perspective. It did not abolish the existing order. Rather, it assumed it and adapted itself to that order. It offered the empire an ideology that supported the existing order and even blessed the pagan cosmos. One scholar has concluded his study of the origin of Christianity's rule as the religion of the state by remarking that "the religion that marked the West was not properly the Christian message."[9] When the leaders of the empire joined the Church, a paganization of Christianity took place, and not a christianization of paganism.[10] The Church, which until A.D. 312 was more of a movement than an institution, became an heir of the empire's institutions: law, organization by diocese and parish, bureaucratic centralization, positions, and titles. The Church-institution accepted political realities and assumed inexorable uniformity. It began on a path of power that continues today and that we must hasten to end.

The key category for understanding the Church is in terms of *potestas* (power). The Church understands itself primarily as the community invested with power (the hierarchy) together with the community deprived of power (the People of God, laity). This Church sees power as the greatest way in which the Gospel will be accepted, understood, and proclaimed. Christ becomes the emperor, the cosmic Lord, and not the Suffering Servant who confronted the powers of this world (including the empire of which the Pope is now heir), not the Jesus who decidedly renounced all earthly power and glory.[11] The Church-institution idealized the past, reading the New Testament *exousia* (authority, power) in terms of juridical and political power, especially the Petrine power of confirming the faith. The words of the gospel, "Whoever hears you, hears me and whoever despises you, despises me and the One who sent me" (Luke 10:16), were interpreted in a missionary context of Church-world rather than hierarchy-community, to the ideological benefit of those who held sacred power.

Until the eleventh century, the Church's power was a power granted by the empire. This began with Constantine, who called the first ecumenical council at Nicea in A.D. 325. He called himself Pope and took his legal framework from the laity. The Church became a feud between emperors who handed out ecclesiastical posts, exercising them in secular fashion. Thus, there arose the dispute between the two powers, sacred and secular, in which each claimed to be the heir of the empire of Augustus. The sacred powers of the Church took to all sorts of cunning schemes in order to justify its claim, including the falsification of documents such as the *Testamentum Constantini* (Testament of Constantine). This only confirms the thesis that power, be it Christian or pagan, sacred or secular, follows the logic of increased desire for power.

In the eleventh century, with Gregory VII, a decisive change took place within the structure of power itself.[12] In his *Dictatus Papae* (1075), the Pope rose up against the secular practices of power which had degenerated into simony and every type of sacrilege and he instituted the ideology of the absolute power of the papacy. Support for this was not the figure of the poor, humble, and weak Jesus but rather God himself, omnipotent Lord of the universe and sole source of power. The Pope was to be understood as the unique reflection of divine power in creation, God's vicar and representative. "Only the Roman Pontiff deserves to be called universal" (2); "His law in a Council commands all bishops, even if it be a minority position, and only he may pronounce the words of deposition" (4); "The Pope is the only man whose feet all princes must kiss" (9); "His dictates may not be reformed by anyone and he alone can reform all others" (18); "The Pope may not be judged by anyone" (19); "The Roman Church has never erred and, as the Scriptures affirm, it cannot err" (22); "The Roman Pontiff, if he has been canonically ordained, becomes holy without a doubt, through the merits of Saint Peter" (23).

The *Summus Pontifex* (Supreme Pontiff) thereby assumed the inheritance of the Roman Empire and became an absolute power, wedding the *sacerdotium* to the *regnum*, the priestly power to the throne. The ideology of "cephalization" was developed in which the head is considered the center and fullness of meaning and power. The expression *kephalē (caput*, head), reserved for Christ in the New Testament, was applied to the Pope, as holder of all values and powers, of God, of Christ, of the Church, of the people, of the empire, of the episcopal college. René Laurentin comments: "The pope came to be identified with Christ. He was thought of less and less as the successor of Peter and more and more as the successor and vicar of Jesus Christ, whom Hervé Nedellec (d. 1323) considered to be the first pope. . . . He became, in the words of St. Catherine of Siena, 'the sweet Christ on earth.' He was identified, verbally at least, with God himself."[13] Absolute power understood in this way caused St. John Bosco to write: "The pope is God on earth. . . . Jesus has set the pope above the prophets, above his precursor . . . above the angels. . . . Jesus has placed the pope on a level with God."[14] What is strange is that this statement was not censored. The exaltation of power, and its exaggeration, is due to power itself in its understanding and exercise.

This ideology of power launched the ecclesiastical battleship that sailed in theological waters until the nineteenth century and still floats in the minds of some of the hierarchy to the present day. The absolute power of the Pope determined the later course of civil and church history, a history that would be the history of this absolute power, of its successes and confirmation, and of the challenges to that power. Either the Church would dominate or it would be dominated.

The absolute power of the institutional Church developed a justification for its rule, just like any other totalitarian power: reason must abdicate its critical function and become a mere instrument of the system; theology became pure and simple *sentire cum Ecclesia*, thinking with the Church. *Ecclesia* is understood as the institution as described in a frighteningly convincing way by official theology under Pius XII and by the curial theologians who prepared the texts for the Second Vatican Council, texts that were later overwhelmingly rejected as not reflecting the living faith of the Church as People of God. In practice, the Church is one enormous diocese in which the Pope, not being able to reach everyone, installs his vicars who share in his absolute power. Dogmas are read juridically and laws, dogmatically.

Unity is understood as conformity and uniformity. Conflict or criticism is seen as something pathological, threatening division and schism. The simplest solution is elimination of critical elements. Typical of every power structure are the court proceedings against anything or anyone not wholly part of the system.[15] The logic of power is the desire for more power, to conserve and preserve itself, to compromise, and, in case of danger, to make concessions in order to survive. This can be verified throughout the history of the Church-institution.

Ecclesiastical power has always been understood as a power of divine legacy. But what is divine in the power of the Church is its origin; the concrete exercise of that power has little or nothing to do with divinity, but rather follows the logic of any human power structure. Many recent sociological studies have pointed out the extreme centralization of the Church's decision-making power.[16]

The Church's appeal to the divine origin of its power does not substantially change the function and pathologies of this type of power. In terms of its bureaucracy, the Church-institution functions as if it were a giant multinational corporation. The headquarters where all ideological and tactical decisions are made is located in Rome with the Pope and the Curia.[17] Dioceses, for all practical purposes, are branches located throughout the world. A relationship of dependence is established between the Curia and the periphery on theological, pastoral, liturgical, juridical, and all other levels. The Second Vatican Council theoretically developed a theology of independence and autonomy for the bishop in his local church, based on an ecclesiology of communion, but there are obstacles at the center in the practical implementation of this understanding.

This type of power has resulted in a wide range of pathological social manifestations, studied by psychology and sociology,[18] such as the lack of creative imagination, of dialogue, of a critical spirit, and an increase in appeals to obedience, submission, renunciation, humility, carrying the cross, discipline, order—values certainly found in the gospels but practiced in such a way as to justify the established powers and in slavish defense of them.

As was pointed out previously, after the eleventh century, the history of the West could only follow one of two paths: the sedimentation of the absolute power of the papacy or the challenge to that power. The latter was to be followed. The institutional Church was made to defend itself against the proponents of freedom. Thus, especially in the sixteenth century, the Church defined itself primarily in terms of those it was against: it was against reform (1521), against revolutions (1789), against values that today are held sacred such as freedom of conscience, condemned in 1846 by Gregory XVI as "madness" (*deliramentum*; DS 2730), freedom of opinion, anathematized as a "most pestilent error" by the same Pope (DS 2731), democracy, and so on.[19] Will the Church-institution, which at Medellín in 1968 spoke out clearly in favor of liberation, also introduce a break in history?

In terms of power, the Church fears all transformations that jeopardize the security of its acquired power. And power itself will never abdicate. It is only shared when it is in jeopardy. The institution always seeks to be on top, with the winners. This explains the facility with which Rome, the center of the institutional Church, ratifies rights and revolutions that have been won through sweat and blood. As Günther Lewy notes, "Once a liberating movement has broken certain chains, the Church will incorporate the newly gained liberties into her ethic of natural law. She will recognize them, as previously she had recognized the validity of the chains."[20] Because of its centralized and authoritarian structure, the Church has no qualms of conscience in accepting authoritarian and even totalitarian regimes as long as its own rights are not attacked. Again quoting Lewy: "'In any crucial situation the behavior of the Catholic Church may be more reliably predicted by reference to its interests as a political organization than by reference to its timeless dogmas.' One may go a step further and say that these dogmas are sufficiently flexible and ambiguous so that the Church can accommodate a variety of political conditions running the gamut from democracy to totalitarian dictatorship."[21] Lewy draws his observations from his detailed study of the Catholic Church and Nazi Germany, showing how the institutional Church, faced with the extremely totalitarian ideology of Nazism, was incapable of separating its ideals and its evangelical message from its interest in survival. The German bishops condemned intrasystemic excesses but made clear its position that "the Catholic religion was no more opposed to the Nazi form of government than to any other," even though it was widely known that genocide was an integral part of the National Socialist doctrine.[22] The Church as institution did not act prophetically if there was any danger of its being eliminated in a particular region. It preferred to survive, though it had to know of the grave violations of human rights such as the extermination of millions of Jews and thousands of Polish intellectuals.

There is a great difference between the Church of the first three centuries and the later Church which rose to power. The primitive Church was prophetic; it joyfully suffered torture and courageously gave its life through martyrdom. It did not care about survival because it believed in the Lord's promise that guaranteed it would not fail. Success or failure, survival or extinction, was not a problem for the Church; it was a problem for God. The bishops were at the forefront, convincing their brothers and sisters to die for the Lord. The later Church was opportunistic; that it would not fail was a question of prudence and compromise that allowed it to survive in the midst of totalitarian regimes, at the expense of gospel demands. The bishop in this later Church does not freely walk in witness to his death; rather, he pushes others, walking behind his flock and often assisting in the death of its prophets, fearful and reticent, calling for fidelity not to Christ but to the institutional Church. To survive, the Church adopts various interpretations of its doctrines, such as those dealing with the use of violence and the right to insurrection. There is a direct line running from Gregory XVI to Pius IX (*Syllabus*) to Leo XIII (*Quod Apostolici Munieris*) to Paul VI (*Populorum Progressio*) that condemns revolutionary violence, even when that violence is provoked by social situations. Such a doctrine is easy to teach when the institution is on friendly terms with the regimes in question. However, when churches are burned and ministers jailed and killed, as in the Mexican Revolution in 1927 and the Spanish Revolution (1936–39), the Church adopts another interpretation of the use of revolutionary violence. Because some members of the Spanish episcopacy supported General Franco, Pius XI made the distinction between just and unjust insurrections. He supported the "recourse to force" as an act of "proper defense" against those who are ruining a nation.[23] Whatever the interpretation, first in one direction and then in another, it always points to the same effort: to strengthen the survival of the institution so that the Gospel may be made present in the world. Is it true that the Gospel needs power, prudence, concessions, the typical tricks of pagan power, all criticized by Jesus (Matt 10:42), or does its strength lie precisely in weakness, renunciation of all security, prophetic courage, as practiced in the Church of the first three centuries?

Such practices of power in the Church, generating ecclesial marginality, tenuous and lifeless communication between its members, as well as religious and evangelical underdevelopment, result in the image of a Church almost neurotically preoccupied with itself and, as such, lacking a real interest in the major problems facing humanity.

But the Church *does* speak out and makes calls to conversion and eventually recognizes its historical errors. Vatican II explicitly stated the need for ongoing conversion in the notion of *Ecclesia semper reformanda* (Church always in need of reform). Unfortunately, conversion is interpreted in such a way that allows the power structure to remain as it is. An intimate and private meaning is given to conversion: the members of the Church must be converted, that is, live a morally holy life and achieve a purity of intentions. This does not touch upon the institution with its structures of ongoing iniquity, discrimination, lack of full participation, and so on. Institutions have a life of their own, independent of the good or ill intentions of individuals within them. If conversion does not reach the institution of the

Church, if it does not call into question the way in which power is exercised, if it does not reach the wider society, then we cannot speak of gospel conversion. We end up with extremely good-willed individuals with pure intentions but who are faithful, loyal, and uncritical toward the institution, who through this institution cause serious damage to people and to the Church. Pascal noted that evil is not so perfectly achieved as when it is done with good will and purity of heart.

Speaking of the reform of the institutional Church, Yves Congar says:

> Our epoch of rapid change and cultural transformation (philosophical ferments and sociological conditions different from those which the Church has accustomed itself until now) calls for a revision of "traditional" forms which goes beyond the level of adaptation or *aggiornamento*, and which would be instead a new creation. It is no longer sufficient to maintain, by adapting it, what has already been; it is necessary to reconstruct it. This kind of reconstruction cannot occur effectively except on the basis of a very determined revision of the historical character of institutions, forms and structures, and of a very genuine spiritual return to the sources.[24]

The Goal of Reform: The Need to Recreate

In order to reform an institution it is necessary to be clear about one's understanding of the institution. The Church as an institution of power would be summed up as follows:

1. As much as it may irritate those in positions of ecclesiastical power, we must repeat that the institutional Church has not passed the test of power. We might have hoped that it would have brought forth a new manner of exercising power according to the call of the Gospel. However, the Church's exercise of power followed the patterns of pagan power in terms of domination, centralization, marginalization, triumphalism, human *hybris* beneath a sacred mantle. Sociologically, Christianity was not sufficiently negative or critical.

> Far too often, particularly in the Constantinian part of its history, Christianity has failed to present the ideals of goodness, justice and love to an unjust society and state. It preferred to side positively with the establishment. It invested with the aura of heavenly justice the unjust masters of society, thereby legitimizing them and giving the many a reason for sacrificing themselves willingly and humbly for the few in the production process as well as on the battlefield. Christianity lost its eschatological salt and became an ideology justifying the establishment. It thereby only intensified the dichotomy between the particular and the universal and prevented their reconciliation in a freer society. In a word, it became reactionary.[25]

It is not enough to say that one must judge history with the criteria of the time. Why, in treating the history of the Church, should not the criteria of the Gospel have greater value?

2. With the conversion of Constantine, Christianity had no other alternative than to assume a historical role in terms of sacred and political power. Inheriting the empire, it had the opportunity to become truly ecumenical and universal. This it did. Christianity is not against power in itself but its diabolical forms which generally show themselves as domination and control of the masses. It lost the opportunity to incarnate a new way of relating through power as pure service for the good of all persons.

3. Despite having continued the pagan form of power, Christianity marked first the West and then the entire world. The history of the world can never be told without mentioning the presence of Christianity. Yet there can be no illusions as to the quality of Christianity present in western culture: it was superficial and contained profoundly anti-Christian elements. Atheism as a cultural phenomenon came from Christianity; the western world gave rise to the great totalitarian ideologies of Nazism, capitalism, Marxism, colonialism, and slavery, with all of their offshoots such as oppression, unjust wars, and colonial rule.

4. Everything seems to indicate that the Church's experience with power is approaching its inevitable end. There are two basic reasons for this: first, Christianity is becoming more and more a dispensable ideology for modern secular, pragmatic, and industrial society. It can no longer serve to legitimate affluent social power structures. Second, Christian consciousness is itself aware of the trouble with ecclesiastical institutions. Cardinal Lorscheider, at the 1974 synod, made the following observations:

> The present ecclesiastical structure must be analyzed and we must ask whether it can and should be otherwise in our time. . . . We do not know how to create the elements of salvation with the means at our disposal. . . . A deeper theological reflection is called for, a reflection on the relationship between the hierarchy and the laity in the womb of the People of God. The exercise of shared coresponsibility must be thought out, developed, and organized, with reference to specific missions within the pastoral plan of the hierarchy. Lay people today are more sensitive to real participation where decisions are being made. There is the desire to not simply offer suggestions to those who decide but to decide together with them.[26]

Those in the hierarchy who do not understand this *kairos* are not learning the lesson of the signs of the times and so stop working toward the future of the Church. Even with all the good will and pure intentions that we do not deny they have, they are drowning in the attempt to renew a type of Church's presence that is neither evangelical nor responsive to the call of the historical moment. The Church finds itself faced with a new society and with new opportunities for presence. With a view to the present and toward the future, there is no time to sing the praises of the past; the institution has already celebrated them.

5. Faced with a new situation, the Church, in the words of Karl Rahner, "must march valiantly toward the new and not yet experienced, to the outer limits, there where Christian doctrine and conscience can travel no further. In the practical life of the Church today, the only fitting theology is a daring theology. . . . What is certain in this day and age is not the past but the future."[27] Who may dare if not Christians, for they know they are led by the Spirit from truth to truth? As long as it is supported by its past and itself, the Church runs the risk of unfaithfulness to the call of the Lord, present in the world as the risen Christ.

6. To recognize the past history of the Church with its exercise of power is not to reject the institution of the Church. The institution is a concrete reality that makes explicit the Christian mysteries and preaches Jesus Christ as liberator, in spite of all internal contradictions. Every Christian must accept this past without running from it, yet at the same time preventing its continuation in the present and future. To accept the past is not to justify it. We must courageously accept it because it is *our* past as much as we are members of the People of God of which the hierarchical institution is a part. Nor does the past allow us to sit back; rather, it calls us to be coresponsible for the future of Christian faith in the world. The cause of Christ and the People of God is too important to leave to the hierarchy. "The institution is not an evil. We might attribute to it St. Paul's words about law: necessary but alone it is insufficient for good and may even become an occasion for sin for anyone who seeks refuge in it."[28]

Only a true gospel love, which is critical and free, can accept the Church with its limitations and errors, because only through loving it are we converted, thus revealing the fascinating beauty of the Church, the bride of Christ and mother to all peoples.

A Return to the Sources:
The Gospel Meaning of Authority

Everything points to the following conclusion: the goal is one of reform, the need to recreate a model for the institutional Church because the model of power has given all it has to give. The attitude of the institution must be one of conversion with everything that term implies: poverty, rejection of false security, acceptance of the inability to control the future, the challenge of faith, trust, and surrender to the Spirit who was given to the Church not to develop an already received and guaranteed deposit of faith but to guarantee fidelity to its essential element, Jesus Christ, in every confrontation between faith and the world (cf. Matt 10:20; John 15:26; 16:8).

The sources of faith need to be reexamined, no longer with the eyes of those with power but with the eyes of all who have abandoned the perspective of power. In the past, ecclesiastical power read and reread the New Testament (almost only the epistles) for the first signs of thinking in terms of power, orthodoxy, tradition, preservation more than creation, moralizing more than prophetic proclamation. The cause of Christ, of the historical Jesus who was poor, weak, powerless, critical of the social and religious status quo of his time, was enshrined and spiritualized by the institution and so divested of its critical power.

For a Church that seeks a new presence in the world and wants to avoid the structures and pitfalls of yesteryear, a very pure rereading of the central message of Jesus Christ, of the gospel understanding of the structures of power and the importance of the Spirit in the Church, is essential. This will be done below in a general way because I have already developed this more thoroughly elsewhere.[29]

Jesus' Fundamental Project of Liberation and Freedom

Jesus did not preach the Church but rather the Kingdom of God that included liberation for the poor, comfort for those who cry, justice, peace, forgiveness, and love. He did not proclaim an established order; he did not call others to be rulers but to be submissive, humble, and loyal. He liberates for freedom and love that allow one to be submissive yet free, critical, and loyal without being servile, that call those in power to be servants and brothers free from the appetite for greater power. Fraternity, open communication with everyone, solidarity with all people, with the little ones, the least of the earth, sinners and even enemies, goodness, undiscriminating love, unlimited forgiveness are the great ideals put forth by Jesus. He does not introduce or bless privileges that give rise to classes and divisions between persons. The *exousia*, that is, the sovereignty, that appears in his attitudes and words is not power in terms of human power. It is the power of love. If he proclaims that he "was given all power in heaven and on earth" (Matt 28:18) and passes this power on to the apostles, we must understand the nature of that power. It is the power of God.

What is the power of God? It is the power of the Father of our Lord Jesus Christ who showed him to be the Father of infinite goodness, revealing an astounding power of the infinite capacity to support and be patient with human persons, the power to love the "ingrates and evil ones" (Luke 6:35). Power is the power to love. The power of love is different in nature from the power of domination; it is fragile, vulnerable, conquering through its weakness and its capacity for giving and forgiveness. Jesus always demonstrated this *exousia* in his life.[30] He renounced power as domination; he preferred to die in weakness rather than use his power to subjugate people to accept his message. In this way he de-divinized power: he no longer made it proof of his transcendence, rejecting requests for proof of miraculous power (Mark 15:32). It is in weakness that the love of God and the God of love are revealed (1 Cor 1:25; 2 Cor 13:4; Phil 2:7).

Criticism of All Dominating Power

It is from the fundamental project of Jesus and the new way of relating that underlies his message that the criticisms he levies against the power structures in his world are to be understood. "You know how those who rule the nations exercise tyranny over them and they practice violence against them. This is not to be among you: on the contrary, if one of you wishes to be great, he must be your servant; and he who desires to be first among you must serve all; because the Son of Man did not come to be served but to serve and to give his life for the redemption of many" (Mark 10:42–44; Luke 22:25–27). These words were provoked by the disputes about power and privilege among the disciples. "Mark the evangelist judges a disciple, bearer of an ecclesial responsibility, follower and representative of Jesus, with dominating powers within the community, to be irreconcilable with the following of Christ on the cross."[31]

The one who represents Christ and his *exousia* must be a servant just as Jesus was. Without this, one is no different from a pagan tyrant. Matthew is equally against any power/domination within the community: "You shall not be called masters because there is only one Master and all of you are brothers. Nor must you call anyone on earth 'father' because you have one Father who is in heaven. Do not call yourselves doctors because only one is your Doctor, Christ" (23:8–11). It is strange to see that the Church institution has developed into exactly that which Christ did not want it to be: from the will for power, hierarchies of teachers, doctors, fathers, fathers of fathers, and servants of servants have all arisen.

The apostles are the bearers of the *paradosis*, the essence of Christ's message and salvific events; this fact gives them special authority; but that authority is not the basis for any privilege, any domination over others' freedom. They must be the servants of the servants. *Exousia* leads to *diakonia*. To live power as service and as servant is the greatest challenge facing the institutional Church. There are tensions and temptations but no ideology contrary to the Gospel can justify what has happened throughout the history of the Church when members of the hierarchy took on titles, honors, secular and sacred powers, often to satisfy primal instincts for possession and self-aggrandizement.

The *exousia* of the apostles, yesterday and today, is not only a diaconal authority of preaching and transmitting the message but also of building up and defending the community. Paul is conscious of the "authority that the Lord gave me to build and not to destroy" (2 Cor 13:10). He is not afraid to conflict with the community and in order to defend it (not punish it) he feels the need to cut off certain members from it (1 Cor 5:3–5). But he never forgets the diaconal sense of his authority: "We do not want to dominate your faith but to contribute to your joy" (2 Cor 1:24; 13:10).[32]

These considerations are extremely important for the functions of unity and government in the ecclesial community. The one in these positions, in relation with the universal Church and in continuity with its history, has legitimate authority. This authority, however, is empty if it is not supported by the example of the humble, poor, weak, and servant Jesus. This authority must be exercised diaconally, like Jesus, full of respect between brothers and sisters and not between lords and subordinates.

Ecclesiastical authority often seeks its legitimation in Christ's words, preserved by Luke: "Whoever hears you hears me, and whoever rejects you rejects me, and whoever rejects me rejects the one who sent me" (10:16). This saying is the missionary commission given to the seventy-two disciples. This missionary context is important for a proper understanding of the text. In mission, people are confronted with the newness of Jesus' message that is not one of power, spectacular revolutionary goals, but one of conversion, love, forgiveness, universal reconciliation, and so on. It is the proclamation of a message that contradicts established human situations and values. The individual is called to conversion. The Gospel is critic and judge of human actions. A conflict arises; some reject the message as well as its messengers. This passage, consequently, speaks of the encounter between the Gospel and the world, and does not regulate the relations between hierarchy and the community of believers. The faithful are also sent out, so these words are also meant for them. To take this text as an argument— whoever rejects anything of the representative of Christ (the hierarchy) rejects Christ himself—would be to use it in an inter-ecclesiastical and juridical sense unforeseen by its missionary context.[33] If the missionary announces Christ and his mystery rather than the individual and the institution, and the missionary is rejected, then he or she will know, as all will know, that it is Christ himself that has not been accepted. This is not the rejection of propositions but the rejection of the one who is evangelizer and proclaimer of the salvation of all people.

The actions of the humanity of Jesus Christ must remain as the critical norm for the Church built upon them. The concrete and consequent living out of this meaning of authority as service would certainly make the Church a place of liberty, fraternity, and open communication between all people, between those charged with the unity of the community and all of its members. The Church would then be the symbol of true liberation and freedom rather than of alienation within a closed and centralized system that excommunicates those who differ with it, sometimes using phrases usually reserved for morally depraved and criminal people.

Ecclesiogenesis: The New Church Born of the Old

Meditating on the Gospels and with a theological reading of the signs of the times, a significant portion of the Church as institution has understood the current challenges for Christian faith and responsibly tries to respond to them. We are seeing the rising of a new Church, born in the heart of the old Church, in the form of *comunidades de base*, communities on the peripheries of our cities, a Church of the poor, comprised of poor people, in the form of bishops, priests, and religious entering into the life of the marginalized, centers of evangelization headed by lay people, and so on.[34] It is a Church that has definitively renounced the centralization of power; unity resides in the idea of Church as People of God, a pilgrim Church, open to the historical march of peoples, a Church that shares in all the risks and enjoys the small victories with a very deep sense of following Jesus Christ, identified with the poor, the rejected, and the disinherited of the earth. This Church is being built day by day, open to new ministries answering the needs of the community and responding to all human life and not just culture, a Church involved in the working world and living out the meaning and joy of the resurrection in the heart of the secular world.

Today we are witnessing a true ecclesiogenesis precisely where the institutional structure shows the most visible signs of disrepair. The Gospel is no longer tied to a classic and consecrated presentation that was inherited from an institutionally glorious past but rather it is being lived as a movement, creating structures that are more in tune with the present. This new way of being Church understands that it does not exist for itself; it is to be a sign of Christ for the world and the place where the Spirit is explicitly active. A sign does not exist for itself but for others. The Church as sign is *from* Christ *for* the world. It never judges itself to be complete but always returns to what it should be, that is, the sacrament of Christ and of the Spirit. The Church thus bubbles with an inner, creative, and self-critical dynamic, with a heart that is sensitive to the presence of the risen Christ and his grace in the world, even before its proclamation of the Gospel.

This new Church, as in all renewal movements, first appears on the periphery. Given the power structure at the center, the periphery is the only place where true creativity and freedom is possible. Faith is born and made present through personal witness; it is not being watched over by the institution. Thus, there is the opportunity for a pure and evangelical authenticity not found within the institution with its bureaucratic preoccupations and its time and energy spent to justify, defend, preserve, and expand its structures.

It is to be expected that the old Church will distrust the new Church on the periphery with its gospel freedoms. It will call it a parallel Church, with its own magisterium, disobedient and disloyal to the center! The new Church will have to be careful to develop intelligent strategies and tactics; it must not be drawn into the center's game of condemnation and suspicion. It will have to be evangelical and understand that the institution can do nothing else but make use of a language that safeguards its own power, that the institution fears any withdrawal from its dictates, viewing such as disloyalty. The new Church will have to remain faithful to its path. It will have to be loyally disobedient. It will have to seek a profound loyalty to the demands of the Gospel; it will also have to listen to the old Church's questioning of the truth of its interpretation of the Gospels. Critically reflecting upon these questions and convinced of its path, it must have the courage to be disobedient to the demands of the center, without anger or complaint, in deep adherence to the desire to be faithful to the Lord, the gospels, and the Spirit—the same desire that is presumed to motivate the institutional Church. This is the root of basic communion. Gospel purity awakens the institution to the Spirit that cannot be channeled along the lines of human interests. For the new Church, its openness to communion with everyone and its attempts at avoiding even the slightest possibility of a break that could destroy unity and charity—though this may lead to isolation, persecution, and condemnation by the institution—is the guarantee of its Christian authenticity inspired by the Gospel.

The future of the institutional Church lies in this small seed that is the new Church growing in the fields of the poor and powerless. It will be an alternative for the incarnation of new ecclesial institutions whose power will be pure service. The papacy, the episcopacy, and the presbyterate will not lose their evangelical ideals of strengthening the brothers and sisters in faith, of being the principal of unity and reconciliation in the community, of being religious leaders able to interpret the meaning of events and desires of all people, especially those of the poor, according to the light of the mystery of Christ. Andrew Greeley describes the function of the papacy in this new situation:

> The pope must, by his personal posture, by the sorts of questions he asks, by the atmosphere he creates in the Church and, last but not least, by the effectiveness of his administration, see that the Christian Church becomes more of the light on the mountain top that it was destined to be—a light bearing witness to the Christian conviction that God is a God of love and that this love is proclaimed by the quality of relationships that men have with one another. . . . He should be the most open, the most loving, the most trusting of all Christians. His confidence in the Christian commitment, his openness to all men, his joy over the Good News, and his trust in

the work of the Spirit must be *transparent*; they must shine forth in his words, in his actions, and in his whole style of leadership. The papacy which is occupied by a man of such transparent convictions will necessarily and inevitably be the most influential leadership position in the world.[35]

What applies to the papacy applies, mutatis mutandis, to lower levels, for example, bishops, priests, and other ministers or leaders charged with the unity and direction of a community. In the main, the past few Popes have approximated these ideal characteristics.

Sara Has Conceived

Can the Church be converted to a more vibrant witness of the Gospel in our world today? It can, because it is happening. But it must renounce a certain type of power. By virtue of its vocation, the Church exists for a future Kingdom and so must proclaim its own provisory character. Its true identity is not in a past that it often vainly tries to restore but in a future that still is to be revealed. If change and human development prepares for and anticipates the Kingdom, as the Council teaches (*Gaudium et Spes*, 34, 39), how much more must change in the Church also prepare and anticipate the new heaven and new earth![36] The "peace of order," stagnation in fixed models, obstinate repetition of past statements compromise the true dimension of openness to the future and eschatological hope proper to Christian faith and instead causes us to forget our condition as pilgrims and strangers on our way to the dynamic rest of God.[37] The Church will be a sign of liberation and will enter into the struggle for liberation with all peoples only insofar as it is converted and becomes more and more an incarnation of the Gospel.

Perhaps the institutional Church, with the experience and prudence of all older people, will smile upon hearing these reflections—like old Sara. She was sterile and believed it impossible for her to conceive. She smiles. Putting ourselves in Abraham's place, we hear God's question: "Why has Sara smiled? Is anything impossible for God?" (Gen 18:14). Smile, Sara, because once sterile you have become fertile, you have become a new creation! Sara has already conceived. There, in Sara's womb, the signs of new life are already beginning to appear: a new Church is being born, in the dark recesses of humanity.

Chapter 6

ROMAN CATHOLICISM:
STRUCTURE, HEALTH, PATHOLOGIES

Catholicism is a theological giant as well as a concretization of the Gospel in history. It is also a historical, political, sociological, and religious reality. As such, it can be analyzed by the various academic and scientific disciplines. Every interpretation is legitimate because it deals with real aspects of Catholicism, but also limited because it is restricted by its own perspective.

From the many possible analyses of Catholicism, the following will be a theological anlysis and interpretation, utilizing the grammar of theological discourse. As important and necessary as this may be, it too is limited. Open to other perspectives, it is an attempt to contribute, from its own perspective, to a better understanding of the complex phenomenon that is Catholicism.

Stages in the Formation of the Question

In the history of theological ideas and ecclesiological controversies, the question "What is Catholicism?" is linked primarily to the Reformation and to the exegetical-historical discussions within Protestant circles in the last century.[1] "Catholic" was considered synonymous with decay and decline. Ernst Troeltsch coined the technical expression *Frühkatholizismus*, primitive Catholicism, to express the decline of the Gospel already evident in the first communities of the New Testament.[2] Later Catholicism was to be built upon this decline.

Catholicism itself did not pose the question. Nor did it feel the need to do so. For the complacent Catholic faith, it was enough to know that what existed was historically continuous with the Gospel and the primitive Church. The rise of Protestantism, questioning this continuity and making the accusation of the deterioration of the Gospel, forced Catholicism to reflect on its identity.

65

Protestantism: A Preconcept in Search of a Concept

The question of the meaning of Catholicism was put forth by Protestants with regard to the legitimacy of their break with Catholicism. They said that the Church of Rome pretends to be the true Church of Christ because it is in continuity with the primitive Church. Luther, in his work *Against Hans Worst* (1541), attempted to show that he and his movement were in perfect continuity with the ancient Church.[3] Therefore, the pretensions of Catholicism were illegitimate, a thesis tantamount to apostasy. This thesis, detailed in the great historical work *Historia Ecclesiae Christi*, published between 1559 and 1574 by a team of authors under the direction of Matthias Flacius Illyricus, consecrated the theory of decay.[4]

The rise of Catholicism occurred from the time of Christ to the first millennium. The reformers believed they were in communion with the Church of the first millennium. For them it was only in the Middle Ages that Catholicism rose as the decline of the true Church. Later, Protestantism pushed back the appearance of Catholicism to the conversion of Constantine; thus, they were in line with the Church of the first three centuries. Harnack established the beginning of Catholicism at the beginning of the second century: "The struggle against gnosticism obliged the Church to fix its doctrine, liturgy, and discipline in formulas and rigid laws and to exclude all who refused to obey it. If we identify as 'Catholic' a Church of doctrines and laws, then it arose in the struggle against gnosticism."[5] In the present century, certain Protestant scholars have even extended the rise of Catholicism to the New Testament. According to them the preoccupation with right doctrine, ecclesial discipline, and the transmission of power, found in the pastoral epistles, demonstrates the unavoidable presence of incipient Catholicism. Others go even further. For example, Haenchen, Conzelmann, Vielhauer, Käsemann, Marxsen, and others do not doubt the presence of Catholicism in Luke and Matthew's gospels. Käsemann says: "Primitive Catholicism in the New Testament stems from the fact that the second coming [of the Son of Man] was no longer awaited. In its place came ecclesiology."[6] The argument contends that this is clear in Luke as well as Matthew. The gospels themselves, as theological expressions of the primitive communities, point to Catholicism because the message, the doctrines, admonitions, and disciplinary measures are fixed there.

Others are even more radical in tracing the rise of Catholicism. They locate it in Jesus Christ himself. He also translated the revelation he received from the Father into a linguistically fixed message, with a determined content, using parallels taken from the surrounding culture. If by "Catholic" we understand the historical, juridical, ideological, social, and other means in which and by which Christianity as the salvation of sinners is made concrete, then we must say that it can be found in the very words and actions of Jesus of Nazareth.

Behind this confessional and polemical question—when did Catholicism arise?—a grave hermeneutical problem of Christian faith is hidden. How does one reconcile the absoluteness of its pretension to continuity with the relativity of its historical approaches? How does one understand the word of God made concrete in human words? How does one find the Gospel within the four gospels? How does one confess the one and same faith within the pluralism of Christian theologies and confessions?

The root of Catholicism is as old as the Church. Adolf Harnack, the great scholar on the history of the first centuries, tackled the problem of the rise of Catholicism.[7] According to him, Catholicism was the result of many forces that slowly converged at the end of the first century. The first force was that of Judaism, present in the way in which the primitive Christian communities were organized juridically in a familial and patriarchal structure. The primitive Church felt it was the heir to the People of God of the Old Testament, a juridically organized community. The law of the People of God was a divine law; thus, law was considered to be divine in the primitive Christian communities. Harnack concludes: "Catholicism as such, in embryonic form, is as old as the Church; it is difficult to find the lack of any of its elements in it."[8]

But if the divine law constituted the essence of later Catholicism, it was still not so for primitive Christianity. The charismatic still dominated over the juridical element inherited from Judaism. Thus, the charismatic structure was another force, personified in the apostles and itinerant prophets. The charismatics died in the second century and the communities were left to leaders who were responsible for order. Because of external circumstances, such as Montanism, a Catholic confederation was created. This gave rise to the notion of apostolic succession that marginalized the charismatic structure of the communities. The bishops, as successors of the apostles, held all religious power and so shaped what would later characterize Catholicism.

Catholicism reached its completion with the third great formative force, Hellenism, with its masterpiece known as dogma, the marrow of the Roman Church. Hellenism is commonly understood as the intellectualization of Christianity resulting from the encounter between the Judeo-Christian message and Greek philosophy. Harnack observes, "Dogma is in its conception and construction the work of the Greek spirit on the terrain of the Gospel."[9] The essence of Catholicism, according to Harnack's definition, is "as much the transformation of Christian faith into revealed doctrine, made up of philosophical-Hellenistic ideals and historical elements, confirmed by the apostles and ratified in power through the sacrament of orders, thus becoming tradition, as it is the identification of the Church of Christ with the empirical Church, the juridical body, led by the apostolic *episcopus.*"[10]

In Harnack's definition, historical elements are mixed with theological elements from the Protestant perspective. From that perspective, Catholicism means the divinization of tradition without recognizing that it is the result of historical development realized by human beings. Christianity is what is divine and true; law, discipline, and doctrinal elements come from that.

Catholicism arose and had to arise out of necessity. Rudolf Sohm, a noted canon lawyer and historian, argued with Harnack[11] and posed the problem in such terms that even today it provokes arguments among ecclesiologists and canon lawyers.[12] Sohm contested Harnack's statement that the presence of a divine law inherited from Judaism existed in the primitive Church. The Church understood itself, in Sohm's view, as *mysterium* or *sacramentum* and as the body of Christ and not as the continuation of the Old Testament People of God. Everything that the community did was understood mystically as the action of the risen Christ who acted through it. There were no sacraments in the modern sense of gestures that communicate grace.[13] Everything was sacramental and an instrument of Christ's activity in his body which is the Church. Why, then, did the seven sacraments and the right to exercise them arise? Sohm answers that they came about and had to come about "from dire necessity."[14] The community had begun to grow. From the body of Christ it became a corporation of Christians. Needs proper to a corporation arose, such as the desire and anxiety for certainty. Faith in the Gospel gave way to faith in divine law. This is how Catholicism irrupted on the historical scene.

> With the rise of divine (Catholic) law, two things came about: *first*, the formal principle of Catholicism, that is, the identification of the visible Church (juridically organized) with Church in the religious sense (Ecclesia). *Second*, the material principle of Catholicism, redemption (justification) achieved through the sacraments (from the Church and priest), juridically determined. Administered they communicate grace, denied they impede it.[15]

Catholicism is thus a human and historical construct, according to Sohm. It is no longer the Church in a theological sense as a creation of the Spirit.[16] The life of Catholicism is part of the life of people with people. The life of the Church, on the other hand, is the spiritual life, the life of the faithful through Christ with God. There is a lot of confusion on the relationship between these "two churches" but the difference between them must be made clear.[17] "The essence of the Church is in contradiction to the essence of law. The Church, in virtue of its essence, cannot tolerate an ecclesial law."[18] The essence of Catholicism consists "in that it does not make the distinction between the Church in a religious sense (Church of Christ) and the Church in a juridical sense. . . . The presence of the distinction represents the Protestant principle, the absence of the distinction represents the Catholic principle."[19]

Sohm touches the heart of the question but abstains from exploring how it came about and how the juridical, doctrinal, and institutional dimensions of the Church should be theologically treated alongside the spiritual (that is, of the Holy Spirit) and transcendent dimensions. It is not enough to contrast them and create two churches. It is necessary—and this is the real problem—to study their relationship. Neither Sohm nor Harnack have contributed to this question. They go no further than a dogmatic affirmation of Protestant tradition: the juridical Church, Catholicism, is the decay and perversion of the Church of the Gospel.

Sohm recognizes, nevertheless, that the law had a positive aspect because it allowed the historical survival of the Church, although it is at the same time the Church's "original sin" and a falsification of Christ's message.[20]

Catholicism is the concrete and historical form of Christianity. In his book *The Social Teaching of the Christian Churches*, Troeltsch dedicates almost one hundred pages to the question of primitive Catholicism.[21] He strongly disagrees with the separation between Catholicism and Christianity made by Sohm and Harnack. Christianity is not an abstract idea. It has always called itself the holy, catholic, and apostolic Church. The essence of Christianity must be sought in this fact and not on some empty, ahistorical level.[22] Troeltsch also argues with Protestant tradition in light of a similar idea. For him, the ancient Church is based on three great pillars: the Gospel, Pauline theology, and primitive Catholicism. These three elements are not chronological but are the principal elements of the organization of the concrete Church. The organization is identified by its religious character and not some social or political ideal. No matter what form the Church may assume, its religious aspect remains. However, it has not always maintained this identity. The distinction made between *ius divinum* and *ius humanum*, divine law and human law, secularized the Church and handed it over to the dynamics of organization.[23] It decayed into a political and no longer specifically religious force. This tendency can be noted even at the beginning of the primitive Church.

The merit of Troeltsch's study lies in having placed the problem in its true hermeneutical context: what concretely exists is not Christianity but Catholicism. Christianity cannot be found outside of history. It only exists in its historical concretizations. Therefore, the distinction between Gospel and Catholicism must not lead to their hypostasis and opposition.

The entire New Testament is primitive Catholicism. The discussion on primitive Catholicism was profoundly modified by the new exegetical methods and the knowledge they made possible. Through form criticism and redaction criticism, the immense theological work beneath the "simple" gospels was brought to light. The Gospel of Jesus Christ is not readily apparent. It is found in four versions, traditions, and theologies. Using the language of both Sohm and Harnack, they should be characterized as Catholic because they are the fruit of a doctrinal, catechetical, and liturgical translation of the Gospel for the conditions and needs of the various Christian communities. Thus, the presence of Catholicism in the four gospels and the entire New Testament is easy to accept.

But then, where is the Gospel of the word of life to be found? The ideas of Joachim Jeremias and others are well known. The Gospel is sought with rigorous historical-exegetical methods to determine the *ipsissima facta et verba Jesu*, the very deeds and words of Jesus. This is what is evangelical; all else is Catholic, that is, interpretation and translation.

However, such an attempt is impossible. On the one hand, we run the risk of making the authentic message of Jesus dependent upon the criteria of historians and exegetes; various messages result from their varied opinions. On the other hand, there is an unavoidable hermeneutical problem: even though the *ipsissima facta et verba* may be historically identified, this is still not the message of Jesus because he interpreted and symbolically translated his messianic message according to the culture of his time. So, hermeneutically, this too should be considered as Catholic and not Gospel.

Other scholars have followed a different path in the search for a canon within the canon.[24] One must be able to identify the Gospel beneath the gospels. That is true revelation which links us to God, the message revealed to the world. Everything else is theological interpretation. The question as to what is Catholicism stems from the fundamental question as to what is the Gospel, the message, the cause of Christ, and what is that one thing without which we lose our relationship to our own salvation. This is the canon within the canon. It cannot be a phrase, a text, or a nucleus of truths for then it would be a historical, cultural, worldly approximation and not the Gospel. The Gospel lives in history and reaches individuals in an incarnated and multiform reality. It cannot be separated from these forms. The Gospel comes together with the gospels, Christianity with Catholicism.

What then is the Gospel, Jesus' cause, the necessary element? We cannot say what it is in categorical terms because, linguistically, the identification of essence is not essential but categorical. The Gospel must be identified within each of its historical Christian forms. As Ernst Käsemann asserts: "The Bible is not the word of God in an objective sense, nor is it the system of a doctrine of faith. It is the result of the history and preaching of primitive Christianity. The Church that canonized the Bible affirms nevertheless that the Church itself becomes the herald of the Gospel."[25] However, it only becomes the true herald of the Gospel insofar as it places itself in reference to the living Christ and is saved by him. The Bible is a Catholic product and only serves this salvific encounter with the living Christ.

With these later considerations, the problem of Catholicism was completely transformed from a pejorative sense to a fundamental one. Catholic means mediation. The Gospel is the reference that this mediation maintains with the living Christ who is accepted and lived as savior. Thus, the historical problem of the birth of Catholicism and its elements (law, traditions, sacraments, etc.) disappears and the hermeneutical question takes over. On this level, Catholics are as "catholic" as Protestants because both are related to the same mediation.

Willi Marxsen, in his work *Primitive Catholicism in the New Testament*,[26] is conscious of the shift and affirms that what characterizes primitive (and later) Catholicism are not any specific statements in the New Testament or even a specific type of writing (Catholic epistles) but rather a dogmatic reading of the texts themselves.[27] This dogmatic approach, without taking into account the historical mediations, asserts that the New Testament is nothing less than the word of God. It utilizes the texts dogmatically to justify doctrines and disciplinary measures in the Church. As such, Catholicism acquires a pejorative connotation as a pathological way of living and understanding the Christian message. However, this tendency is found among Protestants as well as Catholics.

Catholicism: From Pathology to the Search for Normalcy

After having considered the Protestant treatment of the question of what is Catholicism, it is time to turn to the Catholic position. As we have already seen, Catholics *in iure possessionis* (with right of possession) did not sense the need to seek a self-identity that would distinguish them from those who argued against them. They did not act but merely re-acted. Instead of accepting the challenge to deepen their understanding of the relationship of Gospel and history, Christ and Church, salvation and sacraments, they stubbornly affirmed what they already had. Thus, Catholic came to mean conservative, traditionalistic, and reactionary. There was no effort to explore theologically and deepen what they treasured. They forgot that their mediation was a mere mediation; it was presented as something divine, evangelical, and apostolic, and they demanded that it be believed. It is true that everything that refers to the divine, to Christ, and to the apostles is in some way apostolic, Christian, and divine. But it is not so directly or we would be in the immediate presence of the divine in a sort of theophany. It is only divine obliquely inasmuch as the mediation makes the divine or evangelical present in and through it. But official pride won out and gave rise to the post-Tridentine manuals of dogma that persisted until the Second Vatican Council.

The Church presented itself in the following way. Before ascending to heaven, Christ left the Church completely organized with its structures, doctrine, ministries, and sacraments. The Church's task was to keep everything pure. The Church had to remain unalterable in history. It was to be the direct line to the encounter with the Lord in the parousia. Its evolution is linear and its growth simply horizontal. All possible future development is already contained in Christ's commission to the apostles, in Scripture and in tradition. Thus, a specific historical form of the Church from a particular time was justified theologically and consecrated for all times. Everything was instituted by Christ. As Johann Adam Möhler said, "For them, God created the hierarchy. And for the Church, this was more than enough to guarantee it until the end of time."[28]

It is proper to ideology to present as natural what is historical and to present as divine what is human. This is how the human gains an unquestionable value that is imposed on everyone and the historical takes on an element of domination. Therefore, we can speak of the pathological aspect of Catholicism in its capacity for becoming an element for human oppression.

The search for theological normalcy: The evolution of Catholic reflection is based on the continuing destruction of the notion of the Church as issuing forth complete and fully formed from the savior's hands.[29] Historical and exegetical studies have given evidence for the historical evolution of the Church and Catholic dogma. Protestant studies, in particular, have been of undeniable help. However, Catholic research has also been able to demonstrate the same case, above all the writings of Cardinal Newman.

The first Catholic scholar to demonstrate a sensitivity to the problem was Johann Adam Möhler in his book *The Unity of the Church or the Principle of Catholicism*, published in 1825. The author shows developments and forms of the Church in the first three centuries that do not justify a simple explanation for its development. There were historical transformations and novelty. He goes on to demonstrate that the Catholic principle is not characterized by a uniform unalterability of forms but by unity *in* the Church preserved in a plurality of variations. Because of this, Möhler speaks of unity *in* the Church and not unity *of* the Church.

Following from this, it is clear that the existing Church is not only a gift from on high but also the historical construction of a people of faith in dialogue with the surrounding world. Hence, the importance of decision as a constitutive principle of the Church. Erik Peterson, a well-known Protestant theologian and a disciple of Harnack, converted to Catholicism after affirming that the Church exists solely due to the fact that the Jews rejected

Christ and the parousia had been delayed. He could thus formulate the third thesis of his famous essay "The Church": "The Church exists only because of the fact that the twelve apostles, called by the Holy Spirit, decided in the light of the same Holy Spirit to go among the Gentiles."[30] In a very real way, the Church owes its appearance to the decision of the apostles: "It seemed to the Holy Spirit and to us. . . ." (Acts 15:28). Joseph Ratzinger accepted Peterson's theses in his own ecclesiology and states: "The power of decision and dogma belongs to the Church; it begins to exist from a faith in this power and without it becomes totally incomprehensible. All of its biblical tradition is the expression of this faith because Jesus' words were not preserved as relics but because they were part of the Church's actual situation and as such were they interpreted."[31] Peterson is even more emphatic: "A Church without apostolic ecclesial law, without the ability to make dogmatic decisions cannot be called Church."[32]

Heinrich Schlier, another exegete who left Protestantism for Catholicism, also claims that one of the principles of Catholicism, perhaps the most basic, is that of *decision*.[33] God made the decision for Jesus Christ and this divine decision is externalized in word and sacrament in the Church. The Church lives in the measure that it continually decides to accept the divine decision in confronting the decisive challenges of history. It is in this way that Christian faith is constantly incarnated in the world, in ideas, ideologies, and customs.[34] Christian faith does not exist in itself but as a theology or understanding of the world from within ecclesial institutions. The New Testament is the preaching of the Church; it is the product of dogma, liturgy, catechesis, hymnology, and theological traditions and trends in the primitive communities. Catholicism today continues what was started in the New Testament.

The problem of Catholicism is an ecclesiological one: The question regarding Catholicism flows into the ecclesiological one. Is Christianity possible without historical mediation? In other words, can we think of Christianity apart from its appearances in history? The concretization of Christianity in history is called "Catholicism" and "Church." Then, how must we think of Church? The invisible and spiritual Church of Christ on the one hand and the different visible ecclesial forms, human products, on the other can no longer answer the question. The Church is always the concrete and living unity of the divine and the human, of faith and history. The question becomes even more crucial considering the current ecclesiological and ecumenical debates about the relationship between Christ and the Church. Was Jesus thinking of founding a Church organized with ecclesial structures? Or was the complicated structure of the Church born as the historical result of the encounter of many factors, for example, Jesus' message about the Kingdom, certain eschatological structures (the Twelve) present in his actions, his death and resurrection, the delay of the parousia, the coming of the Gentiles to the faith, and so on?

In Catholicism today there are two basic currents of thought: one, more dogmatic, affirms the presence of the Church in the proclamation of the Kingdom and in Jesus' dealings with the Twelve, such that it claims a certain continuity that overcomes the gap created by his death and the destruction of the first communities. The other trend, based on exegetical studies and with a more historical vision, tends to affirm that Jesus did not have in mind the Church as institution but rather that it evolved after the resurrection, particularly as part of the process of de-eschatologization. This perspective dominates the work of theologians such as Rudolf Schnackenburg,[35] Josef Blanck,[36] and Anton Vögtle[37] in the field of biblical exegesis as well as Erik Peterson,[38] Joseph Ratzinger,[39] Hans Küng,[40] and myself[41] in systematic theology.

This perspective sees the Church, as a historical reality, as synonymous with Catholicism. The Church, or Catholicism, is the translation of the Gospel for the concrete life of those who believe, just as the four gospels and the preaching of the apostles was a translation. Church and Catholicism are the results of the actualization of the Gospel in all areas of human life. The question becomes one of understanding the Church that incarnates the Gospel in the world. Gospel, properly understood, is not synonymous with Church. But, neither can it be understood apart from the Church.

Conclusion: Catholicism and the Gospel— Are They the Same?

The systematic questions that have arisen in the history of this problem can be summarized as follows:

1. Catholicism did not come about as the decay of something that, historically, was previously pure and crystal clear, that is, the message of Jesus, the Gospel. Catholicism appeared as a principle of the incarnation of Christianity in history. Catholicism is the mediation of Christianity.

2. The basic question is the understanding of this mediation. On the one hand, it is the Gospel made concrete; on the other, it is not the Gospel. There is a historical identity with the Gospel because it does not exist apart from mediation; it is only through mediation that it is made present in the world. On the other hand, the Gospel is not mediation in that it is not the texts of the four gospels nor is it at the same level as the texts. The Gospel is the impetus and structuring force of Catholicism, the life that creates the structures, the statements and the skeleton that manifest life, living that life but not identified with it. Conscious of this, Catholicism is able to be open and self-transcendent, making room for other possible mediations of

the Gospel. For example, the Roman, Catholic, and apostolic Church is the Church of Christ on the one hand, and on the other, it is not. It is the Church of Christ inasmuch as through it the Church of Christ is present in the world. But at the same time it cannot claim an exclusive identity with the Church of Christ because the Church may also be present in other Christian churches. The Second Vatican Council, overcoming a theological ambiguity present in previous ecclesiologies that tended to identify the Roman Catholic Church with the Church of Christ in a simple and pure fashion, makes the following distinction: "This Church [of Christ], constituted and organized in the world as a society, subsists in the Catholic Church" (*subsistit in*: has its concrete form in the Catholic Church).[42] The Council avoids saying, as was said in previous documents, that it *is* the Church of Christ.

3. Given both the identity and nonidentity of the Church and the Gospel, two styles of Christian life are possible: one enthusiastically accepts historical mediations because they make present the Gospel, Jesus, and his cause. The other will constantly criticize all mediations because it cannot see either the living Gospel or the living Christ in them; rather, it sees only human constructs and so continually seeks the greater purity of the Divine. Both styles of living the Christian faith are grounded in the problem of identity and nonidentity of the Church with the Gospel, of Catholicism with Christianity. Pathologies occur in both cases when either identity or nonidentity is emphasized to the exclusion of the other half of the equation. This seems to be at the root of the problem between Catholicism and Protestantism. What separates them is not so much differing doctrines as different ways of living Christianity.

The Authority of Primitive Catholicism

The above arguments have led to the statement that the entire New Testament as a book is a book of the Church, the historical product of the incarnation of Jesus' message in various cultural circles of the time. This book teaches not only theological doctrines but also the diversity of life in the primitive communities with their ministries and ecclesial structures. It is primitive Catholicism. Epistemologically, it does not differ from later Catholicism. But the Christian churches granted it inalienable authority over other incarnations of the Christian message. It became the indisputable reference for them.

How is this authority to be understood? The answer is not a simple one. There are certain undeniable facts: first, the variations in the message that was translated into four different versions with diverse traditions and ways of choosing, distributing, and presenting the material; second, the multiplicity of theological currents in the synoptic gospels and other New Testament writings; third, the irreducibility of some theological positions: there are contradictions between Matthew and the letter to the Galatians as well as between the letter to the Romans and that of James. There are contradictions within the Pauline corpus itself, for example, between Romans 7:12 and Galatians 3:13 with respect to the value of Judaic law. Yet all of them are contained in the same canon. Therefore, for example, Ernst Käsemann concludes that *historically,* on the level of textual analysis, the New Testament and its diversity of confessions does not ground the unity of the Church.[43] It is not enough for a confession to seek its justification in some New Testament text. The New Testament must be viewed in its totality and not in any one of its many testimonies. The unity of the Church is a theological reality based on hearing and obedience to the one Gospel of Jesus Christ, something beyond the gospel texts. Faith is the determining factor, not history.

The text of the New Testament has special authority not because it is a text but because it is the *first* witness-text of those who were the first witnesses to the word of life. The text, as text, does not have authority except that of the message that it transmits. The message is historically tied to the text which is the key for deciphering the message. Without the witness-text we would lose all historical access to the message and to Jesus who lived among us. Faith, as a historical force, is linked to these first texts but not bound by them. It will continue to read and reread them, interpret and reinterpret them according to current situations and questions. In this way, the message springs forth in a new incarnation, producing the impact of faith experienced by the first witnesses.

The content of the texts also has special authority. The content, like the texts themselves, is linked to culture and history, and so shares historical limits. However, it also serves as a key for deciphering the message, for the reflection that will make clear the veiled truth of Jesus Christ, his liberating message and the salvific event of God-among-us. The Church must have the courage to set dogma for the communitarian formulation of the message that it has understood in faith, lives in love, and witnesses to in hope. It can and must also have the courage to denounce those formulations it judges to be incapable of describing the liberating message of Jesus. Thus, Paul could say that it was impossible to be in communion with the gnostics of I Corinthians; also impossible with the Judaizers who had not understood the newness of Christianity. But the content itself, as representations and not as keys for deciphering the message, cannot be dogmatized and so exclude later history from the task of creating new keys. Dogmatic assertion is legitimate and necessary because of the threat of heresy and perversion of the Christian experience. But it is only a tool that is valid for a specific time and specific circumstances. When the temporal and historical aspect is forgotten and there is the attempt to make it valid for all times, it becomes an impediment to new and equally necessary incarnations of Christianity. The obligation of dogma is linked to the truth that is proclaimed and not to the mode of proclamation.

The text has authority only in the first step of a broader process that gives access to the message. In the later stages of the process, the text must be able to give way to a new text of faith proper to today's world. The text of primitive Catholicism preserves its authority as the first apostolic text, as reference point for all other texts, but it should not be considered as exclusive or as the only possible one in history.

The fact that the New Testament accepts a plurality of theologies and doctrinal positions, even contradictory ones, must be taken seriously. All are contained in one and the same canon and in the one Church itself. This attitude is the basis for living Christian faith. The common reference and desire to be faithful to the single message of Jesus Christ as liberator is what is decisive, and not doctrine (which is only a part of the dialectical process). This attitude is an ongoing call to Catholicism to avoid closing itself in by the glory of its victories or by the brilliance of some newly discovered formulation of doctrine. "Who is Apollo? Who is Paul? Servants through whom you received the faith. And each one is a servant in the measure that God gives to each one.... As for the foundation, no one can offer any other foundation than that which I have offered, which is Jesus Christ" (1 Cor 3:5–11).

What is the truly Catholic attitude? It is to be fundamentally open to everything without exception, something that the New Testament encourages. To be authentically Catholic is to be free and open to the totality of the Gospel.[44] Pathological Catholicism is to follow exclusively certain paths or to hold to only certain currents that express faith. This pathology is evident as much in Roman Catholicism as in Protestantism, as well as in other forms of the incarnated Christian message.

The Identity of Catholicism

The previous reflections have affirmed that Catholicism is a principle of the incarnation of Christianity. It is the historical concretization of the Gospel. It is the objectification of Christian faith.

Primarily, to be Catholic implies an *affirmative* attitude of one who accepts this concretization, embraces the objectification, and affirms a specific path because the individual wants to be Christian. No one can be Christian apart from the world, without words or gestures, without community, without a vital reference point. To be a Christian one must have the courage to accept not only the provisional and historical but also dogma, law, morality, and liturgical discipline. A living being cannot exist without some kind of skeleton. Thus, if a person wants to live as a Christian, one must accept the structures without which there can be no concretization. Limits and structures give rise to feelings of constraint and oppression but if one does not accept these feelings, one cannot enjoy the freedom of the Gospel that creates optimism, the courage to be, and the fullness of the presence of Christianity. There is identity. To be Christian one must be "catholic" in the sense of accepting structures and common references.

Secondarily, to be Catholic implies a *negative* attitude in that objectification is denied and the previously travelled path bypassed, because one wants to be authentically Christian. There is no pure and simple identity between Christianity and Catholicism, between faith and doctrine. The present concretization is only a mediation and as such it hides as well as makes present. It creates a path but also closes off other possibilities. Christianity is a spring that cannot be completely contained within one channel. It is a root that produces more than a single stem and one blossom. It is open. There is room for criticism, for the anger of nonbeing, of absence, of nonidentity. Christianity is not denied in the negative sense but its nonidentification with Christianity is affirmed with a view toward improvement and openness to new ways of doing things. To say yes to one thing, one must say no to others.

Catholicism is, then, a dialectic of affirming both identity and nonidentity. The two affirmations are linked to the concretization of Christianity. To be authentically Christian one must courageously affirm and fearlessly deny in the same dialectical process.

What is the dialectical process that characterizes Catholicism which results in its identity? It must be a category that maintains the unity of the dialectical process and yet also contains the distinction between identity and nonidentity, a category that arises out of the history of the process itself. The term, or category, is that of *sacramentum*.[45] Catholicism is the *sacramentum* of what is Christian.

Sacramentum is one of the oldest words which Catholicism uses to describe itself. It is the translation of the Greek word *mysterion*. *Sacramentum* expresses the basic law of the economy of salvation. Grace does not come like a bolt out of the blue but rather passes through the corporality of this world in order for God to encounter humanity. All of the Christian mysteries are sacramental mysteries because they are communicated and made present through human or cosmic mediation.[46] The Holy Trinity itself is a sacramental mystery in that it was concretely revealed in the historical passage of Jesus Christ.

Identity is affirmed through the sacrament: grace is present in the mediation, the parousia of the mystery is made present (though its inviolable obscurity remains), shining forth through a word, made symbolically corporeal through a gesture, and communicated through a community. Yet, nonidentity is also affirmed in the sacrament. God and his grace are not imprisoned within this or that sacramental expression. The *res sacramenti* (grace) may be granted not only in the particular *sacramentum* (sign) but also in some other. Furthermore, its presence is not epiphanic but rather is mediated in the obscurity of a human gesture, in the opaqueness of a historical word, and in the ambiguities of a community of sinners, all which contain their own substance, grammar, and structures. There is an absence in the sacrament, despite the presence of grace. Mystery is revealed in the sacrament but it is still a mystery. One cannot identify the mystery with the sacrament; there is nonidentity.

Catholicism is composed of this whole dialectical process and to limit it to any one step in that process is to make it pathological. Christianity is manifested in this sacramental circle where the natural and supernatural constitute a dialectical unity. What is Christianity? We do not know. We only know what is shown in the historical process. In other words, only through incarnations, through Catholicism, is the identity of Christianity both revealed and hidden from us.

The identity of Catholicism is found in dialectically accepted, improved, and reaffirmed sacramentality. This sacramentality has been expressed in the great themes of theology in order to characterize Catholicism.[47] For example, the Church, as the organized community of the faithful, is presented as the sacrament of Christ on earth and as the body of the Lord. There is an identity between Christ and the Church because through the Church he comes to us and continues his activity in the world. However, there is also a nonidentity between them because Christ transcends the Church which is only his sign and instrument. The same is true of the seven sacraments. Grace is made visible through the concrete sign present within the community, for there is an identity between the sign and its meaning. But there is also a nonidentity because grace always reserves its freedom apart from concrete signs. The institution represents Christ among the faithful in that it is a prolongation of the sacramentality of Christ. However, the institution possesses its own status, its structures and logic just like any other power structure in the world.

To accept the two dimensions as the expression of one mystery that unites the Church is to accept its sacramentality. Grace, the Gospel, and salvation never remain apart, in themselves, but are a part of the world and its history due to the sacramentality of God and Jesus Christ who, "since the children share in flesh and blood, himself likewise partook of the same nature" (Heb 2:14).

Roman Catholicism: Courageous Affirmation of
Its Sacramental Identity

Given the sacramental dialectic that characterizes Catholicism, there has been the tendency to vigorously emphasize either identity or nonidentity in the sacrament. These tendencies have given rise to two very different styles of Catholicism. It would appear that Roman Christianity (Catholicism) is distinguished by its valiant affirmation of sacramental identity while Protestant Christianity has fearlessly affirmed nonidentity. One emphasizes incarnation, history, and courage in the provisional while the other reveals the freedom of the Gospel, the absolute, and complete discontinuity with the structures of this world. Obviously, one does not exclude the other but rather includes the other; we are dealing with emphases and styles of living the totality of Christianity.

In the first centuries, Catholicism was marked by the desire to accept, assimilate, and impose only the faith, and nothing else. The first historical experiences of Christianity determined its later evolution, much like the way in which childhood experiences affect the entire later development of a person. Every great structural model and historical period served as an incarnation of Christianity, enriching it, committing it, complicating it. Roman Catholicism today is the heir of this complex and ambiguous experience. The seed of the incarnational principle is found in the New Testament, the Judeo-Hellenistic expression of Jesus' message. Christianity made use of existing terms and categories; it could not be otherwise. In the historical process, there is never an absolute beginning. The new is always a synthesis and a different form of what came before.

The principal tendencies of western Roman Catholicism are best described in Clement of Rome's Letter to the Corinthians. According to Klaus Beyschlag, a prominent Protestant scholar:

> Almost everything that constitutes primitive Catholicism as it comes from the West may be found in an analysis of the first letter of Clement: the Judaic basis of the Church in the Old Testament; the apologetic confrontation with Israel; the profound value placed on everything apostolic, especially anything linked to the name of Peter; the dogma of the ecumenical unity of the Church; the primacy of the first article of faith above the second and third; the synthesis between profane and sacred history; the ideal of peace and order in the world; the transformation of apocalyptics into a doctrine of the present; the relative ambiguity of the christological question; the primacy of soteriology, of the synoptic Jesus; the Catholic interpretation of Pauline theology, the message oriented toward the missionary conquest of the world; the organization of the churches by hierarchy and canon law; the synthesis between the hierarchical structure and its charismatic dimension, between Christianity and Church; the concrete norms of Christian life raised to the level of a New Law; the re-

peated sacramental confession; martyrdom interpreted as the daily struggle for perfection within the Church that at the same time is loyal to the
State; the pretension of the Church to sovereignly judge the world.[48]

Such elements serve as the pillars of Roman Catholicism, an observation
that was recently reaffirmed by a noted Catholic historian treating the
subject of faith and religion in the primitive Church.[49]

Entering the world, Christianity did not walk into a religious void. How
did Christianity respond to this situation? Despite the rigorism of a Tatian
or a Marcion who desired a pure Gospel—one wanting it free of pagan and
Hellenistic influences, and the other advocating a Gospel free of Judaism—
the desire for incarnation and identity predominated. Christianity took on
religious elements from the surrounding culture, purified some elements,
integrated some, and rejected others. It achieved a synthesis without losing
its fundamental identity.

Christianity, Judaism, and paganism were not towering abstractions
that confronted one another. Concrete individuals, Jews, pagans, Greeks,
and Romans who loved their respective cultures and the values of their
religious history, converted to the Christian faith. They brought to that
faith all that they were, despite the effort at criticism and purification. As
Paul says: "You do not support the root; the root supports you" (Rom 11:18).
In other words, Christians did not become Greeks or Romans, but rather
Greeks and Romans became Christians. This process was facilitated by the
fact that the Romans were deeply religious and willing to accept sympa-
thetically new rituals,[50] as well as by the fact that paganism itself was undergoing a notable period of spiritualization.[51]

Catholicism presented itself to the world as a religion because the entire
culture was religious. For Judaism it was an *hodos,* a way (Acts 9:2; 19:23),
a sect of Jews who venerated the Nazarene (*hairesis:* Acts 24:5). Ignatius of
Antioch (d. 110) used the term *Christianismos,* Christianity, as opposed to
Judaismos, for the first time.[52] For him, Christianity is synonymous with
Catholicism in the sense that it is being given here. It means the community
of believers with its rites, doctrines, and a concrete way of life. Thus, Ignatius asks that "we learn to live according to Christianity" (*kata christianis-
mon*). However, it was still not recognized as a licit religion.[53] It was juridically inferior and so was subject to repression. This gave rise to the tendency
by apologists to present Christianity as a religion that could serve a useful
function within the empire, just like other religions. They came to present
it as a true philosophy and pedagogy. Minucius Felix, in the *Octavius,* was
able to say: "The people could believe that the Christians would be the
philosophers of the present and that past philosophers had all been Christians."[54]

Defending Christianity as a religion whose acceptance would be advantageous for the empire, they achieved their goal in A.D. 311, with Galerius's edict of tolerance which was the first juridical act that declared Christianity to be a licit religion. Christianity in this case referred to the cultic community; it was this community that was integrated within Roman law. Constantine, in 312, granted immunity to Christian priests and thus made them equal to pagan priests; they also received the same financial assistance from the state. Because of this integration within the religious ranks, Christians no longer suffered negative reactions. They were not only free from persecution but also encouraged by this further victory for "the true religion." Eusebius of Cesarea (d. 339), in his *Praeparatio Evangelica*, interpreted this politico-religious event as the culmination of the history of salvation and the realization of biblical promises.

The incarnation of Christianity as a religion within Roman culture took place in 380 with the law of Theodosius the Great which declared Christianity to be the state religion. It became an obligatory *lex* for everyone; heretics were declared to be "insane" and punished as conspirators against the political and religious order.[55] With the romanization of Christianity some fundamental concepts of the New Testament inevitably took on Roman characteristics. The concepts of faith (*fides*), mystery (*sacramentum*), order (*ordo*), people (*plebs*), and Church (*ecclesia*) acquired a juridical connotation alongside their religious dimensions. For the Romans, the one who oversaw religion was not the priest (who was only a minister) but rather the state and the emperor. With Tertullian, faith came to function as *regula fidei* or simply as *lex*.[56] Roman ideology, in which the *dea Roma* (goddess Roma) was responsible for greatness, was slowly transformed by Ambrose, Prudencius, and Leo the Great into a Christian ideology that presented Christ and Peter and Paul, the princes of the apostles, as the true means to greatness. Leo the Great preached: "Both Apostles were the ones who led you, O Rome, to greatness.... Through the divine religion you will extend your power further than any other profane power."[57]

With a courage never before seen, Catholicism began to assume a cultural and organizational function. It did away with pagan ideology, pagan functions, and pagan rites. It created a few new things, preferring to utilize those it found. This can be seen in the way that Christianity reacted in view of popular pagan religiosity that was, as were the official rituals, very much alive and multifaceted. Those who were converted or crossed over to Christianity because it was *lex civilis*, civil law, brought to the faith their magical cosmology, filled with angels and demons, rites and traditions.[58] These were not eradicated; on the contrary, they were baptized, accepted, and integrated, often without an interior conversion of the faithful. Subjectively, they continued as pagans. Tertullian gives the following account of the religiosity of the people: "Upon leaving the house and upon entering it, at the beginning or end of any task, dressing, putting on shoes, before bathing, before rising or retiring, before any daily act we Christians make the sign of the cross on our foreheads."[59] It is probable that the sign of the cross substituted for magical pagan gestures. There was more transposition than conversion.

This collective phenomenon led St. Augustine to lend a Christian interpretation to pagan rites: "The same reality that is now called Christian was already present among the ancients."[60] For him, the Christian reality was always present in the world under different signs: *mutata sunt sacramenta, sed non fides*! Paganism was another way of expressing the same Christian substance. In this way, there were no fundamental obstacles to accepting its manifestations in culture. This same sacramental optimism is also found in Pope Gregory the Great (d. 604) who, sending missionaries among the Saxons, declared: "You must not destroy the temples of the people, only their idols. Take holy water and pour it over the idols, build altars and place relics there. These well-built temples should be places of sacrifice not of evil spirits but rather of the true God. The people, seeing that their temples are not destroyed, will gladly turn to the knowledge and worship of the true God."[61]

This thinking did not arise because of economic necessity; it was the fruit of a deep sacramental understanding of salvation history that saw God and grace as always utilizing the realities of history for his encounter with human beings.

In spite of this exalted optimism, there was also the need for a discernment of spirits. Not everything was simply accepted and integrated. Augustine, faced with all types of magical formulas and objects, set down the following directives for believers:

> All those things that have no basis in Sacred Scripture nor in the resolutions of the Synods of Bishops nor that have acquired authority through the tradition of the whole Church, but that have appeared in certain times and places in such a pluriformity of appearances such that they do not achieve the sought after goals, must be abolished wherever this is possible. Although they do not contradict the faith, they place a burden upon religion which, according to God's plan, must be free of such enslaving burdens in a simple and clear cultural form.[62]

This entire process must be understood hermeneutically. The incarnation of Christianity, in its first dialectical step, identifies with that which it accepts, values, and perfects. At a second stage, it critically steps back, does not identify itself with the culture, so that it may be free to accept new elements. The first stage characterizes Roman Catholicism, with a desire to accept, to synthesize realities as they are, to conquer and plan for the future. According to Augustine, Christianity says: "I am in all languages: Greek, Syriac, Hebrew; the tongues of all nations are mine because I am one with all peoples"[63] because nothing is separate from the Kingdom of God and, as such, nothing can remain apart from Christianity. It feels called to be yeast and salt for the world. An heir to this spirit, John Henry Newman could say: "Some object: these things are found among the pagans and therefore are not Christian. We prefer to say that these things are found in Christianity and therefore are not pagan."[64] The history of later centuries have confirmed the path already chosen. The aspect of negativity, of the consciousness of nonidentity, arises here and there but never characterizes Roman Catholicism. Rather, it will prove to be the banner of Protestant Christianity.

Pathologies of Roman Catholicism

Catholicism has been described above in terms of its original and healthy tendencies. But, there are also pathological tendencies. One can speak of Catholic and "catholicistic" (the decayed form of Catholicism) tendencies. This differentiation belongs to the history of Catholicism and, as such, must be accepted. Much of what traditional Protestant and cultural criticism has levied against Roman Catholicism is merely a criticism of its catholicistic aspects. This must be accepted by thinking Catholics.

Catholic identity lies in its sacramentality, in the positive mediation through which the Gospel and Christ reach the world. Therefore, institutions, doctrine, law, rites, sacraments, ministries, and other such mediations of Christianity are all valued in Catholicism. It is precisely in such mediations that pathologies may arise. This danger was very apparent to Leo the Great when he preached on the peace between Christianity and the empire: *habet igitur, dilectissimi, pax nostra pericula sua* (our peace has its dangers).[65] And these dangers were not avoided. We can find every imaginable pathology in the history of the Church. An analysis of all the principal ones would take too long. They have already been competently explored by others.[66] We will refer only to the fundamentally pathological structure that is manifested by the absolutizing of the mediation of the Church. Pathologically, the identity between mediation and Christianity is emphasized, thereby hiding, when not reprimanding, the dimension of nonidentity. Thus, the institution of the Church is absolutized in such a way that it tends to substitute itself for Jesus Christ, or to understand itself as his equal. Instead of serving as the sacrament of salvation, it makes itself independent, self-complacent, oppressively imposing itself on others. Catholicism favors word (dogma) and law (canons). The word and the law demand specialists (theologians and canon lawyers), and the need for an elite group of doctors and hierarchs who possess exclusive knowledge of the sacred. They are the only ones versed in this knowledge, with the presumption that it is only through their doctrines, dogmas, rites, and norms that one achieves salvation as a member of the Church.[67] Dogma is one thing and dogmatism quite another, law versus legalism, tradition versus traditionalism, authority versus authoritarianism. Christianity was reduced, in its pathological Catholic understanding, to a simple doctrine of salvation: it became more important to know the truths "required for salvation" (*sicut oportet ad salutem consequendam*) than to be converted to a praxis of following Jesus Christ. Jesus is adored, as are his Holy Land, his words, his history; saints are venerated; martyrs are praised; heroic witness to faith is celebrated; but the principal element is missing: following them and doing what they did. Cultic celebration does not always lead to conversion and very often, instead, leads away from true Christian praxis.

All decisions were centralized in a small hierarchical elite through the absolutizing of doctrine, cultural forms, and the distribution of power within the community. The absolutizing of a form of the Church's presence in society led to the oppression of the faithful. Institutional arthritis led to the lack of imagination, of a critical spirit, of creativity. Anything new was immediately under suspicion and an apology for the ecclesiastical status quo predominated, as did calls for loyalty to the institution rather than to the gospel message and its challenges. The drive for security was much stronger than that for truth and authenticity. Tensions were, and are, frequently suffocated through a repression that often violates the basic human rights that are respected even by officially atheistic societies.

Along with these manifestations, theological-ideological justifications were developed: historical law was assimilated to divine law, and what was cultural was termed "natural law." Thus, the institution was protected by its laws and doctrines against any criticism or attempt at social change. It seemed that everything was neat and tidy. Theologians and saints were to fall into the same illusion. St. Jerome, for example, saw in the fall of the Roman Empire an obvious sign that the end of the world was near (*Ep.* 123:15–17; PL 22:1057–58); Pope Saint Gregory read into the uprisings of his time and in the fall of Rome the signs of the imminent end (*Hom. in Evang.* 1:5; PL 76:1080–81). Actually, the end of one world—its order and power—did arrive. But that world was not the entire world, nor did it involve the entire historical process. History continued and will continue, and other worlds will rise as will other opportunities for the incarnation of faith, making possible the continuing salvific encounter of human persons with God.

The pathology of Roman Catholicism became widespread with the total rejection and expulsion of the negative, critical thinking that had kept alive the consciousness of the Church's nonidentity with the Gospel. The rejection of Protestantism was a historical mistake not only because Luther was excommunicated but because any possibility for true criticism or questioning of the system in the name of the Gospel was also expelled. Catholicism became a total, reactionary, violent, and repressive ideology. There is nothing further from the evangelical spirit than the catholicistic system's pretension to unlimited infallibility, to unquestionability, to absolute certainty. There is nothing further from the Gospel than the encapsulation of Christianity in one unique and exclusive expression, than the inability to recognize the Gospel if it is not expressed through a unique doctrine, a unique liturgy, a unique moral norm, and a unique ecclesiastical organization. Christian experience is replaced by indocrination in the existing system—a system that lives in the inferno of terms and doctrines that are reinterpreted ideologically, again and again, in order to maintain power, an endless chain of interpretations that loses its reference to the one necessary element, the Gospel. The emphasis on the forms of mediation within Catholicism is responsible for its historical sclerosis and its slowness in reading the signs of the times and, in light of them, newly translating and incarnating the liberating message of Jesus Christ.

In conclusion, we want to reiterate that such manifestations are pathologies of a *true* principle, pathologies that cannot destroy the *positive* strength of Catholicism's identity. The negative always rises out of a more fundamental positive; direct and true criticism inspires it to be something better and healthier. Without this perspective, we too would fall into the confusion of identifying Christianity with Catholicism, of confusing the message with its historical concretizations.

Official Roman Catholicism and Popular Catholicism

From the previous reflections, certain inferences may be made in considering the subject of popular Catholicism:

1. It is *Catholicism.* This means that there is great value placed on mediation. Faith is incarnated in the piety of the people. The Gospel is present in the promises made, the processions, the lighted candles, and in the veneration of the saints, making its identity visible through these manifestations. They make the Gospel historical. Thus, there is the basic optimism of Catholicism. There is happiness, joy, and enjoyment in the presence of God's transcendence, and that of Jesus Christ, made present in this popular piety. The realities of this world are accepted as manifesting and communicating (mediating) salvation.

2. It is *popular* Catholicism. Popular, as understood here, is that which is neither official nor belongs to the elite who determine what is Catholic. Popular Catholicism is a different incarnation of official Roman Catholi-

cism, with its own symbolic universe, with a different language and grammar —specifically, that of the people. Thus, it must not be considered as a deviation from official Catholicism.[68] It is simply a different system of translating Christianity within the concrete conditions of human life.[69] Its language is based in primitive thought; its grammar follows the logic of the unconscious. Because of this, a different set of tools is necessary to understand it, different from that based on reflective thought and the rigorous logic of doctrinal systematization with which official Catholicism is analyzed.

3. It is popular *Roman* Catholicism. Although it may possess its own identity, popular Catholicism, by virtue of its popularity, is related to official Roman Catholicism (understood as the People of God). The basic doctrines, the saints, the sacraments, and so on, all come from official Catholicism. It continues to nourish them, to grant or withhold legitimacy. The Catholics of popular Catholicism, themselves, profess that they are part of the official Church (of the clergy). Therefore, one cannot understand popular Catholicism without maintaining the dialectical relationship with official Catholicism. Official Catholicism controls the words, the doctrines, and the laws but leaves the practices to the people. They possess a creativity that allows the religious experience to be freely expressed. This experience, at the same time, will nourish official theology as well as encourage the renewal of official institutions. It will open up new ways of expressing the presence of official Catholicism in the culture of the time. It is often the case that great renewal movements, new forms of piety, great prophets, saints, and mystics emerge from a popular environment where the experience of God and Jesus Christ, free of the superegos of official doctrine, point out a new mediation. Without popular Catholicism, official Catholicism does not *live*; without official Catholicism, popular Catholicism is not *legitimized* in its Catholic character.

4. Popular Catholicism can also manifest pathologies. Owing to its very structure, it is more subject to deviations because there is a predominance of experience over criticism, of symbols that are born in the subconscious over concepts that are developed through conscious reason. Archetypes of the religious experience of humanity often arise from the collective subconscious, endangering Christian identity. For example, the desire for security and certainty often gives rise to superstitious and magical practices. Popular Catholicism can mean a true interior liberation that feeds the courage for survival, that maintains a firm hope against all hope, and that preserves the clarity of the transcendent meaning of life. However, by ignoring a criticism of its practices it may be infiltrated by the practices of the oppressors of the people, who, with their ideological interpretation of human conflicts and their manipulation of religion, try to maintain a rela-

tionship of force and injustice. Thus, there is the need for an accurate analysis of what is popular and what is antipopular in popular Catholicism.

Conclusion: Roman Catholicism—
More Traditional, Less Traditionalistic

Catholicism—from the above analysis—basically signifies an optimistic attitude toward historical realities, a disposition of openness, of willingness to accept various cultural forms, traditions, and ways of life to express the faith and the Gospel. This attitude constitutes the great Catholic tradition; it is its glory and its banner. This tradition overflowed with the happiness and joy of Catholics, and history was made under its banner. Everywhere it was planted Catholic culture was born, with its monuments, its churches, its sacred art, and its literature. Alongside this positive dimension was also a pathological dimension that must never be repressed, but always kept in mind.

In view of this past Catholic attitude, today's Catholicism, so entrenched in a particular incarnation that it is ready to defend against all changes that are more than mere modernizations of the structure itself, must strive to regain its purer tradition, opening itself to new lessons, and to accept, critically, new religious experiences. Catholicism today is not sufficiently Roman Catholic in the sense described above. It is Catholicistic and reactionary, unfaithful to its grand tradition and obsessed by its lesser and more recent traditions. It is insufficiently traditional and too traditionalistic. Because neither very Catholic nor very traditional, it has great difficulty being generously open to popular Catholicism and allowing itself to be renewed by the Christian experience that is being lived by the People of God.

Chapter 7

IN FAVOR OF SYNCRETISM:
THE CATHOLICITY OF CATHOLICISM

Catholicism implies a courage for incarnation, an acceptance of heterogeneous elements and their subsequent integration within the criteria of a specifically Catholic ethos. Catholicity as the synonym of universality is only possible and attainable through the process of syncretism from which catholicity itself results.

This question has become very real ever since the Second Vatican Council, given the Church's openness to other religions and the extraordinary value placed on culture. This is not simply a religious or cultural ecumenism but rather an invitation to allow the Gospel to penetrate areas that until now have been left apart from or outside of it. Some question whether this new openness is just another strategy for Catholicism to strengthen its hold while maintaining its historical influence. If that were the case, the serious interest in syncretism would be spurious and incidental. The case may be, rather, that we are dealing with the "law of incarnation" proper to Catholicism, whose present reality and future destiny are determined by its capacity to syncretize. From this perspective, syncretism appears as something positive, a normal process for Catholicism.

What Is Syncretism?

The value of syncretism depends on the viewpoint of the observer.[1] If the observer sits in the privileged places within Catholicism—understanding it as a signed, sealed, and delivered masterpiece—then he or she will consider syncretism to be a threat to be avoided at all costs. If, however, he or she is situated on a lower level, amid conflicts and challenges, in the midst of the people who live their faith together with other religious expressions, on a level that understands Catholicism as a living reality and therefore open to other elements and the attempt to synthesize them, then syncretism is seen as a normal and natural process.

Our understanding of syncretism has always come from those who have been afraid of it: the defenders of theological and institutional knowledge.

They have always treated syncretism pejoratively. The former secretary of the World Council of Churches saw syncretism as the temptation of the century because, he thought, the human soul is not *naturaliter christiana* but *naturaliter syncretista* and so syncretism is more dangerous than atheism. Even Vatican II echoes this alarm and warns "against all types of syncretism and false particularism" (*Ad Gentes*, 22).

What, then, is syncretism? How are we to understand it? There are different definitions:

Syncretism as addition: One is said to be speaking of syncretism in the case where a religion is not yet developed as a fully distinct religion but rather is the addition or alternation of different beliefs, each part with its own structures, rites, and places of worship. Thus, for example, one might attend a Catholic liturgy, afterward go to a spiritualist, and later pray at the church of the Jehovah's Witnesses. This is the simple addition or joining of disparate elements without interrelating them. They are united only by the personal experience of the believer whose own diffused and undefined religiosity values these religious expressions. This, obviously, is the pejorative sense of syncretism, lacking a specific identity.

Syncretism as accommodation: This occurs when the religion of a dominated people is adapted to the religion of those who dominate, be it as a means for survival or as part of a strategy for resistance. For example, the religions of native peoples accommodated and adapted to the institutions, feasts, rites, and beliefs of colonial Catholicism. This process does not necessarily mean the destruction of the original religion's identity but it does involve the adoption of certain elements that may be incompatible with its ethos, sowing the seeds of conflict and tension within the religious experience of the dominated peoples.

Syncretism as mixture: All syncretism implies a mixture of some kind, but it is important to determine the type of mixture. In this case it is understood as a superficial mixture of elements and their juxtaposition, such as occured within the Roman pantheon: gods and goddesses from Asia, Egypt, Syria, Persia, and all of the conquered peoples sit among the Roman gods in the same temple. There is no external unity, only the diffused interior unity of the believer who feels the tremendous power of the Divine manifested in so many different types of gods. There is neither systematization, that may satisfy one's profound religious needs; nor religious vision of the world. There is a simple profusion of gods with very contradictory characteristics. Syncretism in this sense is synonymous with dilution and confusion.

Syncretism as agreement: "According to this understanding there is no one unique revelation in history; rather, there are diverse paths for encountering the divine reality. All formulations of truth and religious experience are, by their nature, inadequate expressions; it is necessary to harmonize them as much as possible and thereby create a universal religion for all humanity."[2] The first sentence is not the problem; it is perfectly sustainable, especially from a historical-salvific perspective. The difficulty arises with the desire to create an agreement of formulations, rites, and expressions with a view toward a single religion that is useful to all. This vision ignores the very structure of religion, its experience and identity, and is concerned only with external levels. It feeds the illusion that the harmonization of expression also harmonizes radical experiences. This understanding of syncretism is superficial and lacks organic wholeness.

Syncretism as translation: When one religion uses the categories, cultural expressions, and traditions of another religion to communicate and translate its own essential message, one is said to be speaking of syncretism. Only those elements that are compatible with the identity of the host religion are utilized. This is a process that is common to all universal religions.

Syncretism as adaptation: This is a long, almost imperceptible process in the development of religions. A religion first is exposed to different religious expressions and then assimilates them, interprets them, and recasts them according to its own identity. This is not a blind acceptance; it involves adaptation and conversion which often leads to periods of crisis and uncertainty as to whether the religion's true identity is being preserved or diluted.

This historical process involves a necessary ingredient whereby the dominant religion is able to "digest" the acquired elements and make them its own. This is a vital and organic process, similar to what happens when we eat: no matter how diverse the food may be, it is ingested and adapted for human life. But there are those foods that are indigestible and that produce adverse side effects. The same holds true when religion enters into history and is exposed to its environmental influences. It not only receives; it works with what it receives and imparts its own seal. All of the great religions in history, those that have reached a high level of development, have been the results of an immense process of syncretization.

But the process never ends. A religion, like Christianity, preserves and enriches its universality as long as it is capable of speaking all languages, incarnating itself in all cultures. This, we propose, is valid syncretism (although it too, at times, may be pathological). It is a process that includes the other definitions of syncretism while, at the same time, going beyond them.

The legitimacy of syncretism as the life process of a religion needs to be demonstrated. Its relevance for the world today is obvious given the deep religious sensitivity of so many people as well as the richness of existing religious expressions, for example, from the third world, from indigenous peoples, from colonial-medieval Christianity, from reformed and modernized Christianity, from various Christian denominations. Through this process, Catholicism can, by opening itself to this religious wealth, create a whole new image.

Christianity as One Huge Syncretism

Ruling Catholic opinion claims that syncretism only exists in other religions. Christianity, being a revealed religion, cannot be syncretic. It received its primary structural elements from its divine founder, Jesus Christ. Biblical Judaism itself is the historical revelation of Yahweh. This interpretation comes from the dominant religion, and it is spelled out in a wholly ideological discourse that considers all other religious manifestations either as preparations for it—and as such, essentially imperfect—or as its disintegration (such as popular Catholicism or the churches of the various reform movements).

This claim by official Catholicism has been discarded by scholars of various disciplines interested in the religious phenomenon, especially that of Christianity. They show that it is as syncretic as any other religion. The Old and New Testaments are both composed of syncretic writings that have assumed the surrounding influences of their own and other cultures. The New Testament texts contain Judaic, Judeo-Christian, Greek, Roman, gnostic, stoic, and many other elements—elements not simply juxtaposed but assimilated, starting always from a strong Christian identity with particular christological criteria.

The result is not a religion that issued forth from the hands of God or Christ and was received by us in its present form. In reality, it is a cultural product, the activity of human beings influenced by God's intervention. On one hand, it is a gift from God and so, rightly, has a supernatural origin; and on the other, it is a human construct, whose many steps and stages may be studied and described. God's gift is faith and divine revelation made definitive in Jesus Christ. But all of this was witnessed to and lived within preexisting religious and cultural boundaries. The Church as a structure is as syncretic as any other religious expression.

Pure Christianity does not exist, never has existed, never can exist.[3] The Divine is always made present through human mediations which are always dialectical. They are divine in the reality of history (identity), revealing divine identity while, at the same time, hiding it because of their intrinsic limitations (nonidentity). What exists concretely is always the Church, that is, the historical-cultural expression and religious objectification of Christianity.

Many historians of Christian origins have shown that Catholicism is a grandiose and infinitely complex syncretism.[4] There are two attitudes in the Church: one, the self-affirmation of its own identity, especially through apologetics aimed at demonstrating its specifically Christian essence; the other, an openness and sympathy to the values that existed before the advent of the Christian message, accepting them redemptively by expressing the message through them and from within them, giving rise to a new syncretism.

Syncretism, then, is not necessarily evil nor does it represent a pathology of pure religion. It is a normal condition of the incarnation, expression, and objectification of a religious faith or expression. It may give rise to pathologies. Fundamentally, it emerges as a universal phenomenon constitutive of all religious expression.

Theological Legitimacy of Religious Syncretism

The Church's own theological understanding is the basis for the validity and legitimacy of syncretism. It also provides the limitations necessary for it not to degenerate into a pathology that may compromise the essence of Christian faith. The positive aspects of syncretism can be described by some of the key categories of Catholic (Christian) theology, for example, the universal history of salvation, faith and religion, and the essential catholicity of the divine message.

The Offer of Universal Salvation

The substance of Christian faith is the declaration that God, as creator of the universe, is also savior of the universe. He offers himself as human salvation and human fulfillment to all peoples collectively and to each person individually. He does not deny himself to anyone. Perdition is the exclusive result of a freedom that denies the salvific love of God. God's love is concrete: it does not remain a universal and abstract concept; it reaches out to touch the individual where that person is, using the elements of the person's life, culture, and religion as mediations. In other words, the universal salvific will of God is historicized and incarnated in the rites, doctrines, and traditions of a religion, in the ethical codes of a society, in the various forms of social interaction. Thus, the history of salvation is the history of God's self-communication to humanity; a corresponding revelation also allows all people to have knowledge of the existential truth that sets them on the path of salvation.

In this historical-salvific perspective, religion, by no means a merely human construct, has a supernatural *origin* because its initiative comes from God. Religion is humanity's response to the divine invitation—divine proposal and human response forming an inseparable unity. Religion is, then, essentially syncretic because it is made up of the incarnation and historicization of universal salvation together with the experience of saving grace.[5]

At this level, syncretism is clearly positive in terms of theology; the organization of elements or their origin is of little importance. Concrete religious realities serve as communicating sacraments and expressions of grace. The first Christian apologists saw the presence of the word that "illuminates each man that comes into this world" (John 1:9) in the religious and cultural values of the Roman Empire; they called them "seeds of the word" (*logoi spermatikoi*).[6] Many of them repeated the words of Seneca: "*Quod verum est, meum est. . . . Sciant omnes quae optima sunt, esse communia*" ("What is true is mine. . . . Know that the best things are common to us all").[7] Justin Martyr claimed: "Everything good that has been said, no matter by whom, is Christian."[8]

The question of syncretism becomes truly acute when Christianity became the official religion and all were obliged by law to be Christians. The various religious groups became Christian and brought to the Christian communities every sort of rite, belief, doctrine, and religious custom. Theologians at the time, besides attempting to purify these new elements in light of the demands of the gospels and the specific identity of Christianity, promoted an interpretation of these religions in terms of the history of salvation. They saw the mystery of Christ present and actual from the beginning of the world; the universal Church covers all of history, from Abel to the last of the elect, taking different forms in each age and culture but always communicating the same saving grace.[9] Augustine maintained that "the same reality that is now called Christian was already present in ancient times."[10] Origen, believing in the presence of the universal word in humanity, was of the opinion that one should pay attention, not to the rites and ceremonies of the pagans so much as to their attempt to encounter the Divine.[11]

This optimistic interpretation allowed for the development of the grand Catholic syncretism: feasts, rites, traditions, and religious teachings were assimilated, incorporated, and reinterpreted within the Christian horizon, becoming part of the symbolic wealth of the Catholic Church. The Second Vatican Council, with its theological appreciation of non-Christian religions, relies on the same argumentation; it sees "a secret presence of God" (*Ad Gentes*, 9), "a hidden seed of the Word" (*Nostra Aetate*, 2) in the true elements of these religions.[12]

When we refer to the universal history of salvation we must think not only of God's gratuitous offer but also of the element of human acceptance or rejection. Salvation is never a matter of fate; it is never an imposition, but rather a proposition made in view of the individual's freedom. There is always the possibility of rejection. The history of sin in the world is the incarnation of human rejection of the divine invitation.

Our present situation is profoundly ambiguous. In the words of St. Augustine, *"Omnis homo Adam, omnis homo Christus,"* each person is at one and the same time Adam and Christ, sinner and just.[13] No mediation is pure and free of the contamination of sin. Biblical Judaism and the Church are presented as the mediations of both saints and sinners. Only in Jesus Christ is there the absolute encounter of God's offer with complete acceptance by the human person. Jesus alone is the *novissimus Adam*, totally uncontaminated creation. That is why he is venerated as the presence of eschatological reality which is anticipated in time. In other words, religious syncretism not only speaks of the love of God but also hides, represses, and obstructs it when the individual is overemphasized, confusing the mediation with divine reality, leading to a slavery to ritualism that forgets the primacy of God and his grace. In spite of this danger, Christian faith has always affirmed the superabundance of God's self-communication over the abundance of sin; that is, no matter how pathological syncretism may become, despite the magic, superstition, and ritualism, the grace of God is not totally obstructed. God finds a path to the heart in order to redeem it, in spite of human failings.

Theology must also be prevented from considering the faults of paganism, and even of Christianity itself, as the work of Satan alone. The human search for the Transcendent, for a transhistoric salvation, is never totally frustrated. Yet, the consciousness of the history of sin and perdition demands a constantly critical spirit that is capable of discerning the symbolic from the diabolic in all religious expressions.[14]

Religion as the Syncretic Expression of Faith

The question of syncretism is raised in the discussion regarding the relationship between faith and religion. This discussion is a particular favorite among Protestants given an excessive passion for a gospel purity that counterposes faith and religion as, for example, do Barth and Bonhoeffer. They see religion as a human effort aimed at guaranteeing salvation, and faith as a free gift from God. Catholic understanding of religion as a mediation distinguishes faith and religion but also understands that, on the level of praxis, both form an indissoluble and unmistakable unity. The justifiable desire to distinguish them does not legitimate dividing that which, in concrete life, is always one. A quick review of the stages involved in the religious act will allow us to see the overlap of faith and religion as well as the appearance of syncretism within this interaction.[15]

First, the *homo religiosus* uncovers the ontological dimension of existence, that is, a dimension that belongs to the basic structure of human beings, prior to any reflection or religious act. The religious act itself discovers existence as an openness to the Transcendent or to Transcendent Being. However, this experience of life as openness can be described in terms that are not necessarily linked to a particular religious confession. In this first stage of reflection, every individual discovers himself or herself in reference to and related to a reality whose meaning is not yet deciphered. One exists freely, colliding with Mystery (with something unknown).

The theologian sees a form of God's presence in this vacuum and anxiety; the cry of the individual is nothing but the echo of God's voice.[16]

At a second stage—the stage of freedom—the individual freely accepts or rejects the reference to the Transcendent. One may accept existence as it is experienced phenomenologically, accepting one's reference to a Mystery that polarizes that existence and naming it. Life is then understood as grounded; life is cultivated in reference to the Mystery that is revealed, and even more so when one is open to that Mystery. However, the individual may also deny this existence, leaving questions unanswered, fleeing from life or even structuring one's response to existence with a variety of absolutes that leave the individual dissatisfied.

This is the responsorial structure of existence. Existence is to be called; it can do nothing but respond either positively or negatively; there must be some response. There are four levels or aspects to this response:[17]

—*as a cry for help* in the face of threatening situations: the Transcendent appears as the savior from illnesses, emotional problems, existential fears;

—*as a desire for fulfillment* in which the Transcendent is seen as the one who realizes the secret desires of the heart in terms of infinite happiness, eternal love, total reconciliation;

—*as an attitude of respect* in which the radical otherness of the Transcendent is recognized. This has nothing to do with the individual's needs but rather is the result of a recognition that all existence is directed toward that Mystery;

—*as gift to the Other* in which the religious individual reaches out and surrenders in trust to the designs of Mystery. Life is dedicated to the Transcendent, and love, the source of existence, is consecrated to it, resulting in the crystal-clear work of disinterested freedom that we call love.

All of these steps in the responsorial expression of existence show a gradual maturity: one passes from a self-interested response to one that is a response of disinterested love. This is all one process that touches the entire human person, feelings, life threats, the heart's secret desires, and the true realm of freedom which is the giving of oneself to another. Each step or stage develops its own image of Mystery (God). One should mention now that there is always the possibility of a magical image of God, one who attends to the vital needs of individuals. This danger and other deviations are present whenever the process is detained in a particular stage. There is the need for constant criticism, for continual conversion to the Absolute, questioning all models and images, and so freeing the religious experience from the accusation of illusion or alienation from true existence.

The third stage is that of objectification. The individual is essentially a corporal being who lives together with others in the world. One's experiences are expressed through psychic, intellectual, material, social, cultural, and other realities. Openness to and acceptance of the Transcendent never take places in a vacuum but takes shape through mediations and a symbolic universe which has its roots in the concrete world of the person and the community, in one's social class, conflicts, searches, and so forth. Theology calls faith the acceptance of the transcendental openness to Mystery and it calls religion the historico-cultural expression of that openness. "Religion is expressed and institutionalized faith; and faith is the core and essence of religion."[18]

It is on this level of expression that the phenomenon of syncretism appears. To find expression, the experience uses tools that it finds in culture and society. Faith is expressed in the *sociological* dimension: religion appears with its institutions, traditions, customs, sacred powers. Faith is made visible on a *corporal* and *material* level through rites and symbols. It roots itself in human *affectivity*, meeting the desires for fulfillment, reconciliation, immortality, and happiness. It manifests itself in the *ethical-praxis* dimension by establishing codes of conduct and ideals that direct personal and social practices. It is expressed on the *intellectual* level, which articulates the doctrinal understanding of faith with creeds and dogmas.

This entire complex of elements comprising religion is a true syncretism. All of the elements serve as mediations for faith and form the sacramental-symbolic universe of religion. Because it is a cultural phenomenon, this symbolic complex is open to scientific inquiry that detects reflections of social conflicts, the origins of images, and the psychosocial structures of the expressions of faith. However, the nucleus that gives rise to religion—faith—escapes scientific analysis. Scientific analysis leads to phenomenology; the faith that underlies religion cannot be made objective because it is the fruit of freedom. Faith is a fundamental experience and cannot be reduced to any other.

Catholicity as Identity in Plurality

The true concept of the catholicity of the Church leads to a positive understanding of syncretism. Catholicity is not primarily a *geographic* concept, that is, a Church present everywhere in the world; nor is it a *statistical* concept, that is, a quantitatively more numerous Church. It is not a *sociological* concept, a Church incarnated in various cultures; nor is it a *historical* concept or a Church that preserves its historical continuity. Catholicity lies within the very identity of the Church that is preserved, confirmed, and manifested "for everyone, always and everywhere." The identity of the Church is in the unity of its faith in God the Father who sent his Son, with the power of the Holy Spirit, to save all people; it is a faith that is mediated through the Church, the universal sacrament of salvation. One faith, one God, one Lord, one Spirit, one Gospel, one baptism, one eucharist: this is the catholicity, the unity, and the universality of the Church.[19]

This identity is objectified within the parameters of a given time and place. The universal (catholic) Church is made concrete in particular churches that, within the cultural, linguistic, psychological, and social classes of a particular region, live and witness to the same oneness of faith. Catholicity is a characteristic of each particular Church inasmuch as each Church, through its particularity and not in spite of it, is open to the universality present in other churches as well.

The catholicity of the Church is the power to be incarnated, without losing its identity, in the most diverse cultures. To be catholic is not to simply expand the ecclesiastical system but to live and witness to the same faith in Jesus Christ, savior and liberator, within a particular culture. "In order to be able to offer all [men] the mystery of salvation and the life brought by God, the Church must become part of all these groups for the same motive which led Christ to bind Himself, in virtue of His Incarnation, to the definite social and cultural conditions of those human beings among whom He dwelt" (Ad Gentes, 10).[20] The Church would not be catholic if it were not African, Chinese, European, Latin American. Paul VI, in his message Africae Terrarum, said: "Many customs and rites, previously thought to be eccentric and primitive, today, in light of ethnological knowledge, show themselves to be integral elements of particular social systems worthy of study and respect" (7). Valuing the African culture, apparently polytheistic, he affirmed:

> The spiritual vision of life is a constant and all-pervading foundation in African tradition. This is not simply an "animistic" tradition in the sense given this term in the history of religions at the end of the last century. Rather, it is a deeper, wider, and more universal concept according to which all creatures and creation itself are linked to the invisible world, the world of the spirit. The human person, in particular, is never thought of as simply material, limited to an earthly life, but rather the presence and efficacy of another spiritual element is recognized, causing human life to be related to the life beyond. From this spiritual concept, a most important common element becomes one of God as the first and ultimate cause of all things. This concept, perceived more than analyzed and lived more than thought, is expressed in a very different way from one culture to another. In reality, God's presence penetrates African life as the presence of a superior, personal, and mysterious being. He is called upon in the most solemn and critical moments of life, when the intercession of any

other intermediary is judged useless. Almost always, free of a fear of omnipotence, God is invoked as Father. Prayers directed to Him, individually or collectively, are spontaneous and at times emotional. Among the forms of sacrifice, the sacrifice of first fruits stands out because of its purity of meaning.[14]

The text ends by stating that "the Church greatly respects the moral and religious values of the African tradition, not only because of its significance but also because it sees in them the providential basis upon which to spread the gospel message and to further the building of a new society in Christ" (14).

From the above reflection comes the realization that syncretism achieves the concrete essence of the Church. On the one hand, the Christian faith expressed within a certain culture shares in that culture's destiny, its glories and miseries, the dreams that are expressed, as well as the limitations of the means by which those dreams are realized. On the other hand, faced with other cultures in which the Christian faith has yet to be made objective, and in order to make its mission understood while respecting the good that God himself has made possible within these cultures, the Church must develop new syncretisms and thus incarnate anew the Christian message. Syncretism is not only inevitable but is positively the historical and concrete way in which God comes to people and saves them. The question is not whether or not there is syncretism in the Church. The problem is in the type of syncretism that exists at present and which one should be sought. Which syncretism truly translates the Christian message and which one destroys it? The need is to establish criteria, however problematic this may seem to be.

True and False Syncretism

The establishment of criteria is always conditioned by the position from which praxis is rooted and theory is expressed. There is no neutral or extrinsic position; rather, criteria rise out of concrete situations.[21] This does not eliminate the possibility of developing criteria; it only makes us conscious of their relativity. We will develop two types of criteria: some internal to the very question of syncretism; others involving the self-understanding of the Christian faith.

Criteria Intrinsic to Syncretism

These criteria emerge from the balance that must be maintained between the component elements of syncretism. Religious syncretism arises when faith is expressed in its sociocultural state as a religion. Religion can never take on substantive value; it does not have autonomy because it is essentially functional. In this respect two deviations may occur: religion without faith or faith without religion. Obviously, these deviations are never complete, because the ideal type belongs to the realm of utopia; in reality, the elements are intertwined. Yet, the substantive primacy of faith over the functional character of religion must be maintained. This fundamental and universal criterion (applicable to any religious expression) is the warning for possible and actual deviations.

One pathology is found in religion without faith. This is a religion that is closed in upon itself. On the sociological level it appears as the belief in salvation achieved through the simple observance of rites and norms, and through socioreligious incorporation. The need for ongoing conversion is avoided. On the corporal level rites and symbols are magical; exact and mechanical recitation is enough to infallibly produce the desired results. The symbols do not give way to Mystery but idolatrously substitute for it, breaking it down to various mysteries. On the psychological level religion compensates for human frustrations and generates a false sense of security. It is reduced to a psychological function and is closed to the mystery of God. On the intellectual level it falls into an attempted gnosis, striving to enclose Mystery within formulas and dogmas, preserved in their literal purity. On the ethical level is legalism and pharisaism where justification is found in good works alone.

In this way, religion ceases to be a mediation for faith; it is presented as the ultimate structure for the religious individual. By not leading the individual to the orbit of faith, freedom, and the transcendent Mystery, religion becomes an oppressor of human consciousness.

There is also an inverse pathology wherein faith tries to keep itself so pure and open to the Mystery of God that it sees no use for religion. Religion is viewed as destroying Mystery because it objectifies it. Rather than protecting Mystery, this preoccupation seriously affects the individual, denying the person's essential rootedness in the corporal world. Thus, a denial of the sociological dimension of religion (for example, institutions) reduces faith to an inoperable individualism and privatization. The destruction of material manifestations such as rites and symbols results in agnosticism and an iconoclastic attitude. The rejection of the emotional dimensions present in religion leaves it empty and abstract, dehumanizing the person of faith. The negation of the doctrinal development of faith opens the way for an uncontrolled and subjective living of faith, devoid of common references, leaving Mystery to the mercy of the changing tastes of individuals. The breakdown of an ethical commitment leads human praxis into anarchy and social irresponsibility.

Faith does not find its proper expression in these deviations; it demands an impossible purity as if the individual were not part of the world. The balance is found in the dialectical tension between the faith that nourishes religion and the religion that expresses, concretizes, and shapes the historicity of faith. Religion finds its meaning when it is not separated from faith; faith, in turn, has meaning in breaking through the barriers of objectifications, maintaining its transcendence while still possessing an incarnational intentionality.

These two universal criteria warn us of the fact that there are more than a few pathologies in the Church. Yet, pathology is not only pathology but also refers to normalcy.

Criteria from Christian Self-Understanding

The question arises as to those criteria that are specific to Christianity and which are born from Christian identity. Which syncretism is true or false for Christian faith? One must remember what has already been said about the simultaneity of sin and grace throughout the history of salvation; the same applies to Christian syncretism. A syncretism that held only truth has never existed and, if it had, would have been an eschatological event. At the present time, the wheat is mixed with the chaff. The truth of Christian syncretism is relative and cannot pretend to be otherwise. It will have to tolerate deviations that, alone, are unavoidable but which should be such that they do not adulterate Christian identity to such an extent that it is no longer discernible.

Christian syncretism is understood to be the syncretism that arises from the essential core of Christian faith that is embodied in the symbolic framework of another culture. This presupposes that the culture is converted in such a way that it ceases to be what it was, at its roots, and becomes an expression of the Christian faith. This does not happen without conversion. Otherwise Christian identity is corrupted and absorbed by the identity of each culture.

For this reason, in any missionary activity, the first step must be the reaffirmation of the Christian faith, distinguishing it from other religious expressions. The Gospel is proclaimed, inviting all to conversion. Once conversion has taken place, the process of syncretism is begun. In this second stage Christian identity borrows "from the customs and traditions of their people, from their wisdom and their learning, from their arts and sciences . . . all those things which can contribute to the glory of their Creator, the revelation of the Savior's grace, or the proper arrangement of Christian life" (*Ad Gentes*, 22). A true syncretism is always begun with Christian identity as its substantial nucleus.

The opposite may take place, that is, a religion may enter into contact with Christianity and, instead of being converted, may convert Christianity to its own self-identity. It may syncretize elements of the Christian religion with its own. It does not become Christian by incorporating Christian elements. It continues to be pagan and thus is a pagan syncretism with Christian connotations. Certain investigations have revealed this phenomenon among various religions, such as the *yoruba* religion in Brazil. They accommodated, assimilated, and transformed Christian elements while preserving their own identity. Christianity did not convert them; it was converted.[22]

This does not mean that these religions have no theological value. It simply means that they must be understood within the history of universal salvation and not within the intrasystemic parameters of Christianity—as if they were manifestations of Christianity, like popular Catholicism. These religions make concrete, in their own way, God's offer of salvation. They cannot yet be called Christian, nor do they call themselves by that name, but rather, because of the salvific plan of the Father in Christ, they are anonymously Christian. Although they may have syncretized Christian elements within their systems, they are still theologically at the advent, at the stage previous to the explicitly Christian event.

The Church is in a missionary stance with respect to these religions; it will have to proclaim the identity of the Christian faith and work for their conversion to this identity. Once this task is accomplished, the Church will be able to syncretize all of the wealth of these religions that is compatible with the Christian faith. But the question remains as to what is specific to the Christian identity.

Christian identity: There is no such thing as a chemically pure Christian identity; it is always syncretized. Therefore, it is difficult to discuss it and also set aside its historical objectification in western Greco-Roman-European culture. Christian identity is not theory but experience, a way of life. This experience is linked to the experience of Jesus of Nazareth, his life, death and resurrection, coming to us through the New Testament witnesses. In the life of this powerless man, the apostolic faith understood that it was faced with the total and definitive self-communication of God (incarnation) such as he is. And God revealed himself in the man Jesus as Father, Son, and Holy Spirit.[23]

As God totally present in Jesus, he is the full salvation of the individual. In effect, through his resurrection he made visible the realization of the utopia of the Kingdom of God and the joyful freedom of life that is called to life and not death. Whoever has so much importance for the end of history must also have had it for the beginning of history. Creation (protology) comes from God with a view toward this ultimate good (eschatology) through the mediation of Jesus Christ and his Spirit.

The absolute Mystery, then, is called Father, who sent his Son to fulfill, liberate, and redirect all things toward oneness in him, through the power of the Holy Spirit. Universal paternity implies universal fraternity. All of this can be stated and accepted because of the sacramental mediation of the community of Christian faith which began with the faith of the apostles and continues uninterrupted to the present day in what we call the Church. But to share in the salvation offered in Jesus Christ it is not enough to be incorporated into this ecclesial community; one needs to live the same experience of Jesus Christ, an experience of sonship and deep fraternity. This is the ethic of following Christ that leads to community and allows us to share in the salvation offered through him.

This experience, narrated through praxis, is what constitutes Christian identity. It must be able to be identified in any religious and cultural syncretism. Otherwise it is not right to speak of an *essentially* Christian syncretism.

The Catholic attitude of openness to syncretism: What has been the historical experience of this Christian identity? Without criticizing it too severely, two basic tendencies are revealed. On the one hand is deep sympathy, an openness to the religious wealth that it encountered, assimilating, transforming, or accommodating that wealth, leading to a compromise of the identity of the Christian faith. This is the experience of Christianity in a Catholic vein. The other tendency is critical, yet expands the very system that is syncretized, purifying, rejecting, and maintaining the demand for a purity of faith. This is the Christianity of Protestantism.

Both tendencies are found together, be it within Roman Catholicism or Protestantism; different emphases give rise to diverse styles of living out the Christian identity.[24] Both have their support in the Bible and in tradition. On the one hand, we hear: "What you worship in ignorance I intend to make known to you" (Acts 17:23); "Test everything and keep what is good" (1 Thes 5:21). Yet we must also remember: "Do not trust every spirit but put the spirits to the test to see whether they come from God" (1 John 4:1); "Remain in that which has been from the beginning" (1 John 1:1–4; 2:7–24; 2 John 5) because there are positions that water down Christ and his message (1 John 4:1–6; 1 Cor 13:3); "guard what has been given to you; avoid idle discussions about false knowledge because some have gone beyond Christ" (1 Tim 6:20–21;1:3–4; 2 Tim 1:13–14; 4:2–4). Tradition testifies to the deep sympathy toward existing religions, accepting everything possible from them. Other times one may find simple substitution: instead of pagan amulets, metal crosses are used; instead of formulas for curing illnesses, words and phrases from Scripture, as well as their style, are employed.[25]

But there has also been a real attempt at true syncretism, by excluding all magic, superstition, and polytheism. The Synod of Ancyra (314) ordained that wizards and others who followed pagan customs, those who gave hospitality to magicians, were all subject to excommunication for a period of five years. The Synod of Elvira (312) set forth in canon 6 that should anyone kill another through magical arts, he or she was to be excluded from the Christian community for life. The Synod of Laodicea in the second half of the fourth century mandated in canon 36 that "priests and other clergy may not be magicians, wizards, necromancers or astrologers. They may not fabricate protective amulets, which are chains for the soul and offer no protection for life. We therefore order that those who carry such things be expelled from the Church."[26] We read in an explanation of the creed written between 360 and 400: "Do not allow anyone, in case of sickness, pain or worry, to seek a medicine man or anyone who wears phylacteries. Never do such a thing nor allow anyone else to do so."[27]

On the subject of syncretism, Augustine made the distinction between what faith teaches and what faith tolerates.[28] As we have already seen, he established some criteria that are useful even today:

> All those things that have no basis in Sacred Scripture nor in the resolutions of the Synods of Bishops nor that have acquired authority through the tradition of the whole Church, but that have appeared in certain times and places in such a pluriformity of appearances such that they do not achieve the sought after goals, must be abolished wherever this is possible. Although they do not contradict the faith, they place a burden upon religion which, according to God's plan, must be free of such enslaving burdens in a simple and clear cultural form.[29]

The above enables us to point out the fundamental criteria of Christian praxis in the process of syncretization. First, Scripture itself is a criterion. The Scriptures already represent a purification within Judaism and primitive Christianity, given inadequate formulations and practices surrounding the Mystery of God and human dignity. Second, Christian praxis is supported by the tradition of the universal Church that has passed many elements through a sieve and preserved what best expressed the Christian experience. Third, there is the criterion of the decisions of the episcopal synods that have discerned critically the objectifications developed by the People of God. Finally, there is the argument of the tradition of the prophets and of Jesus in the defense of human freedom and spontaneity in the cultural universe: neither be hypocritical (Matt 6:5) nor advocate lengthy and wordy prayers (Matt 6:7) nor burden others with a religious weight of countless norms, laws, and rituals (Matt 23:4). Synthesizing all of this, one can say that everything that aids liberty, love, faith, and theological hope represents true syncretism and incarnates the liberating message of God in history.

It is clear that we are not speaking of Christian identity in terms of the universalization of a *concept* of identity, as has been the case when faith has been identified with doctrine. Doctrinal Christianity does not tolerate syncretism; its one-time syncretization is dogmatized and new teachings are not recognized. Logically, this understanding must do away with the reality of history. For history to continue identity cannot be thought of in terms of a universal concept; it must be understood as an ever new, repeated, and preserved experience that is expressed in different ways depending on the age, place, social class, and geopolitical situation. The Christian experience, understood as catholic, is open to universality; it does not choose only one culture in which it is to be incarnated; every culture is worthy of the salvation won by Jesus Christ and of having that salvation proclaimed within it.

Two fundamental criteria: There are two fundamental criteria present in the Scriptures and also taken up by Jesus. The identity of the Christian experience is primarily the experience of absolute Mystery that communicated itself in grace, love, and forgiveness to humanity in the concrete reality of a human person (Incarnation). However, more than preserving this identity, it must be expressed in terms of spiritual worship and an ethical commitment that gives witness in life to the truth of this understanding.

Spiritual worship: At the core of every religion is the encounter with God. Every religion, with its symbolic universe, seeks nothing other than to lead the individual to the Divine and so make a salvific encounter possible. Biblical tradition calls this spiritual worship. Spiritual, in this sense, has nothing to do with the opposite of material; it has to do with the worship of the heart, the consecration of the whole person. God does not want things from the human person, like sacrifices, prayers, rites, or sacraments. He wants the individual's heart, one's life, a contrite, humble, open, serving, loving heart. The purpose or function of religion is to create and give expression to this oblative attitude, and not substitute itself for it. When one looks only for ceremonies and rituals, one is seeking him or herself; one is not seeking God. If one is seeking God primarily instead of rites, then the rites have meaning as expressions of the individual's search and as celebrations of the person's encounter with God. Overemphasizing ritual, music, and symbolism leads to a bastardization of religion and causes it to lose its true purpose for faith and experience. Christ and the prophets are adamant in the defense of religion whose truth does not lie in its material expressions but in the translation of the individual's response to and acceptance of God (cf. Mark 12:33; Matt 23:23–25; 15:1–23; 12:7; John 2:13–22; 4:21–24).

Ethical commitment: True worship and ethical commitment are one and the same. One is led to others in the same way that one is led to God. God's cause implies the cause of humanity and vice versa. The prophets highlighted the connection of the commandments of the first tablet (having to do with God) to those of the second tablet (pertaining to one's neighbor).

The violation of the sacred law of humanity is included in the violation of the sacrosanct law of God. Whoever lives the law of love and practices the law of justice is in communion with God. Whoever says that he loves God and yet hates his neighbor (1 John 4:20) is a liar and his worship is nothing more than idolatry. A religion that is at home with misery caused by injustice and the violation of human rights can no longer express the true faith and is no longer the reflection of an experience of the encounter with the Divine. Jesus' "woe" applies to this type of false religion: "it does not worry about the heart of the Law: justice, mercy, and good faith" (Matt 23:23; cf. Matt 5:23–24; 9:13; 10:7; 21:12–13); in the words of the prophet Micah: "You have been told, O man, what is good and what the Lord requires of you: only to do what is right and to love goodness, and to walk humbly with your God" (6:8). The God of Jesus Christ does not free the individual from this obligation; he demands that one be a participant in the building of concrete relationships of justice, fraternity, and love between persons, because this is the sure path toward God and salvation.

These criteria aid the discernment between true and false syncretism, whether it is within the Church itself or in the encounter with other cultural or religious expressions. True faith redeems religion and false syncretism, making them also true. Because faith expresses the dimension of transcendence and universality as well as the acceptance of the living God who enters concretely into history, it is open to him in any of his concrete mediations. This is how faith develops its syncretisms that express this encounter with God.

There is the growing conviction that the present Christian and Catholic syncretism is incapable of doing justice to other cultures. Speaking of the *ubandista* religion of black Brazilians, Bonaventura Kloppenburg rightly states: "Neither the official Catholicism of Rome nor the pure Protestantism of the reformers nor the orthodox spiritualism of Allan Kardec seems to allow sufficient room for the religious needs of the people. There is a growing popular protest against all imported religious forms that are insufficiently adapted to the indigenous situation."[30] One comes to the conclusion that the future of Christianity depends on its ability to formulate new syncretisms. Its present cultural expression, from Greco-Roman-Germanic culture, belongs to a glorious past. The present seems to indicate that it will be definitively replaced by the new cultures that surround us.

A Pedagogy of Flexibility

The new syncretism that is now necessary is not possible without the preservation of the Christian identity. Yet, it has nothing to do with adaptation either. This new syncretism demands a missionary and evangelizing zeal that is directed toward conversion to Jesus Christ as God who communicated himself to humanity. This conversion is only possible if Christian faith has the courage to give up its own syncretism and risk a new one, accepting, assimilating, integrating, and purifying the values found in the religions of other cultures. Without this truly paschal experience, a new Church will not be born, just as the first Church of the apostles was not born without the experience of resurrection. A clear consciousness of this challenge seems to be absent at the present time. The Church seems to find it easier to expand the reigning ecclesial system rather than allow and prepare for the birth of another. So the challenge is not being met but simply postponed.

For this new experience to come about, as in all new life, flexibility is necessary. In ancient theology, flexibility (*katabasis*) was a basic theological category. God was infinitely flexible toward humanity, accepting its reality with its undeniable limitations and onerous ambiguities. It was not in spite of them but rather in and through them that he redeemed us. The resulting Church clothed itself in a courageous flexibility toward the Greeks, Romans, and barbarians, accepting their languages, customs, rituals, and religious expressions. It did not demand any more than faith in Jesus Christ the savior. The early Church believed that he then would go on to conquer the hearts of individuals as well as their religions until they reached the fullness of the truth hidden in the confession that Jesus Christ is the savior.

Christian consciousness will have to give witness to a similar flexibility, placing toleration before condemnation, encouraging true Christian experience before watching out for its liturgical and doctrinal formulations. To trust in the religious experience of indigenous peoples is to surrender oneself to the Spirit who is wiser than all ecclesial prudence and who knows the true paths far better than the theological search for the purity of Christian identity. If pastoral activity is not united with prophecy, if contemplation is not allied with the meaning of reality, the Church will find it difficult to drum up the courage necessary to be stripped and then clothed in a new sacred mantle.

Just as God accepted humanity as he found it, so also must Christian faith seek out individuals where and how they are culturally. It is out of this situation that a pedagogy for growth and maturity in the faith must begin.[31] The deeper this faith is, the more open it is to the true syncretism in which God and Jesus Christ Liberator do not appear as the object that will satisfy the heavy burden of the search for security and power, but rather as the heart of life and love that attracts and penetrates all things and all persons.

Chapter 8

CHARACTERISTICS OF THE CHURCH IN A CLASS SOCIETY

In this chapter we will attempt to identify the principal characteristics of the Church as it is found in the base, the grassroots, among those who are not in power. This will be the new face of the Church that, in its own way, traces the new features of the face of Christ insofar as the Church professes to be the sacrament of Christ.

Preoccupation with the characteristics of the Church (in ecclesiology one speaks of notes and properties) is ancient, evident in St. Epiphanius (315–403) and Cyril of Jerusalem (313–86) who, during the First Council of Constantinople (381), influenced the development of the creed which is still prayed in the Church today.[1] Four basic characteristics of the Church are enumerated in this creed: "We believe in one, holy, catholic, and apostolic Church." These characteristics were offered as the criteria for discerning the true Church of Christ.

What Is Meant by "Characteristics of the Church"?

The desire to establish criteria for the true Church comes from apologetics and true confessional agreement. Where and in what group do we find the true Church of Christ? How is the true Church distinguished from the false one? This question was crucial in the sixteenth century with the ecclesiological controversies of Huss and Luther. These theologians made the academic distinction between notes and properties.[2] *Notes*, as the word suggests (what makes a thing notable or perceptible), are those qualities of the Church that (a) are accessible to every spirit (even primitive ones), (b) would therefore have to be more widely recognized than even the Church itself and so be able to lead to a knowledge of the true Church, and (c) must be inseparable from the true Church to such a degree that they cannot be found outside of it. *Properties* are those qualities that belong to the Church yet do not lead to the knowledge of the true Church at first glance because they can be discovered apart from the Church, such as the quality of being without defect, of being necessary for salvation, and so on.

108

The notes that characterize the Church are the four described above: unity, holiness, catholicity, and apostolicity. Later, especially with the polemic against the Waldensian heresy in the thirteenth century (under Pope Innocent III), together with the ecclesiologists at the end of the nineteenth century, a fifth note was added: Roman. The Church is one, holy, catholic, apostolic, and Roman.

The argument of the path of notes (*per viam notarum*) was almost dismissed because of the difficulty of proving that the notes are found exclusively within the Roman Catholic Church.[3] The result was the concentration of the argument in the most discernible note: its Romanism. Yet this alone did not guarantee the true Church because there was the impression of speaking of some other Church.

The purpose here of dealing with the characteristics of the Church is not rooted in polemics; there is no need to argue that the new forms of the Church that are irrupting throughout the world, especially among the *comunidades eclesiales de base* in Latin America, are part of the true Church of Christ. The presumption is already accepted; they are truly the Church of Christ and the apostles on the grassroots level. Nor is the academic and essentially fruitless distinction between notes and properties really necessary. They are mentioned solely to provide a contact between traditional ecclesiology and the present Church being born among the peoples of the world, the Church that is born of the Spirit of God in the midst of social reality. The first medieval scholars of the Church spoke of the *conditiones Ecclesiae*, the tangible conditions of the Church. Whoever observes the current ecclesial events, a true ecclesiogenesis, with the eyes of faith must ask: What relevant traces can be seen? How do the characteristics of the *comunidades eclesiales de base* and other base communities speak to us of the characteristics of Jesus Christ and his message? This is the basis for the present reflection, because the function of the Church is to make visible, and historical, the salvific meaning of Jesus Christ and his mission and, doing so, become the sacrament-sign and sacrament-instrument of liberation.

However, it is first necessary to situate the Church as it is socially organized within the world. This is fundamental because of the consciousness that the Church is in the world and not the world within the Church, a position canonized by *Gaudium et Spes*. Failing to do so—as happens in almost every book on ecclesiology, including recent ones like Hans Küng's *The Church*[4]—hinders the true understanding of the Church and opens the way for an idealism that hides from the complex reality of the Church. The real situation is one of a Church in a class society. How are we to understand such a Church? In order to understand the growing movement of popular Catholicism and base ecclesial communities, one must understand the present reality of a Church involved in a society of low, middle, and upper classes. Otherwise the Church that is born of the people, from the base, cannot be understood.

The Church Allied with the Ruling Class[5]

There are two dimensions in the Church, each one having its own nature but also mutually related: the Church as religious-ecclesiastical realm (institution) and the Church as ecclesial-sacramental realm (sacrament, sign, and instrument of salvation). By religious-ecclesiastical realm one understands the complex of ecclesiastical institutions as well as the group of religious "actors" who interact among themselves and with the institutions.[6] Because both are dimensions of the one Church they must be well-defined in order to avoid any real or linguistic parallels, because the basic premise is that the ecclesiastical realm is the support for the sacramental-ecclesial realm. The institution is the vehicle for the sacrament; the social visibility of the Church makes grace and the reign of God tangible.

In order to identify the characteristics of the Church, the religious-ecclesiastical realm must be considered. To what extent do the visible characteristics of the Church reveal the invisible characteristics of the salvation of the Gospel and the person of Jesus Christ? The religious-ecclesiastical realm is not a preestablished structure of practices, actors, institutions, and teachings that refer to God, Christ, and the Church as sacrament. It is the result of a process, the product of a systematizing that is shaped by two primary forces: society, with its concrete procedures, and the Christian experience, with its content of revelation. In other words, the Church was not ready-made in heaven; it is the fruit of a definite history and, at the same time, the product of a faith that in its own way assimilates the events of history.

The Religious-Ecclesiastical Realm and Society

The Church does not operate in a vacuum but in a society that is situated in history. This means that the Church, like it or not, is limited and shaped by a social context, with a population and limited structured resources that have a certain character. The religious-ecclesiastical realm is a part of the social realm which influences it in a dialectical manner. A premise taken here—and it is far too difficult to prove here—is that the organization of a society revolves around its means of production. By means of production we understand the manner in which a certain populace is organized in relation to accessible material resources necessary to develop the goods that maintain its existence and reproduction, be it biological or cultural reproduction.

This organization is infrastructural, and the rest of society is built upon it. It is *constant* because it meets ever present needs; it is *universal* because it is common to all societies and all ages; and, it is *fundamental* because, in the final analysis, this organization is the condition for the possibility of all other initiatives. The Church is also conditioned, limited, and oriented by a specific means of production. In other words, the means of production determines which religious-ecclesiastical activities are impossible, undesirable, intolerable, acceptable, necessary, and primary; that is, it determines the characteristics of the Church.[7] However, religious-ecclesiastical actions are not mere social products with a religious label. They have their own specific nature but when they are expressed in a social context, they are affected, limited, and oriented by the means of production peculiar to the type of society in which they are expressed.

There are various means of production, some more balanced than others. The western world is comprised largely of societies organized around unbalanced means of production, organized around the capitalist system which is characterized by the private ownership of the means of production in the hands of a few, by the unequal distribution of opportunities for work, and by the unequal distribution of the products of that labor. This unbalanced system gives rise to class societies, wherein there are relationships of domination and power between the classes as well as conflicts of interest. There is marked inequality in terms of food, clothing, lifestyles, sanitary conditions, employment, leisure, and so on. Such a class structure limits and determines all activity within the society, independent of an individual's intentions, and this also includes religious-ecclesiastical activity. The faithful in the Church occupy objectively different social positions according to their social class. They perceive reality in a way that corresponds to their social condition, and so they interpret and live the gospel message out of the needs, interests, and behavior of their particular class. Thus, actions that are possible or impossible, tolerable, recommended, necessary, or demanded vary from one social class to another.

Yet, the actions of a social class are not automatic, mechanical, or static. Every class finds itself in a continual process of progress (or regress), depending on its place in the social division of labor. Just as the means of production are unequal, so also is the class dynamic in that it is conflictive and unbalanced, with unequal forces struggling with each other.

In a class society there is always a dominant class (or group of classes) that is responsible for the growth of the whole society. This dominant class always strives to consolidate, deepen, and widen its power, persuading those who are dominated to accept their domination, conquering them through ideological agreement.[8] But the domination is never total. Because it is achieved through a more or less lengthy process, there remains the resistance of the dominated along with their strategies for survival and the strengthening of their lost power. There is ongoing conflict between dominators and dominated, whether it is open or latent. This resistance imposes limitations on the ruling class, for without them the subordinated classes may become revolutionary classes.

The dominant classes, in their strategy for power, try to incorporate the Church in the widening, consolidation, and legitimation of their dominion, especially in order to gain the acceptance of their rule by all individuals and groups. The religious-ecclesiastical realm is strongly pressured to organize itself in such a way that it is adjusted to the interests of the ruling classes, a pressure that takes the form of economic, juridical, political, cultural, and even repressive measures. In this way, the Church serves a conservative and legitimating function for the ruling classes.

However, it is not preordained that the Church accommodate itself to the ruling classes. The subordinated classes also solicit the Church to aid them in their search for greater power and autonomy in the face of the domination they suffer. They ask the Church to support and justify the breakdown of the ruling classes and lend itself to revolutionary service. Yet, the faithful are present on both sides; the Church is inevitably affected by class conflicts and so may either serve a revolutionary function or serve as a strengthening force for the ruling classes. These two possibilities are not free choices or options. They are dependent upon the rapport that the religious-ecclesiastical realm has established with the various classes throughout the sociohistorical process. It may happen that the Church has reproduced the structures of the ruling classes within itself, thereby creating an equally unbalanced structure that reflects the dominant social realm.

This clearly is not a mechanical reproduction because there is always the relative autonomy of the religious-ecclesiastical realm. To say that it is relatively autonomous is to say that it is not totally determined by the social realm, but neither is it completely independent. Because of its specific nature—the Christian experience, its objective expression in theory and practice, the institutional character by which it reproduces, preserves, and spreads that experience, especially the institution of the hierarchy—the religious-ecclesiastical realm immediately assimilates and reworks social structures and influences.

Throughout its history, the Church has defined itself at times with the ruling classes and at other times with the lower classes. The unequal social structure, revolving around ownership of the means of production, slowly came to predominate within the Church itself.[9] An unbalanced structure in the means of "religious" production was created; in socioanalytical language (so as not to give a moral connotation), there has also been a gradual expropriation of the means of religious production from the Christian people by the clergy. In the early years, the Christian people as a whole shared in the power of the Church, in decisions, in the choosing of ministers; later they were simply consulted; finally, in terms of power, they were totally marginalized, dispossessed of their power.

Just as there was a social division of labor, an ecclesiastical division of religious labor was introduced. A group of functionaries and experts was created, responsible for attending to the religious needs of all through the exclusive production of the symbolic goods to be consumed by the now dispossessed people. It is impossible to go into all of the internal conflicts of religious power (e.g., hierarchy-laity, low clergy–high clergy) or all of the forms of ideological consensus that have been created through the centuries that have resulted in the fact that ecclesiastical functionaries today hold a monopoly on the legitimate exercise of religious power.[10] It is clear that a Church so structurally unbalanced is in harmony with the social realm that possesses the same biased means of production. The Church has often become the legitimating religious ideology for the imperial social order.

The way in which the Church has been present to the lower classes will be dealt with later when exploring local churches and especially the base ecclesial communities.

Christian Experience and Revelation

The other formative force in the religious-ecclesiastical realm is the Christian experience with its content of revelation. This is widely known. What must be affirmed is the irreducibility of the experience of Christian faith witnessed to and preserved by the founding texts which are the Christian Scriptures read and reread throughout history (tradition). They are the narration of the story of a being in whom the apostles perceived the ultimate meaning of humanity and the world (salvation). The pillars that support the Christian faith and that constitute the inspirational wellspring for the Church are the actions of the dead and risen Jesus and his message of love, hope, fraternity, mutual service, and trusting surrender to the Father. This is the core of faith, not an interpretation, the criteria that continually judge the Church, its practices, its rhetoric, and its means of religious production.

The religious-ecclesiastical realm contains an undeniable contradiction; on the one hand, it has historically been characterized by an unbalanced means of symbolic production, aiding capitalist society; on the other, its basic ideals call for a balanced, shared, and fraternal means of production. Because the Church lives this contradiction, there is always the possibility of the irruption of prophets and the liberational spirit that will cause the Church to approach those groups that seek more just relationships in history and that are organized in a revolutionary way. This is exactly what is happening at the grassroots level in the Church.

Unbalanced Means of Religious Production

The Church has been active in the consolidation of the ruling classes, tending to act as a conserving and legitimating agent; it has become a multiclass religious-ecclesiastical realm that reflects the conflicts that crisscross the social fabric. At the same time, it has formed its own ruling class with all power in the hands of the Pope, bishops, and priests. The four basic characteristics (notes) of the Church are presented within this unbalanced ecclesiastical system of religious production.

Unity is presented as the uniformity of one doctrine, one discourse, one liturgy, one ecclesiastical order (canon law), one morality, and, if possible, one language (Latin). The unification of the symbolic order reproduces the cohesiveness of the social ruling classes, hiding and transfiguring both social and intraecclesiastical conflicts. The unity of the Church is defined as the communion of the people with the hierarchy and that communion of the hierarchy with the people. Communication and all discourse is, at the same time, united and ambiguous: united in order to hide the conflicts that, by their nature, would result in a diversity of statements; ambiguous so as to meet diverse needs and thus preserve a united power. These united and ambiguous statements are generally limited to nonconflictive subjects, favoring harmony and the explicit denial of the importance, or even existence, of class divisions, denying the legitimacy of the struggles in search of liberation through constant appeals to the supernatural and to moral observance. The unification of classes within the same Church is merely symbolic, to the advantage of the dominant classes in a sociopolitical manner.

Holiness is defined as the way in which the faithful within the Church comply with the ethos set by the ruling hierarchy. The great virtues of the holy Catholic person are obedience, ecclesiastical submission, and humility, all in reference to the Church, that is, one is baptized in order to serve the Church. As a result, almost all of the modern saints are saints of the system: priests, bishops, and religious; there are few lay people and even these few were captured by the central ruling power. The prophet and the reformer who, in the name of faith, criticizes or proposes a change in the power relations within the Church is subjected to every type of symbolic violence (canonical proceedings, excommunication) and never is said to characterize holiness in the Church.

Apostolicity, in an unbalanced Church structure, is only applied to a single class, to the bishops as successors of the apostles; it is not considered to be a characteristic of the whole Church. Apostolic succession is reduced to the succession of the apostolic power and not to apostolic teaching, as was the original meaning of the term. It hides the fact that, in the words of Paul VI, "the lay person, like the bishop, is a successor of the Apostles."[11]

Catholicity is strictly defined together with unity (uniformity); it leans toward quantitative aspects: one and the same Church present in the entire world (*per totum orbem terrarum diffusa*). Catholicity is not defined by its concrete elements such as its incarnation in various local cultures and churches, but rather by its abstract elements like the same hierarchy, the same sacraments, and the same theology.

In order to make a theological judgment of this unbalanced structure of the Church, we must ask: To what degree does it make visible and carry on the relevant experience of Jesus Christ and the apostles, serving as a herald for the ideals of fraternity, participation, and communion present in Jesus' practices and message? In the interest of brevity, this question cannot be answered here. Yet its importance must be recognized; there is a general feeling throughout the ecclesial body that perceives the contradiction between the unequally structured religious-ecclesiastical realm and the person and message of Christ and the apostles. Everywhere the call is heard for an internal restructuring of the Church in order for it to be more faithful to its origins and better carry out its particular mission of establishing theological order, through the creation of mediations of more participatory, more balanced, and, therefore, more just power.

The Church and the Lower Classes

The Church is not doomed to carry out a purely preservative mission, contrary to the view held by orthodox Marxism; rather, because of its ideals and origins (the dangerous and subversive memory of Jesus of Nazareth crucified under Pontius Pilate), its mission is revolutionary. But this is dependent upon certain social conditions as well as the Church's own internal structure. Given a certain break with the ruling class(es), the Church may find itself allied with the lower classes in their struggles against domination, especially with those groups possessing a religious vision of the world. These groups, such as those in Latin America with a strong religious heritage and culture, tend to create a *strategy of liberation*, one that must begin with an independent and alternative view of the world contrary to that held by the ruling powers. This prior condition is necessary to create the objective conditions for the true transformation of their own subordinate existence.

This is where the religious-ecclesiastical realm becomes relevant. If it helps in the development of a religious view of the world that reflects the liberational interests of these groups, opposing the dominant classes, it will be carrying out a revolutionary function. The religious interests of the base are geared toward legitimating its search for liberation, and to counterlegitimate and denaturalize the domination they suffer. The religious-ecclesiastical realm can offer this legitimation, given certain concrete internal and external conditions, whether it be because it understands the justice of their struggles or because it sees them in agreement with gospel ideals.

Generally, religion is not the principal means for reproducing the capitalist system. In the predominantly religious lower classes, the development of an independent and alternative Christian view, opposed to that of the ruling classes, leads to a liberating process that will have historical success as long as it achieves a certain degree of class consciousness, organization, and mobilization. Theologically, this vision recaptures the historical person of Jesus of Nazareth who favored the poor and felt them to be the first beneficiaries of the Kingdom of God. This theology recovers the original meaning of his life and death, as a life committed to the cause of the humble in whom the cause of God was being frustrated, as a death caused by a conflict motivated by the dominant classes of the time. In this light, the principal symbols of faith are reinterpreted and their liberating dimensions are unveiled, dimensions that are objectively present but that are repressed by a religious structure that is allied with the ruling social class.

It is evident that such a recovery of the original meaning of Christianity does not mean a break with ruling ecclesiastical traditions. Normally, it is the task of the religious intellectual to bring about a new mending of the eventual tears in that tradition. On the one hand, through a link with the lower classes the intellectual helps them perceive, systematize, and express their great desires for liberation while, on the other, accepting them within the religious (theological) task of the Church, demonstrating their coherence with the fundamental ideals of Jesus and the apostles. Thus, important pieces of the ecclesiastical institution can be allied with the base, raising the possibility of a popular Church with popular characteristics.

This is the phenomenon that is taking place with the base ecclesial communities in Latin America: a true ecclesiogenesis, the genesis of a new Church, but one that is not apart from the Church of the apostles and tradition, taking place in the base of the Church and in the grassroots of society, that is, among the lower classes who are religiously as well as socially deprived of power. This novelty must be understood analytically; these communities mean a break with the monopoly of social and religious power and the inauguration of a new religious and social process for restructuring both the Church and society, with a different social division of labor as well as an alternative religious division of ecclesiastical labor.[12]

According to one view of this new Church from the base, one can point out fifteen characteristics of this Church; Robert Bellarmine, in 1591, described fifteen characteristics of the Church of the ruling classes. The coincidence is not without significance.

1. A Church as People of God: The term "people" is not taken in the sense of nation, lumping everyone together indiscriminately and thus hiding internal differences, but rather in the sense of people/lower class, defined as those who are excluded from participation in society and reduced to the mass, a thing instead of persons. "People" is an analytical term and also an axiological category. Analytically it defines a group in opposition to another, while axiologically it proposes a value to be lived by all persons. In other words, all are called to be people and not just a subordinate class. Human beings achieve this in the measure to which, through the mediation of communities, they cease to be a mass, develop self-consciousness, lay out a historical plan for justice and participation for all (and not only for themselves), and teach practices that lead to the prompt realization of this utopia.[13]

The liberational strategy of the people is rooted in the overcoming of the present monopolistic structure of civil and sacred power and directed toward a new society with the greatest possible participation. This people becomes the People of God in the measure to which, forming communities of faith, hope, and love inspired by Jesus' message of complete fraternity, they try to make concrete the reality of a people comprised of free, fraternal, and participating individuals. This historical reality is not only a product of a balanced social movement, but theologically it signifies the anticipation of and preparation for the Kingdom of God and the eschatological People of God.

The base communities form this people on the move; their existence launches a challenge to the hierarchy, that has monopolized all sacred power, to understand itself in terms of service and not as power for power's sake,[14] as a mediation for justice, fraternity, and coordination, leaving aside all monopolistic and marginalizing structures. In Latin America, as elsewhere, there is a vast network of base ecclesial communities alongside a diocesan and parochial structure, a Church of the laity together with a Church exclusively led by the clergy, revealing the tension that exists and persists within the Church. Through this tension, however, more equal relationships may develop, allowing a greater participation by all in both the production and benefit of religious "goods."

2. A Church of the poor and weak: The majority of the members of the base communities (at least in Latin America) are poor and physically weak due to the harsh expropriation of their labor. The communities are taking measures to insure the opportunity for the members' efforts and labor to be brought together in common, through the formation of political parties and other community initiatives.

The fact of being poor and weak is not only a sociological fact; through the eyes of faith, it is a theological event. The poor individual signifies an epiphany of the Lord; that individual's miserable existence is a challenge thrown at God himself who once resolved to intervene in order to reestablish justice. Poverty expresses a failure of justice when poverty is not spontaneous but comes about due to a system that expropriates everything from the individual person. The poor are the natural bearers of the utopia of the Kingdom of God; they are the ones who have hope, and the future belongs to them.

3. *A Church of the dispossessed*: The vast majority of base ecclesial communities are involved in some form of dispute regarding lands from which they have been or are threatened with being expelled. They are also often involved in disputes concerning wages, employment, health, housing, school, and/or labor. It is easy to see that the present capitalist, elitist society was not made for them; nothing is for their use: not laws nor the courts nor the political machinery nor the mass media. They are truly dispossessed; until recently they have been the objects of the Church's and society's mercy. They were not viewed positively but were the objects of political handouts and as people to be used for popular festivals.

Now they are getting together; they are forming communities; they are gaining a critical and transforming consciousness in terms of both the Church and society. They are taking history into their own hands, becoming masters of their own destiny. The ecclesial community is the principle behind the discovery of the dignity inherent in the human person, a dignity debased by the ruling classes, which is leading to an emphasis on the rights of the poor. They are discovering that they are the subjects of rights and laws as citizens, that they are the image and likeness of God, children of the Father, temples of the Holy Spirit, and destined for complete personalization at the end of history, yet also anticipating that reality in the present through their practices of freedom.

The base ecclesial communities are, in our view, the correct expression of the Church, expecially for those who are the victims of capitalistic greed, rather than the traditional, hierarchical Church with its classical and modern associations, such as the St. Vincent de Paul Society and the Cursillo, charismatic renewal and marriage encounter movements, that encourage a class society by sharing in the plan of the ruling classes.

4. *A Church of the laity:* Lay, in its original Greek meaning, signifies a member of the People of God. Thus, the priest, bishop, and Pope are also lay people. However, in the ecclesiastical division of labor, lay means all those who do not share sacred power, all those who do not produce the symbolic goods that presently create the ecclesial community; they receive what has been produced by the body of ecclesial functionaries and blindly carry out their decisions. In the base communities, almost entirely made up of lay people, one sees the true creation of an ecclesial reality, of com-

munal witness, of organization and missionary responsibility. The lay people take the word in their own hands, create symbols and rites, and rebuild the Church with grassroot materials.

5. *Church as the* koinonia *of power:* Sacred power lies within the entire community, and not only in the hands of a few. The base community is not anarchical, in the sense of no organization or leadership, but rather opposes the current model of the monopolization of power in the hands of a body of specialists above and outside the community. The roles of leadership and coordination are shared and so power becomes a function of the community rather than of one single person. Power in itself is not rejected, only its monopolization and expropriation by the "elite." Because of this basic stance, there are more than a few communities that avoid all vocabulary that denotes authoritarianism and the concentration of power in a single individual or group.

6. *A Church that ministers:* The base ecclesial communities, because of their communitarian more than societal character, facilitate the sharing of power. The various positions within the community are not predetermined by the attempt to preserve a preexisting structure but are responses to needs as they arise. The entire community is ministerial, not only some of its members, thus avoiding the current division of religious labor: hierarchy–making decisions–laity following orders. Theologically the Church is Christ's representative and its ministers are the representatives of the Church; they are also Christ's representatives in the measure in which they are churches. Therefore, power lies within the entire community and that power is expressed in different ways according to various needs, even'the power of the Supreme Pontiff. Thus, the services are never above and outside of the Church but within it, as the expressions of the Church's sacramentality in service to the entire ecclesial community.

7. *A Church of the diaspora:* The base communities represent, sociologically and historically, the first successful experience of the Church with popular roots, outside institutional Christianity. Institutional Christianity means a particular relationship between the Church and civil society, carried on through the state and the ruling social and cultural structures of a given nation; the Church sides with the dominant classes in order to be able to exercise its power within civil society.[15] In 1960 the historical conditions first appeared for a Church born of the people, of the dominated classes. The tension is not between an official Church and a popular Church but between institutional Christianity (the Church incarnated in the ruling classes) and the popular Church.

The base ecclesial communities are the Church within society (in the lower classes) and not society within the Church. They are a Christian diaspora spread throughout the social fabric. Beyond their theological and eschatological significance, they also take on political value: they aid in the rebuilding of civil society which is being torn apart constantly by class division and the assaults of the ruling antipopular classes. These communities encourage a spirituality of mutual aid, teaching a communitarian and solidary praxis, preparing the way for new social interaction.

8. *A liberator Church:* Through the Christian community, as is happening with the base ecclesial communities, the people are able to enter into politics, understood as commitment to and practice in search of the common good and social justice. Christianity is the religion of the people; through it they understand and organize their world. A Christianity that is expressed through the expectations and demands of the oppressed is liberational, and the base community emerges as the means for that liberation. The only motivation for political commitment is the Gospel and the life of Jesus, leading the communities to struggle for liberation from injustice. This faith is not free from its political obligations; it gains its true dimension in the liberating process of a society that gives birth to less iniquitous forms of interaction, pointing toward a liberation that transcends history and yet is historically awaited in the here and now.

9. *A Church that sacramentalizes present liberations:* The community does not only celebrate the word of God and the official sacraments (when it has them) but also celebrates, in the light of faith, life itself, including the gains and losses of the entire group. It knows how to act out its problems and solutions; it liturgizes the popular, and popularizes the liturgical. The community learns to discover God in life, in its events, in its struggles. It is beginning to recover from the sacramental amnesia of the Church, brought about by the limitation of the entire sacramental structure to the seven sacraments, at the Council of Trent.[16]

10. *A Church that continues the grand tradition:* Jesus, the apostles, and the first Christian communities were of the people; they were poor and from the lower classes. The memory of its humble beginnings has never been lost in the Church, but with the institutionalization of Christianity these beginnings were set aside. The liberating message of Jesus was expropriated by the ruling classes for their own purposes. The base ecclesial communities are in harmony with the Church of the Acts of the Apostles, with the Church of the martyrs, with all of the prophetic movements that have again accepted the evangelical dimensions of poverty, service, renunciation of all pomp and glory, and activity among the marginalized. This Church of the people, of the poor, has always existed but its history is almost never told; it is being continued within the experience of today's Christian communities in the base. Not only are they reproducing past structures but also creating new ones in response to the historical demands of today. This grassroots Church is an event of people who gather together

around the word of God more than an institution with preestablished structures. It is not that the community is indifferent to sacraments, doctrine, and the hierarchy; they simply are not its raison d'être. The basis of these communities is the word of God that is heard and reread within the context of their real problems; they are held together by their faith, their communitarian projects, their helping one another, and their celebrations.

11. A Church in communion with the Church-at-large: The Church at the base is not a Church that parallels the larger institution; the antagonism is not between institution and community but between institutional Christianity (the Church as associated with the ruling powers of a class society) and the popular Church (identified with the grassroots). The Church at large, structured as a network of institutional services, converges with the Church as a network of base communities. The latter receives the symbolic "capital" of faith from the former, its link with tradition and its dimension of universality. The Church at large participates in the life of the people and is thus linked with the most urgent causes of humanity in terms of justice, dignity, and social participation. The two are actually one and the same Church, the Church of the fathers of faith, made concrete in different social strata, dealing with particular problems. The base is not allergic to the presence of bishops and priests; on the contrary, it calls out to them and demands a new style of ministry that is simpler, more evangelical, more practical, and one that expresses the concerns of the people. Because of these base communities, the entire Church is currently making a more decided choice for the liberation of the oppressed, for the defense of human rights, and for a global transformation of society leading to more human structures.

12. A Church that fosters unity from its mission of liberation: Theological tradition has understood the unity of the Church as being built upon three pillars: one faith (*vinculum symbolicum*), the same sacraments (*vinculum liturgicum*), and the same hierarchical government (*vinculum sociale*). The Latin Church emphasized hierarchical government as the fundamental principle of unity: *unus grex sub uno pastore* (one people under one pastor). The Eastern Orthodox Church accentuated the sacrament as the creative principle of unity and as the expression of that unity, especially the sacrament of the eucharist (*una eucharistia, unus grex*). In the *comunidades eclesiales de base*, unity stems from mission. It possesses the same faith, receives and administers the same sacraments, and is in communion with the greater Church that is hierarchically structured; but its inner unity is created and nourished by a reference to something external to it, that is, mission.

The context of conflict and struggle concretely shapes the mission of the Church, to reflect and live faith in a liberating manner, committed to the humble, struggling for their dignity, and helping to create a common life more in line with gospel criteria. This option is becoming all the more unavoidable in every base community, whether they be rural or urban groups. Divisions are not normally created at the level of faith, sacraments, or leadership; they come about on the level of one's commitment to reality. We might say that unity is built on this option for reality: *una optio, unus grex* (one option, one people).

13. *A Church with a new expression of catholicity:* Unity facilitates the understanding of universality. The base communities have a clear call as a social class but, at the same time, they make it clear that they have a universal vocation for the justice, rights, and participation of all people everywhere. The rights of all come through the mediation of the recovered and protected rights of the poor. The concerns taken up by these communities are universal, and they become universal in the measure in which the communities accept the universality of these concerns.[17] Thus, these communities are not closed in on their own class interests; everyone, no matter of what class, who opts for justice and identifies with the struggles of the community will find a place there. Struggling for economic, social, and political liberation which opens the way for total liberation in the Kingdom of God, the community is at the service of a universal cause.

Capitalism, as a system of unbalanced social interchange, is an impediment to the universality of the Church as long as it only works for the interests of a single class. A democratic and socialist society would seem to offer better objective conditions for a fuller expression of the Church's catholicity. In other words, catholicity—in a capitalistic system—runs the risk of remaining intentional, utilizing the same symbols with varying content depending on the class situation. Rich and poor alike receive communion together in Church, but they do not share in the factory. If there were communion (sharing) in the factory, the eucharistic communion would express not only the eschatological communion at the end of time but also the real communion present in society now.

14. *A completely apostolic Church:* We are in the habit of understanding apostolicity as a characteristic of bishops, the successors of the apostles. However, this concept is a recent development. Originally the apostle was the one who was sent out, as Jesus is described in the New Testament (Heb 3:1). It is very probable that Jesus did not apply the term to the Twelve.[18] Upon being sent out into the world to continue his mission of revelation and proclamation, the Twelve became apostles. But the term is not limited to the Twelve; Paul is called an apostle. In fact, every baptized person receives the task of announcing and giving witness to the news of God in Jesus Christ and so becomes an apostle, a continuation of the sending out of the first apostles. The first twelve remain those who deciphered the mystery of Jesus as the

incarnated Son of God. We are tied to this apostolic faith and its teaching through the founding texts and the living memory of the communities of faith. Because of their function as translators and "decipherers," the apostles became the coordinators of these communities. Therefore, all who exercise this function of coordination are successors of the apostles.

The difficulty with the current understanding of apostolic succession arose when the original twelve apostles were considered individually. The symbolic meaning of the number "twelve" as a designation of the messianic community (the new Israel), and its collegiality, was lost. The fact is that the apostles were not sent out individually; it was the group, the *collegium*, the *community* of the Twelve, that is, the first small *ecclesia* gathered around Jesus, that was sent out. As such, it is the entire community that is apostolic, and not only certain holders of sacred power.

The base ecclesial communities recover this original meaning of apostolicity inasmuch as the community, as community, senses itself as sent out to be the carrier of the orthodox doctrine of faith, sharing the various services brought forth by the Spirit, living an apostolic life through the following of Jesus, his attitudes, his message, and the hope for the Kingdom that has been deposited in the heart of the person of faith. Apostolic succession is not limited to hierarchical function, which divides the community. Everyone is a bearer of the teachings of Jesus Christ and all share in the three basic tasks: to give witness, to sanctify, and to be responsible for the unity and life of the community.

15. *A Church striving for a new type of holiness:* The saint is not only the ascetic, the faithful observer of divine and ecclesiastical laws, the one who has penetrated and interiorized the mystery of God and his human appearance in Jesus Christ. The base communities have created the possibility for another type of holiness, that of the militant. Beyond fighting against one's own passions, the militant fights against exploitation and exclusive accumulation of wealth in an effort to build more communitarian and balanced social structures. New virtues are expressed in terms of class solidarity, participation in communal decisions, mutual aid, criticism of the abuses of power, defamation and persecution in the cause of justice,[19] unjust imprisonment, loss of employment, boycotts, and the criticism of private ownership that lacks social responsibility. The communities find models in those persons who have suffered honorably because of their commitment to the community and to the Gospel, keeping alive the names of their confessors and martyrs, remembering them in their community celebrations.

The Credibility of Christian Hope

All of the above features, and others could be mentioned, characterize the new ecclesial experience that is taking place at the base of the Church and society. All of them reveal a new spirit of greater fidelity to the liberational origins of the gospel message as well as to the transcendent destiny of the world. Faith is not alienated from the world nor does it create a community apart from other people; it is the ferment of indefatigable hope and love, supporting the strength of the weak and the certainty of the search for justice and fraternity. Interest in heaven does not allow us to forget the earth; heaven depends precisely upon what we do on and with the earth. A Church committed to the dispossessed of this world lends credibility to the reality that faith proclaims and that hope promises. It reveals the face of Christ, beckoning those who are discontented with the present world order. The base ecclesial communities springing up throughout the world prove that it is possible to be Christian without being conservative, that one can be a person of faith while at the same time committed to society and its future, that one can hope in eternity without losing one's foothold in the struggle for a better tomorrow, even here and now in our own day and age.

Chapter 9

THE BASE ECCLESIAL COMMUNITY:
A BRIEF SKETCH

Base ecclesial communities (sometimes referred to as basic Christian communities) are a phenomenon that has its origin in Latin America, where they were given their name *comunidades eclesiales de base* because they are communities primarily comprised of lower-class, grassroots people, the base of society, as opposed to the pinnacle of power in the social pyramid. The bishops meeting at Puebla in 1979 hailed them as a "reason for joy and hope" (96, 262, 1309), as "centers of evangelization and moving forces of liberation" (96). To understand this phenomenon that holds so much promise for the future of faith in history, the following sketch is offered. There are five basic points that characterize the base ecclesial community.

1. An Oppressed yet Believing People

The communitarian spirit is a part of modern life. In addition to the large social structures, there are also small groups of people who want to live more immediate and fraternal relationships. The base ecclesial communities are an expression of this desire. There is the added fact that the institution of the Church, in many parts of the world, is in crisis due to the lack of ministers ordained through the sacrament of orders. Without these ministers communities of faith are left to themselves, and run the risk of falling apart and disappearing. The birth of the base ecclesial communities represents a way out of this crisis. In these communities the lay person takes on the task of spreading the Gospel and keeping faith alive. It is also important to note that the members of these communities are generally poor and from the base of society (the lower classes) and from the base of the Church (the laity).

The base ecclesial community is generally made up of fifteen to twenty families. They get together once or twice a week to hear the word of God, to share their problems in common, and to solve those problems through the inspiration of the Gospel. They share their comments on the biblical

125

passages, create their own prayers, and decide as a group what their tasks should be. After centuries of silence, the People of God are beginning to speak. They are no longer just parishioners in their parish; they have their own ecclesiological value; they are recreating the Church of God.

It is true that the Church is Christ's gift which we gratefully receive. Yet the Church is also a human response to faith. The Church is the People of God, born of a believing and, in many parts of the world, oppressed people through the Holy Spirit of God. They are a community of the faithful in which the risen Christ is present. This is the realization of the mystery of the universal Church in the grassroots, in this humble and small group of men, women, and children, often very poor but filled with faith, hope, love, and communion with other Christians. The base ecclesial community makes concrete the true Church of Jesus Christ.

On the one hand is the institutional Church with its dioceses and bishops, with its parishes and sacred ministers, its chapels and churches; on the other is a growing network of base ecclesial communities (especially in Latin America and Brazil in particular, where there are over 70,000 such communities), reaching countless Christians who live out their faith in these communities. These are two expressions of the one Church of Christ and of the apostles. The institutional Church supports and encourages the base ecclesial communities; through them it is able to enter the popular sector and be made concrete by sharing in the painful passion as well as the hopes of the people. These ecclesial communities, in turn, are in communion with the institutional Church; they want their bishop, their priests and religious. In this way, the communities are put in touch with the grand apostolic tradition, guarantee their catholicity, and reaffirm the unity of the Church.

The more the Church is open to the people, the more it becomes the People of God. The more that the poor and oppressed of our societies come together in the name of Christ to hear his word of salvation and liberation, the more they concretely are, in a very real historical sense, the Church of Jesus Christ. There is no real conflict between the ecclesial institution and the ecclesial communities. Conflict does not exist because a large part of the ecclesial institution has joined the communities, including many cardinals, bishops, and pastors. The real tension exists between a Church that has opted for the people, for the poor and their liberation, and other groups in that same Church that have not made this option or who have not made it concrete or who persist in keeping to the strictly sacramental and devotional character of faith.

The base ecclesial community is a blessing from God for our present day and is also the response that faith gives to the challenges of an oppressed and believing people.

2. Born from the Word of God

The Gospel is the calling card of the base ecclesial community. The Gospel is heard, shared, and believed in the community, and it is in its light that the participants reflect on the problems of their life. This is a typical feature of the community; the Gospel is always confronted with life, with the concrete situation of the community. It is not simply a marvelous and consoling message; above all, it is light and leaven. The Gospel is seen as good news, as a message of hope, promise, and joy from the real situations of the poor.

The relationship between Gospel and life takes shape through a slow and difficult process within the community. Initially, the word is brought to bear on the problems of the group, such as the illness of one of the members or unemployment. In time, the group begins to take into account the social question of their surroundings, be it their street or the neighborhood. There may be problems of water, electricity, sewers, paved streets, clinics, schools, and so forth. Later, the group begins to take a political stance toward the social system. The current organization of society is brought into question. At this level of consciousness they begin to participate in the struggles of the people through labor unions, various people's movements, political parties, and the like.

Yet, for the people of the base, faith is the great doorway into social problems. Their social commitment comes from the vision of faith. Their faith is not changed but rather, faced with the facts of life, it is strengthened, doubled, and shows itself for what it is, a leaven of liberation.

The Gospel is shared in absolute freedom in the base eccesial community. Everyone is given the chance to speak and to give their opinion about a given fact or situation. Surprisingly, the popular exegesis of the community comes very close to the ancient exegesis of the fathers of the Church. It is an exegesis that goes beyond the words and captures the living, spiritual meaning of the text. The gospel passage serves as the inspiration for the group's reflection on life, where the word of God is actually heard.

3. A New Way of Being Church

The base ecclesial community is not only a means for evangelization in popular settings. It is much more. It is a new way of being Church and of concretizing the mystery of salvation that is lived in common. The Church is not only the institution with its sacred scriptures, hierarchy, sacramental structures, canon law, liturgical norms, orthodoxy, and moral imperatives. All of that is important, but the Church is also an *event*. It emerges, is born, and is continually reshaped whenever individuals meet to hear the word of God, believe in it, and vow together to follow Jesus Christ, inspired by the Holy Spirit. This is what happens in the base ecclesial communities. The group may meet under a huge tree and every week they are found there, reading the sacred texts, sharing their commentaries, praying, talking of life, and making decisions about common projects. It is an event, and the Church of Jesus and the Holy Spirit takes shape under that tree.

The principal characteristic of this way of being Church is community. Everyone is a true brother and sister; all share in common tasks. This is the starting point. Everyone is fundamentally equal, yet not everyone can do all the things necessary within the community. Therefore, there are co-ordinators (often women) who are responsible for order and presiding over the celebrations and sacramental aspects of the community. The Church of the first centuries was understood primarily as *communitas fidelium*, the community of the faithful, with the participation of all members in all things. It slowly became a hierarchical Church, and the possession of sacred power was the basis of its structure, not the community. This organization was historically necessary, but it left no room for the responsible participation of all people in the affairs of the Church. In the base ecclesial community there is the possibility for greater participation and balance in the various ecclesial functions. Lay people are discovering their importance; they, too, are successors of the apostles in that they have inherited the apostolic teachings and are coresponsible for the unity of faith and the community. Apostolicity is not the characteristic only of certain members of the Church, such as the Pope and bishops, but is a characteristic of the entire Church, and this apostolicity is shared in different ways within the Church. Lay people are rediscovering their apostolic and missionary significance through the ecclesial communities. Very often one community establishes other communities and helps them in their growth and development.

The communitarian way of living out faith gives rise to the creation of many lay ministries. In Latin America, these ministries are called services, which is essentially the meaning that Paul gives to "charisms." All services are understood as gifts of the Holy Spirit. There are those who know how to visit and comfort the sick; they are given the task of gathering information and visitation. Others are educated and some teach about human rights and labor laws, some prepare the children for the sacraments, and still others deal with family problems and the like. All of these functions are respected, encouraged, and coordinated in order that everything tend toward service of the whole community. The Church, then, more than an organization, becomes a living organism that is recreated, nourished, and renewed from the base.

4. Sign and Instrument of Liberation

The base ecclesial community is not and cannot be an underground organization or sect. It is a community that is open to the world and society. The reading and common sharing of the Gospel leads the community to social action. All of the problems the members suffer are brought to the base ecclesial community. The group then questions the causes and consequences of these very real problems. In this way, the community serves an undeniably critical and demystifying function. The members of the community learn to live the truth. In the community, it is no longer possible to hide reality. Everything is named for what it is: exploitation is exploitation; torture is torture; dictatorship is dictatorship. The institutional Church has played a great role by conscientizing the people as to their rights, giving them the tools to analyze their situation, and by denouncing the injustices they suffer.

Furthermore, a new type of society is taught within the community. One learns to overcome the unjust relationships that dominate the larger society. How? Through the direct participation of all the members of the group, the sharing of responsibilities, leadership, and decision-making, through the exercise of power as service.

The base ecclesial communities are socially active communities. In some places they are the only channel for popular expression and mobilization. They organize memorials, group projects, community activities, neighborhood credit unions, efforts to resist land takeovers, and many other concerns of the people. Where popular organizations already exist, the base ecclesial community does not try to compete. Rather, it identifies with those movements, sharing members and leadership, support and criticism. The primary concern of the base ecclesial community is *not* the organization of social movements but the formation or strengthening of *popular* movements.

In many places the base ecclesial community poses a threat to the established social order. The communities are repressed, persecuted, and have their saints and martyrs. But this does not seem to have diminished their strength. On the contrary, base ecclesial communities are growing more numerous, stronger, and more courageous because of this consciously accepted suffering.

5. A Celebration of Faith and Life

Christian faith is not only defined in terms of its dimension of commitment and liberation. It has its time for celebrating that liberation. It celebrates the liberation that God achieved for us in Jesus Christ; his presence through the word and the sacraments is celebrated and the faithful are comforted by his promises. The base ecclesial communities have developed this dimension of celebration. Their misery and the seriousness of their struggles have not taken away from the feast where the people breathe freely and enjoy their freedom and joy.

There is a great value placed upon popular religiosity, the devotions to the particular saints of the people, the processions, and other popular feasts. These expressions are not considered to be the deterioration of official, orthodox, and liturgical Catholicism. They are taken to be the way in which the people, within their own categories, have accepted Jesus' message, ruled not so much by the logic of ideas and analytical reasoning as by the logic of the subconscious and the symbolic. Popular religiosity is as valuable as other expressions of faith. It was through this popular religiosity that God visited his poor people. It was through their prayers, their saints, their feasts in honor of the Virgin and the various mysteries of Christ that the people have been able to resist centuries of political and economic oppression and ecclesial marginalization. Through their own religiosity the people, in many parts of the world, have been able to discover the meaning of life, keep their faith alive, and nourish their trust while in a society that has denied them their rights, dignity, and participation. All of this is now leading the Church to reinterpret its traditional pastoral practices that had little appreciation for the religious expressions of the people.

The base ecclesial communities not only strengthen the faith of the people, which would be enough in itself, but also foster creativity in the search for the proper expression of living out faith. The unity between faith and life finds a place in the community and so the presence of God in life is celebrated there. When the community prays, its "prayers of the faithful" recall all of the problems, oppressions, oppressors, hardships as well as victories, successes, and ongoing projects of the community. Not only are the official sacraments celebrated but the sacramental dimension of all life is cause for celebration because the community sees God's grace impregnating the concrete events of its life together. The community has this fine sense of the religious dimension to be found in all stages of human life, and so community gatherings are never completely profane or devoid of God's presence.

Liturgical creativity is also given its place in the community. The people appreciate the canonical, official liturgy but they also create their own rituals, spontaneously enacting the word of God, organizing great celebrations that center around the Bible and include significant regional objects or foods. It is at these times that faith is given its finest expression. A people that knows how to celebrate is a people with hope. They are no longer a wholly oppressed people but a people who march toward their liberation.

Chapter 10

UNDERLYING ECCLESIOLOGIES
OF THE
BASE ECCLESIAL COMMUNITIES

People, especially the poor, are organizing themselves in order to live their faith in a communal way. They are not repeating the past nor are they reforming present structures. A new future is dawning, something unforeseen during the past centuries of ecclesial rule. We are dealing with a true ecclesiogenesis, that is, the genesis of a Church that is born of the faith of the people.

The theologian trying to explain this phenomenon must be one who first listens and learns. Practice precedes theoretical systematizing; always reality first and reflection later. Reality is the reflected experience of the community. If theology does not listen and learn from these communities, it will cloud rather than illumine the paths of the new Church that is being born from the old.

The chart below outlines the basic ecclesiologies underlying the base ecclesial community. These ecclesiologies are constantly undergoing changes and development, and represent various overlapping stages in the growth of the community. At various stages in the life of the community one ecclesiology may be accented more than another, yet they all are present to some extent. Almost all of the communities have taken or are taking the following path:

REALITY	GOAL	REFLECTION	PRAXIS
Clericalism: a Church of the priests	Church of the people not *for* the people but a Church *with* them	Church as People of God	Open dialogue, equality, listening to the people, participation. The priests change.
Imposing Church: anonymous, no questions, no information; institution, obedience to laws.	Fraternity, dialogue, services; horizontal relationships, coresponsibility	Church communion, community of faith and love; sacrament-sign	The people change, communicate and express themselves in the liturgy, undertaking services. Community not of obedience but of love.
Alienation: Church is only rites and sacraments; allied with the rich	Seeking out the poor; an incarnated Church denounces injustices, defends the exploited and is conscious of human rights.	Prophetic Church; liberator, community of Abraham; sacrament-instrument of of liberation	Social commitment; groups for conscientization and reflection on human rights, formation of base ecclesial community

Church as People of God

Immediately after the council, the term Church as People of God was discovered. This was a tremendous change from the past. But the change did not affect the people; in fact, they wondered why it took the Church so long to discover something so obviously crucial, evident to anyone reading Christ's message. The priest was the one who changed. He was no longer distant from the people; he became incarnated among the people. This process, by and large, was one of secularization. The priest abandoned almost all of the sacred signs with which he was invested, such as his cassock and cloister; the liturgy was simplified and his house open to the people. The question today is whether the priest has gone too far; the people themselves are not nearly as secularized.

The people value their own popular religiosity while the priest diminished his own piety and that of the Church. He conscientized the people; in the process, he destroyed a great deal of popular religiosity. He brought the people back to the Church but they did not surrender. Today, the popular signs are being reevaluated. The sacred is accepted as one form, together with legitimate secularization, through which God is made explicitly present. But the real problems with this category do not lie on this level.

The true difficulty involves the theological implications present in the basic statement: the Church is the People of God. There is a fundamental equality in the Church. All are People of God. All share in Christ, directly and without mediation. Therefore, all share in the services of teaching, sanctifying, and organizing the community. All are sent out on a mission; all are responsible for the unity of the community; all must be sanctified.

If all are equal, then it is not necessary for everyone to do every task. In the building up of the same community, diverse services arise in response to the concrete necessities manifested in the community. A special office of giving unity to all of the services so as to maintain harmony is the function of the priest on the local level and of the bishop on the regional level. These are functions of unification and not of sanctification, unity in worship, organization, and the passing on of faith.

The concept of Church as People of God inverts the relationships with regard to ministries. In classical ecclesiology there is a Church that only takes the hierarchy into account. The following diagram illustrates the differences:

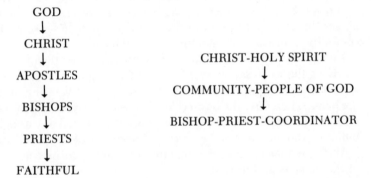

GOD
↓
CHRIST
↓
APOSTLES
↓
BISHOPS
↓
PRIESTS
↓
FAITHFUL

CHRIST-HOLY SPIRIT
↓
COMMUNITY-PEOPLE OF GOD
↓
BISHOP-PRIEST-COORDINATOR

In this conception, the faithful have only the right to receive. The bishops and priests receive all religious "capital," produce the religious "goods," and the people consume them. This is a monarchical model, common in the history of the Church.

In this model, everything revolves around the People of God. The services and offices come after the community. This is a fraternal and communitarian model, flexible in that the services conform to needs as they arise.

Anyone who opts for the Church as People of God must take it to its logical conclusion: to be a living Church, with flexible and appropriate ministries, without theological privileges. It is interesting to note that chapter 2 of *Lumen Gentium*, which treats of the People of God, comes before the chapter on the hierarchy, illustrating in itself a new understanding of ministry. This new understanding enables one to understand, theologically, the various services that are rendered within the community as manifestations of the risen Christ. Caring for the sick, helping to explain the Scriptures in the Bible study groups, conscientizing the community as to human rights, presiding over the community, are all true ministries.

Courage is needed to create this popular Church and to let it grow. It is a Church of the people, with the values of the people, with their language, liturgical expressions, and popular religiosity. Until very recently the Church has been a Church only of priests *for* the people; it is now beginning to be a Church *of* the people.

Church as Community and Sign of Liberation

The Church as community has given the opportunity for a new experience of the life of faith, allowing the people participation not only in the liturgy but also in decisions, committed to maintaining the Church and adding to its growth. There has been a positive decentralization of the Church; the base ecclesial communities are more than simple chapels. They have their own autonomy and values. The liturgy becomes an expression of faith and not the carrying out of a sacred ritual. The word is no longer the private property of the priest; the people share it. Tithing becomes the expression of commitment to the community.

Living the primary sacrament, the Church, is the previous condition for receiving the seven sacraments. One might imagine a hand with seven fingers; it makes no sense to want the fingers without wanting or implicating the hand. Therefore, the base ecclesial community places great value on the formation of stable leadership, be it through a council or through a trained monitor who guarantees the unity and harmony of the community.

With the idea of Church as community, one must be conscious of some of the dangers and limitations.

What is the meaning of this community of faith? It is important that the community deepen the essential values of Christianity, fraternity, mutual care, solidarity, participation in all of the concerns of the community, sharing information, grassroots decision-making, and so on.

It is important that a spirituality of faith be fostered, one of adherence to Jesus Christ made present in the community and adherence to the Holy Spirit present in the various services or charisms, creating deep and lasting expressions of faith able to be sustained during difficulties and possible persecution. Without this community-created spirituality, the individual believer will not have the strength to undergo the inevitable confrontations or persecution, even imprisonment, that accompany his or her commitment grounded in faith.

This spirituality is essential. It is a step that cannot be overlooked or substituted by social commitment or the concern for human rights. It must be always present to nourish faith, to build strength, and to make the risen Christ present in the world.

The danger lies in thinking that Christianity is found fundamentally in its communitarian aspects, in the liturgy or in intimate and familial sharing. If it remains on the level of communitarian religious identity, the group tends to duplicate the services of society, establishing schools and health clinics or food banks. It is important to do these things when they do not exist. But this is not the only reason for the group's existence. The group exists within the world. It is not a miniature world where everyone participates, where everyone knows one another. It is part of a world open to conflicts, class struggles, exploitation, where religion is often used to calm the soul so that everything runs smoothly, the way things have always been done; it is part of a world where the powers on top exploit the suffering people below.

An intrasystemic liberation is possible. Positions change, people suffer a little bit less, and there is some progress because necessary assistance is acquired, but the walls that oppress and imprison the whole world are not torn down. One can adapt one's freedom within a prison; one accepts the limitations and learns to live with them. That may be considered progress but the prison remains a reality. Problems arise when the individual, excited by the progress achieved within the prison, forgets about the prison itself. One must become conscious of the prison and work to make sure that there are no more prisons and no more imprisoned people, that all are freed. The base ecclesial community must not be satisfied with its progress within the prison; it must begin the lengthy process by which the prison is dismantled and transformed in such a way that the prison no longer exists.

This process of liberation demands a much more detailed analysis of society: how the production of wealth functions, how wealth is distributed, the place of individuals in relation to capital, employment, and participation. The community that is awakened to this reality is already conscious of the violations of human rights, of structural poverty, of the social injustices that are the fruits of the organization of an entire system that is often presented as good, Christian, democratic, and so forth. Christian faith awakens one to social justice, to the true meaning of the global liberation of Jesus Christ that demands the transformation, the conversion, not only of the individual but also of structures.

Church as Prophet and Instrument of Liberation
At this stage the base ecclesial community is already conscious of its mission in the world. It is not enough to be concerned with the internal problems of the community if global misery and exploitation abound. The com-

munity then begins to study the mechanisms of oppression in detail. Yet, the ecclesial community does not look at it simply as a sociological fact. It is interpreted as social sin, as injustice that offends both God and neighbor. Jesus Christ wants to liberate all persons from these situations and to lead all to a freer, more fraternal society filled with divine grace.

Therefore, the community, in its reflection, cannot restrict itself to what is specifically Christian, that is, to the reflection on faith, charity, grace, sin, marriage, the sacraments, or the mystery of Jesus Christ. These are unavoidable subjects but alone are not enough. Nor can it limit itself to the examination of communitarian concerns such as self-help, health, participation in community efforts, liturgy, and the like.

The group must arrive at the reflection upon social and structural problems that profoundly affect the community, such as justice, exploitation, poverty, marginalization, participation, freedom of speech, of action, and of choice. This hits reality where it counts, where transformation can begin that improves not only the community but also the surrounding world, preparing it for an even greater transformation.

This is where specific problems arise. One must reflect on the means that make both Christian faith and love a truly transforming power. Belief is not enough. New liberating praxis is also necessary.

Scientific analysis of reality is necessary. Scientific does not mean the use of technical words and detailed research. It does mean the knowledge of what lies behind the phenomenon. For example, we see a shack and we know there is poverty. Scientifically, one discovers the cause or causes that create this poverty. One finds that it is not laziness or the lack of opportunity but that the cause is the distribution of employment among individuals. To know scientifically is to lead the members of the community to understand the mechanism of the society in which they live, how the state functions, not giving everyone the opportunity for work and defending the interests of those who own the means of production, that is, the mass media, the police, laws, unions, political parties, and so forth. Knowing this, the people are able to be critical.

Faced with the organization and imperialism of the established social system, people tend to feel impotent, that there is no way out. To fight this feeling there must be the hope and deep faith that justice and participation have more of a future than does exploitation. Therefore, there is the need for the base ecclesial communities not to remain on the level of social problems but to move beyond them into a deepening of faith, hope, love, trust, and patience lest they lose hope and turn to violence and terrorist tactics. Terror is an act of desperation and bitterness, the fruit of an insatiable thirst for justice without the corresponding sense of history, without patience, without a sense of opportunity. The feeling of impotence must be overcome because it tears the individual apart. Conscientization that results in the feeling of impotence is irresponsible and undermines the Church, causing the committed to go elsewhere.

Liberation is the fruit of a long process. There are steps that must be taken, and these begin with the praxis of the community itself, a praxis that liberates. The community itself must not be an oppressor but a symbol of freedom of speech, of action, of participation. Otherwise how can it be a sign and instrument for liberation?

This new praxis leads to a change in the attitudes of the members of the community, and not just a change in their actions. These attitudes may lead to persecution. The system of oppression has accused many of the faithful, many priests, and even bishops of the traditional Church of going too far in judging the system. These persons are defamed as subversives. In order to face this possible repression one must have a deep spirituality of faith in, and imitation of, Jesus Christ and the apostles. The feeling of solidarity must be fostered within the community. In Latin America, when a member of a base ecclesial community is imprisoned (as happens so often), the others care for the prisoner's family, seek legal assistance, and support and encourage the prisoner through visits and various other means, as was done in the early Church.

In order to survive in a world that does not appear able to be transformed, the communities combine commitment with prudence, risk measured with courage. They act against the forces of oppression without unnecessarily provoking them. They have created a sprituality of martyrdom, accepting persecution, defamation, imprisonment, and even death itself, for the one who truly follows Jesus Christ. This is not an easy thing to do. It demands a great deal of conviction and strength.

We must ask God's forgiveness for our lack of courage.

Chapter 11

ECCLESIA DOCENS
versus ECCLESIA DISCENS

This is a very complex subject and, in order to achieve a true critical consciousness, it demands sociological, psychosocial, and ideological treatment, as well as a specifically theological one. There has been a great deal of violence and domination by some Christians over others owing to the acceptance of one Church that speaks and teaches and another Church that listens and obeys, all done in the name of a truth that only a select body of priests is presumed to possess. Truth is meant to liberate and not oppress (John 8:32). Therefore, to safeguard this distinction between *Ecclesia docens* and *Ecclesia discens*, it is necessary to highlight the various mediations that support it.

First Thesis: The entire Church (communitas fidelium) is the
Ecclesia discens.
There is only one God, one revelation, one liberating act of the Father in Christ through the Spirit, one eternal life and one eschatology. In view of this salvific event, the only religiously responsible attitude is that of faith. Faith is humanity's response to the wonders of God (*magnalia Dei*); faith consists in saying yes and amen, in the biblical sense, to the divine initiative. Faith presupposes silence, listening, acceptance. The Church is born from this response of faith; it is the community of those who have given a response to God's offer. As such, the entire Church is *Ecclesia discens*, student of the one teacher, Jesus Christ (Matt 23:8; 10:24; 13:13) and disciple "of the Spirit of truth that will teach the entire truth" (John 16:13), and that because of God "we do not need anyone to teach us" (1 John 2:27). If anyone in the Church (Pope or bishops, especially) does not consider himself primarily as a member of the Church *discens*, he ceases to be a sacramental member of the *communitas fidelium* because that person has lost what theologically constitutes the Church, that is, faith.

The distinction between *Ecclesia docens* and *Ecclesia discens* is only valid, if it must be, provided that *discens* (Church as hearer of the word) is

138

emphasized over *docens* (Church as witness of evangelical events). "You alone are holy, you alone are the Most High, Jesus Christ." "You alone are teacher" is implied in this praise, and everyone is a disciple who even today hears the call "Come and follow me" (Mark 10:21). The Spirit continues "announcing to us the things of the future" (John 16:13) and "teaching us all things" (John 14:26).

Second Thesis: The entire Church (*communitas fidelium*) is the Ecclesia docens.

The primary mission of the community of faith is to cause others to also say yes and amen to God. This is the mission of making disciples (Matt 28:19). Peter's first sermon in Acts illustrates the docent or teaching practice of one who listened and accepted the saving acts of God: "Listen . . . listen to what I have to say. . . . This is the Jesus God has raised up and we are his witnesses" (Acts 2:14, 22, 32). This is the faith that speaks and gives witness after having heard and accepted. It speaks so that others may also "live in communion with us" (1 John 1:4), continually enlarging the community of those who believe. Because of the faith expressed through baptism, all are submerged in the mystery of Christ and so are made bearers of the Spirit (cf. Rom 8:9; 1 Cor 3:16, 19), and all are sent out to give witness. As such, all are the *Ecclesia docens* who proclaim to others what God has done for the benefit of all.

Third Thesis: Docens and discens are two functions, not divisions, in the Church.

Within the community of faith, there is a time for listening and a time for speaking, a time for learning of revelation and a time for witnessing to revelation. *Docens* and *discens* are two aspects of the one community; they are two adjectives that describe two practices of the whole community. They are not two nouns that split the community. To be *docens* and *discens* springs from two functions of the same Church and are not two parts or divisions within the Church.

There is mutual teaching within the Church. There is the time in which the hierarchy must hear and listen to the Scriptures, attentive to the signs of the times, a time to pay attention to the cry of the poor rising to heaven and to discern the will of God for all; there is the time when the lay person has to speak and witness to the truth of the Gospel within the social system in which that person lives, even when it leads to the beatitude of persecution. The hierarchy becomes a member of the *Ecclesia discens* and the laity becomes a member of the *Ecclesia docens*. Each one is teacher and disciple of the other and all are followers of the Gospel. Jesus' call must be understood in the coexistence and simultaneity of these two functions. No one is to be called master, teacher, father, or spiritual director because all are brothers and sisters (cf. Matt 23:8–10).

Fourth Thesis: The distinction between Ecclesia docens and
Ecclesia discens is theologically valid only after the
socioanalytic reflection on the religious division of labor has
been done.

In spite of the basic equality within the Church because all are brothers and sisters and disciples, there is a time when the Church assumes in a particular way the function of teaching. This is not teaching as the term is generally understood or teaching in the sense of giving witness. The Church refers to this particular function as official and authentic teaching, the *power* of teaching with which the Pope and bishops feel particularly invested. The hierarchy of power comes with the power of teaching.

Theological and canonical manuals affirm that the Church of Christ is, by divine institution, essentially hierarchical. This means that "there exists, due to the divine will of its founder, a discrimination by which some persons have been called to exercise the essential powers, to the exclusion of others, according to the law established by Christ himself."[1] Christ, it is argued, is the messiah-teacher, giver of all power. He transmitted all of this power to the apostles (Matt 28:18–20) in such a way that "whoever hears you, hears me and whoever rejects you, rejects me" (cf. Luke 10:16). This is an epiphanical view of the Church, structured completely and directly by the will of its founder.

This interpretation is based on a literal reading of the texts as they were codified, without considering their development and the theologies reflected in their various forms. Furthermore, those who make such statements are the very ones with an interest at stake. To guarantee the validity of an authentic magisterium, the epiphanical view of the rise of the Church must be superseded by a theological conception that takes into account the various mediations present in the affirmation that Jesus founded the Church.

First, one must incorporate the historical-critical results of exegesis. We are told that the Church, in some way, was at the center of Jesus' attention; yet, the elements concerning the structure of the community are mimimal.[2] This does not mean that the affirmation concerning Jesus' foundation of the Church has no meaning. The contributions of critical exegesis cannot be disregarded.

Second, one must consider the socioreligious facts concerning the rise of hierarchies[3] and the religious division of labor.[4] The great religions, like Christianity, are associated with the appearance of cities, which introduced the division between urban and rural, and the first social division between manual and intellectual labor. Max Weber is credited with having demonstrated that urbanization contributed to the rationalization of religion, making possible the rise of a body of experts charged with the preservation, codification, and official exegesis of the religious "capital" common to all the faithful. Thus, two Churches, one *docens* and one *discens*, flourished. "The priests, directly, are responsible for the rationalization of religion and they derive their legitimacy from a theology built on a dogma whose validity and perpetuation guarantee their existence."[5] The hierarchy rises out of the community of equals, charged with a *diakonia* for everyone: to produce and reproduce a global coherent vision of Christian faith.

A theological reflection that fails to recognize these facts runs the risk of being ideological and clouding what can be clarified with historically verifiable reasons. In other words, although Christ may not have said anything about the power of authentic teaching, there still would have been a magisterial aspect to the Church. Theologically, the founding will of Christ does not exclude but includes the normal process by which a religious community guarantees fidelity to its original identity, that is, by means of a body of experts in communion with all believers.

Emile Durkheim demonstrated that the division of labor does not necessarily lead to the substantialization of function but, rather, an internal solidarity can be maintained with the grassroots, the common base, granting it a useful and necessary service of preservation, codification, amplification, and clarification.[6] So the distinction between *Ecclesia docens* and *discens* is justified so long as it preserves its usefulness for the community of brothers and sisters. It is a distinction within the community and not apart from and above the community.

This dialectic is best expressed by Matthew: the power of binding and loosing lies within the whole community (18:18), yet this power is a particular function of the principle of unity in the community, that is, Peter (16:19). In the early Church, it is said, the *potestas sacra* (sacred power) was given to the whole community in general and to the bishops and priests in particular.[7] The bearer of this power is the community and the magisterial function rises from it as a means of expression.

Fifth Thesis: The dichotomy of Ecclesia docens and discens is the result of a pathological view of the Church's reality.
All holiness, historically, can become pathological. This occurred with the present topic. There were times, especially beginning with the Gregorian reform, in which the Church was primarily the clergy. From then on the *Ecclesia docens* tended to be a separate sociological state. The creation of a body of experts dichotomized the community. It brought about an expropriation of religious power and the majority became merely lay people, di-

vested of the power to produce symbolic goods, relegated to being specta-
tors in the life of the Church. The rigid separation between clergy and laity
was emphasized by Gregory XVI (1831–46): "No one can deny that the
Church is an unequal society in which God destined some to be governors
and others to be servants. The latter are the laity; the former, the clergy."
Pius X is even more rigid: "Only the college of pastors have the right and
authority to lead and govern. The masses have no right or authority except
that of being governed, like an obedient flock that follows its Shepherd."[8]

Paulo Freire has demonstrated the pathological character of this type of
relationship which dehumanizes both parties.[9] On the one hand is the *Ecclesia docens* that knows all and interprets all; on the other is the lay person
who knows nothing, produces nothing, and receives everything, that is,
the *Ecclesia discens*. The hierarchy learns nothing from its contact with
the laity and the latter are given no ecclesial space to display their wealth.
Thus, the ontological vocation of every person is denied, that is, to be a
participant and not a mere spectator in the history of salvation.

Happily, Vatican II brought things back into perspective, recovering its
theologically threatened health. The Church is fundamentally the People of
God. All share in the magisterial role of Christ, even the laity (*Lumen Gentium*, 35). The hierarchy, as a part of this people, enjoys an official role but
always in service to the entire Christian community (*Lumen Gentium*, 25).

*Sixth Thesis: Dialectical interaction is the healthy distinction
between Ecclesia docens and Ecclesia discens.*

All power, to be legitimate and to safeguard its evangelical function, must
know its limits. Otherwise it yields to the temptation of all power, that is,
to become absolute, the pure and simple oppression of all others. In the history of the Church the faulty identification of *discens* and *docens* to the
benefit of the *docens* (the hierarchy) led to authoritarian situations unac-
ceptable to gospel values (Luke 22:25–28). It was a one-way street where
the hierarchy teaches the people who only listen. A two-way street is necessary, from the *discens* to the *docens* and from the *docens* to the *discens*. In
order to do this, the following rules must be observed:

1. *Open dialogue on both sides*: everyone must listen, especially those
who must speak authentically, and all must have a guaranteed opportunity
to speak; there must be an exchange of knowledge without domination on
the part of any one side and with mutual respect, because the Spirit abides
in all persons.

2. *Mutual criticism*: this is necessary to prevent absolutization and domination. "Only by developing a permanently critical attitude can men
overcome a posture of adjustment to become integrated with the spirit of
the time,"[10] or discern the true will for the Church in the signs of the times.

3. *A reference to the external*: the Church does not exist for itself but in service to the world that must be evangelized and saved. Both the *Ecclesia docens* and *Ecclesia discens* must maintain a reference to the world and to the Spirit that blows over the world as well as the Church. This vertical and horizontal interaction is how a healthy and valid relationship is guaranteed between authentic speaking and obedient listening within one and the same Church.

Chapter 12

AN ALTERNATIVE VIEW:
THE CHURCH AS
SACRAMENT OF THE HOLY SPIRIT

The theology of the Latin Church teaches that every idea and description of the Church should be based in christology. The New Testament itself clearly suggests this when it speaks of the Church as the body of Christ or when the risen Christ says to Saul: "I am Jesus whom you are persecuting" (Acts 9:5; cf. John 17:18; 20:21). The Church has always understood itself as the continuation of Christ and his mission. The First Vatican Council taught and summarized the common doctrine of tradition: "The eternal Shepherd and bishop of our souls, desiring to perennialize the salvific work of redemption, decreed that the holy Church be raised up" (DS 3050). Vatican II states that "to accomplish so great a work, Christ is always present in His Church, especially in her liturgical celebrations" (*Sacrosanctum Concilium* 7).

The nexus between Christ and Church is so deep that Pius XII, in his encyclical on the mystical body of Christ, was able to affirm that whoever sees the Church sees Christ, that the Church is Christ himself. Obviously, such statements should not be taken literally.[1] The Church is not hypostatically united to the Logos as was the humanity of Jesus. The Church is at one and the same time saint and sinner, always in need of conversion and reform.

The Incarnation—Model of the Church?
Expressions such as "the Church is Christ continued," "the Church is one with Christ," highlight the continuity of a function. Just as Christ achieved salvation for all persons, the Church must prolong that mission throughout the centuries. It has the same mission as Christ. Yet, traditional theology has taken Jesus Christ as the model for understanding the whole Church. Both have parallels, that is, there is a human and divine nature in Christ just as the Church is both human and divine. But there is a primary limita-

144

tion in this understanding of Christ and the Church. Christ has been almost exclusively understood in terms of his incarnation as a man with a body, soul, and divinity. The physical body of Christ has been the comparative model for the Church, the mystical body of Christ. Just as the body has various members and diverse functions, so also does the Church have many members with diverse functions. It is from this comparison that the official documents of the magisterium, such as the encyclical *Satis Cognitum* of Leo XIII and *Mystici Corporis Christi* of Pius XII, have deduced the visibility, unity, and plurality in and of the Church.

The human body is limited and well-defined. The Church, as the body of Christ, is also well-defined and limited so that members are clearly defined (one is either a member or nonmember) as are the institutions that must maintain the Church's unity and strength in the world. Such a concept of Church is the logical consequence of the model of the physical body of Christ.

However, this christology and consequent ecclesiology is, basically, too narrow. These theological disciplines, by solely considering the physical body of Christ as the model for the Church, fail to take into account the decisive event of the resurrection. Through the resurrection the body of Jesus Christ was not simply brought back to life. It was completely fulfilled and liberated from every temporal and spatial limitation. He was no longer simply a carnal body, that is, a body subject to an earthly condition, a prisoner to the conditions of space and time, the need to eat and drink, and the limitations of ambiguous communication through word and gesture. His resurrection transformed Jesus' carnal body into a spiritual body (cf. 1 Cor 14:44ff).[2] A spiritual body is the new reality of the risen Jesus, now free from the limitations of earthly existence, enthroned in eternity and in the limitless arena of divine life, liberated from space and time. Through the resurrection the limits of the carnal Jesus fell away, bringing forth a global relationship to all of reality. The risen Jesus became the cosmic Christ of the letters to the Ephesians, Colossians, the prologue to the Fourth Gospel, and the letter to the Hebrews (1:2, 10–13; 2:8–9).[3] The body of the risen and pneumatic (spiritual) Christ can no longer be considered as a physically definable entity from which we can deduce the limits of the Church, the body of Christ. Therefore, the expression of the Church as the body of Christ must be carefully defined. When Saint Paul uses this expression, he has in mind the pneumatic and risen body of Christ and not his physical body. Paul identifies the risen Christ with the Spirit (2 Cor 3:17). So, the Church must be thought of in terms of the risen Christ, identified with the Spirit, rather than in terms of the carnal Jesus. The Church has a christological origin; it also has, in particular, a pneumatological one (pneuma-Spirit). Inasmuch as the Church comes from the Holy Spirit, the Spirit of

Christ, it has a dynamic and functional dimension; it is defined in terms of energy, charism, and the progress of the world because the "Spirit blows where it wills" (John 3:7) and "where the Spirit of the Lord is, there is freedom" (2 Cor 3:17). The christological and pneumatological origin of the Church merits greater reflection.

The Church, Founded by Christ and the Apostles, Led by the Holy Spirit

Common teaching states that Christ founded the Church. This truth is part of the inheritance of Christian and ecclesial faith. However, the way in which Christ desired and founded his Church must be clearly established. Not all of the institutional elements of the Church can be traced back to Jesus. He did not preach the Church but rather the Kingdom of God.[4] He preached a total and global transformation of the old world that, through divine intervention, would become the new world, where sin, sickness, hatred, and all of the alienating forces that affect both human life and the entire cosmos are defeated. In his preaching and practice of the Kingdom of God, Christ introduced elements that later would form the basis for the Church, such as the gathering of the twelve apostles (Mark 3:13–19), the institution of baptism, and the eucharistic supper. But these elements do not constitute the entire reality of the Church. The Church exists only because the Kingdom was not accepted by the Jewish people and Jesus was rejected by them. If the Kingdom preached by Christ had been realized, there would be no need for the Church. Essentially, the Church substitutes for the Kingdom and must, theologically, define itself as an instrument for the full realization of the Kingdom and as the sign of a true yet still imperfect realization of this Kingdom in the world.

Furthermore, the Church exists because the end of the world is no longer imminent. There is a history of faith and of the acceptance of Jesus and his message. In the beginning the apostles and disciples awaited the proximate irruption of the Kingdom of God with the glorious and definitive coming of the Son of Man (the risen Jesus). They set out to convert the people, preaching the same message of Jesus: the Kingdom and its closeness. But the stubbornness of the people, the martyrdom of James, and the imprisonment and escape of Peter led them to lose hope in the imminent irruption of the Kingdom. They turned to the pagans and, prompted by the Spirit, the apostles took a decisive step. They took the elements introduced by the historical Jesus (his message, his summoning of the Twelve, baptism, eucharist, etc.) and founded the concrete Church. Its essential elements were from Christ. However, in its concrete and historical form, the Church was supported not only by Jesus' words but also by the decisions of the apostles, inspired by the Holy Spirit. Tradition has always held that the Church was founded on Pentecost. Yet, the Church has both a pneumatological *and* christological foundation.

The Church as institution is not based on the incarnation of the Word but rather in the faith in the power of the apostles, inspired by the Holy Spirit, that caused them to move from eschatology and the end-times to the present situation of the Church, translating the teachings about the Kingdom into a doctrine about the Church. The Church arose from a historical decision by the apostles, enlightened by the Holy Spirit. The Church, born of a decision, will continue to exist only if Christians and all people of faith in the risen Christ and his Spirit continually renew this decision and incarnate the Church in ever new situations. The Church is not a completely defined and established entity; it is always open to new situations and cultural encounters, and within these realities, it must incarnate and proclaim the liberating message of Jesus Christ.

Is there a source for the unity of the Church beyond Christ and the Holy Spirit? Such a point of unity can be highlighted both biblically and dogmatically.

The Basic Unity between Christology and Pneumatology

From a reflection on the New Testament come two basic propositions: first, the carnal Jesus was the presence of the Holy Spirit in the world; second, the Holy Spirit in the Church is the presence of the pneumatic (risen) Christ in the world. A third proposition is contained in these first two: the Holy Spirit proceeds from the Father and the Son, a dogma that was defined by the Council of Constantinople in 381. This means that the Holy Spirit, by origin, shares something of the Son as well as the Father. This very abstract statement will become clear later. It is necessary to give the foundation for these three propositions.[5]

The Carnal Jesus: Presence of the Holy Spirit in the World

This comes from the theology of Luke. For him, Jesus was not just filled with the Holy Spirit; he is Lord, possessing the Spirit completely, a permanent bearer of the Spirit (Luke 4:1, 14, 18; Acts 10:38). He is not "led by the Spirit" but follows his own path "in the Spirit" (Luke 4:14, contrary to Mark 1:27). From the beginning Jesus is the work of the Spirit and is anointed by the Spirit (Luke 1:35; 4:18–21; Acts 4:27; cf. Matt 1:18; Heb 1:9; 2 Cor 1:21; 1 John 2:22).[6] Luke does not recognize a growth of the Spirit in Jesus, as was the case with John the Baptist. Jesus fully possesses the Spirit, but the manifestations of the Spirit become more and more clear until the Spirit is corporally visible (Luke 3:22; Acts 2:3–6; 4:31). The miracles are, for Luke, signs of Jesus' own power as one who is filled with the Spirit, rather than signs of the Spirit only, as they are for Mark and Matthew (Luke 5:17;

6:19). "Jesus did not have the Spirit. He was the Spirit. What Moses had, Jesus was. Paul identified Christ with the Spirit (2 Cor 3:17). Jesus himself was the great Sacrament and Sign of divine life and the Spirit. He was not a prophet who spoke in the name of the Spirit but was the Spirit itself in human form."[7]

For the Old Testament, as well as for Matthew and Mark, the Spirit is the strength of God that invades a person and gives that person a power that otherwise would not be possible. In the theology of Luke, Jesus always had the fullness of the power of the Holy Spirit and whatever he did was done through his own power. Through Jesus Christ the Spirit is communicated to the community (Luke 24:49; Acts 2:33). The Spirit is the one who instituted the missionary Church (Acts 15:28), established its functions (Acts 20:28), and it was through the Spirit that canonical decrees were established (Acts 15:28) and tasks distributed (Acts 6:6; 13:2). The Spirit is characteristic of the Church. Anyone who schemes sins against and is judged by the Spirit (Acts 5). The Acts of the Apostles serves to show that the Church is filled with the Spirit of Christ and that it is the outlet for the activity of the risen Lord.

The Holy Spirit in the Church: Presence of the Risen Christ

This is the fundamental thesis of Pauline theology. It deepens the Lukan understanding outlined above. The Christian life is a life according to the Spirit, disallowing a complete definition with the world (cf. Rom 12:2). It is to live in the new reality brought about by the resurrection of Jesus, a reality that inaugurates the new heaven and the new earth, making each person a new creature (1 Cor 5:17). For Paul, the risen Lord is identified with the Spirit: "The Lord is the Spirit. And where the Spirit is, there is freedom." (2 Cor 3:17; parallel ideas in Rom 1:1–5; 1 Cor 15:45; 6:17; Rom 8:9–11.) This text has been one of the most difficult theological and exegetical riddles.[8] Recent exegesis has uncovered a meaning that is extremely rich for the present ecclesiological reflection.[9]

Paul had no intention of identifying two personal beings, the Son and the Holy Spirit. He did not have an explicitly developed theology of the Trinity as we do today. By saying "The Lord is the Spirit," Paul is expressing the *nature of the risen Lord*.[10] How does the risen Lord live today? For Paul, the answer is clear: The risen Lord lives in the form of the Spirit.[11] The resurrection made Christ, instead of earthly and carnal, a living spirit (1 Cor 15:45). Living in the Spirit, or in Christ, is always the opposite of living in the flesh, according to the flesh, or in the carnal body. Living in the flesh is to live within limits, enclosed, in tribulation, in weakness, and in temptation. Jesus of Nazareth lived according to the flesh, with all of the pejorative connotations of the term. But this carnal nature was completely transformed by the resurrection. Now he lives according to the Spirit (*en pneumati*, in Greek, an expression used nineteen times by Paul), sometimes referred to as a glorious body or a spiritual body (1 Cor 15:44).

Living according to the Spirit is not to live without the body and only in the spirit; it means to live with both body and soul, completely filled with God, to be a whole person but without limitations, weaknesses, tribulations, or the threat of death. It is to be clothed in corporality for which space, time, and the world are no longer limitations but pure openness and communion, with God and with all of reality.

The Spirit always comes from God (1 Cor 2:12). Thus, this nature is always determined by God. The risen Jesus now exists in the form of the Spirit; therefore, the Lord is the Spirit, and "whoever is joined to the Lord becomes one in Spirit with him" (1 Cor 6:17). The Spirit is the "material" of the risen body of the Lord (cf. 1 Cor 15:35ff).[12] The presence of the risen Lord in the Church is the presence of the Holy Spirit. This presence is unlimited and fills all things, just as the Spirit hovered over the primitive chaos that preceded the creative act of God, acting in plants and animals, speaking through prophets, raising up heroes, creating and sustaining all life. This is the nature that the risen Jesus assumed.

One Person in Two Persons

The basic unity between the risen Lord and the Holy Spirit finds its ultimate foundation in the intratrinitarian reality. The Spirit is the breath of (coming from) the Father and the Son, as a unique principle (DS 704). The Spirit is one person in two persons, sharing the unity of the same nature. Using the words of Thomas Aquinas, the Spirit is the common nexus of both persons.[13] If the Son was sent, as he was for the consummation and liberation of humanity and the cosmos, it follows that the Spirit was also sent. Some theologians have gone so far as to speak of the incarnation of the Holy Spirit.[14]

Just as in the Trinity the Spirit is one person in two persons, so in the economy of salvation is it one person in many persons, that is, in all those filled with grace, especially in all Christians. Just as in the Trinity the Spirit is the principle of unity between the Father and the Son, so in creation is it the principle of union, communion, and reconciliation of all persons with others and with God. The Holy Spirit "makes the Church the Sacrament of intratrinitarian relationships. What happens in trinitarian life finds its echo in the intimate life of the Church. In the deep recesses of the Church, the intradivine works are made visible."[15]

Accepting this, it is left to explore the way in which the Church is the sacrament of the Holy Spirit, which is the Spirit of Christ.

The Church—Sacrament of the Holy Spirit

The above reflections serve as a means for describing the reality of the Church. The Church must be thought of not so much as beginning with the risen Christ, now in the form of the Spirit, but rather as beginning with the Holy Spirit, as the force and means by which the Lord remains present in history and so continues his work of inaugurating a new world.[16] The Church is the sacrament, sign, and instrument of the now living and risen Christ, that is, the Holy Spirit.[17]

The Symbolism of Pentecost: The Spirit in the Church

Luke, relating the story of Pentecost (Acts 2:1-13), wants to demonstrate how the Church came about and how it is impregnated with the Spirit of Christ. On that day the new activity and presence of Christ in the world, through his Spirit, was made visible to all. What does the real presence of the Spirit of Christ mean concretely for the Church? It was evident for Luke and for the whole of the primitive Church: it means the inauguration of the time of fulfillment, when individuals could consider themselves as redeemed brothers and sisters, awaiting the final end. Yet, while waiting they live the reality made manifest by the resurrection. Luke describes these realities with a Judaic symbolism that needs to be clearly understood.[18]

There was the belief at the time that in the end-times (of total fulfillment) the Spirit would descend upon all persons and everyone would prophesy. Luke tells how the Spirit, on the day of Pentecost, descended upon the disciples and upon all who were with them in prayer (Acts 2:1-4). He thus shares the truth that with the risen Jesus, and with the Church, all have entered the final phase of revelation. There is no longer any waiting for God. God, in Jesus, gives us the definitive yes and amen, and has already saved us (cf. 2 Cor 1:20).

It was also the belief at the time that the confusion of languages created by humanity's pride (see Gen 11) would be abolished and overcome. It was to be a time of reconciliation and fraternal communion. Language would no longer be cause for separation or misunderstanding. In narrating the Pentecost event, Luke has the Spirit descend as tongues of flame. All are present: Arabs, Jews, Romans, and so forth, understanding Peter's words in their own tongue.

The message of the Church is thus destined to reestablish the primitive unity of the human race and the mutual accord between human beings. The *shalom* of God reigns in the Church, that is, peace, friendship, and the fraternal spirit of understanding. Vatican II stated that the Church is the "visible sacrament of saving unity," "a lasting and sure seed of unity . . . for the whole human race" (*Lumen Gentium*, 9). Yet it is more than that. Luke is interested in bringing out the universal character of the Church—a

Church brought about to speak all tongues that will continue to grow until it is able to be expressed in all languages. Therefore, he takes pains to enumerate the twelve diverse peoples who hear the good news of Christ in their native tongues. According to Eastern understanding, known to Luke and his listeners, each people was consecrated to a sign of the zodiac. The peoples cited by him (Acts 2:9–11): Parthians, Medes, Elamites, and the others, correspond exactly, even in their order of mention, to the signs of the zodiac. Luke wanted to express the truth that the Church has a cosmic dimension, is destined for all the peoples of the earth, and so its mission, like Christ's has a universal character.

The story of Pentecost, with its clamorous descent of the Holy Spirit, is laden with theological meaning, expressed in a symbolic language known to its listeners. Understanding this language, the basic message is clear: the Church is the sacrament of the Holy Spirit, the Spirit of Christ, the risen Christ himself active in the world. Through the Spirit the Church arose to lead the world to its ultimate perfection in God. As St. Irenaeus said, "Where the Church is, there is the Spirit of God and where the Spirit of God is, there is the Church and all grace."[19] The Church lives because of the Spirit. In the same way the Lukan text of the Our Father in its Caesarean version has much more meaning, reading "May your Spirit come upon us and purify us" instead of "Thy kingdom come" (Luke 11:2). Many renowned exegetes consider this variant reading in Luke's gospel to be older and to well express the theological understanding that Luke had of the Church and its relationship to the Holy Spirit.[20]

The Cosmic Church as the Body of the Risen Christ

The pneumatic character of the Church is best seen by analyzing the expression "The Church is the body of Christ." As pointed out above, this expression will lead to theological confusion if the term *body* is taken in its carnal sense rather than in its pneumatic meaning. As has already been shown, Christ became spiritual, rather than carnal, through the resurrection (cf. 1 Cor 15:45); that is, his nature of body, soul, and divinity is no longer limited to a particular place or time but is, as Spirit, free of all these earthly constraints and acquires a cosmic dimension, open to the totality of all reality. His is a "spiritual body" (1 Cor 15:44). As such, he is present in all things. He is "all in all things" (Col 3:11) and nothing that exists is far from his presence. As an ancient text stated, "quoting" the risen Christ: "lift a stone and I am under it; split a log and I am within it. I will be with you until the end of time."[21] The risen Christ tore down all barriers that separate people (Eph 2:15–18), abolishing the separation between races, religions, between the sacred and the profane. No longer is there any limit to his ineffable and pneumatic existence.

Where does this reality of Christ appear? For Paul, the local Church constitutes the social manifestation of the risen Christ, especially when the eucharistic supper is celebrated. It is in eating the body of the risen Lord that the People of God, gathered together, also become the body of Christ, "in one Spirit all of us were baptized . . . and all of us were given to drink of the one Spirit" (1 Cor 12:13).

However, if the pneumatic (risen) Christ knows no limitations, neither may his body, the Church, confine itself to the limitations of its own dogma, its rituals, its liturgy, or its canon law. The Church has the same boundaries as the risen Christ; and these dimensions are cosmic in nature. Its functions and mysteries, its structures and services must always be open to the Spirit that blows where it will, as a dynamic force in the world. Therefore, all people of faith, in the Spirit, must be members of the Church and must have their place within its visible structures. No one is outside of the Church because there is no longer an "outside," because no one is outside of the reality of God and the risen Christ. Yet, individuals may elect to reject this reality. Even so, they do not cease to be a part of this reality. There is always the possibility of their conversion, accepting the salvation that has already been won for them.

The Holy Spirit and Structure: Sign or Counter-sign?

The pneumatic element belongs to the institutional structure of the Church. Due to a prompting of the Holy Spirit (the risen Christ), the apostles decided to go out on a mission and give concrete form to the Church, embracing elements and realities that the carnal Jesus had introduced. The Church must continually repeat this apostolic decision and, facing new situations, find those expressions and institutions that truly communicate his message, thus achieving Christ's salvation for all peoples. This is where the question arises: Are the Church's decisions, those made in the past, so absolute that they are untouchable, even when they seem to no longer apply? If we take the writings of the New Testament seriously, we can see that the apostles and disciples took great freedom in introducing new institutions and translating the message of Christ into other languages and philosophies.[22]

The founders of the Church kept in mind that it was not so important to look to the past and repeat what Christ said and did, but to look to the present and allow themselves to be inspired by the Holy Spirit and the risen Christ, making decisions that would best lend themselves to salvation and to the passing on of Christ's project. This is why John and Paul are considered the princes of Christian liberty. They did not preach the message of Christ only in the linguistic and cultural language used by Christ, speaking of the world and the apocalypse in the terms of later Judaism: they had the courage to translate Christ's message for the mentality of the Greek world. For example, we know that the essential content of Jesus' preaching was centered on the coming of the Kingdom of God. John, who wrote his gospel around A.D. 90 to an audience of Greeks and others steeped in the gnostic mindset, did not proclaim the message of Christ in terms of the Kingdom of Heaven but rather translated it into existential terminology, such as meaning (Logos-word), bread, life, living water, way, truth, door, and the like. Similarly, Paul translated the fundamental concept of following Christ as "being in Christ."

Neither Paul nor John fell into a doctrinal fixation, alleging that such and such words were actually spoken by the word of life but rather, with a basic fidelity to the spirit of Christ and his message, they translated those words into concepts and expressions that their hearers could understand, accept, and thus be converted to faith in Jesus Christ the savior. The same can be said about ecclesiastical institutions. Only if they are open to an ongoing perfection, reform, and adaptation will they be of service to the Spirit in the Church and in the world. Otherwise they run the risk of becoming conservative and an oppressive power contrary to the liberating development of grace and faith. All of the institutions and theological language within the Church can and must be sacraments (signs and instruments) of the Spirit through which the risen Christ acts and is made present in the historical reality of all persons. If they are too rigid and if they reject their function for faith and grace, they may become *counter*-signs of the Kingdom and of the presence of the living Lord in the world. They must be like the chalice, serving the precious wine of the Spirit but not substituting for it, gathered in the humbleness of a human sign that it may be made present and tasted by all peoples.

Chapter 13

AN ALTERNATIVE STRUCTURE: CHARISM AS THE ORGANIZING PRINCIPLE

The Church as the sacrament of the Holy Spirit implies a consideration of the resurrection and every element of creativity and harmony as primary, beyond institutions, in the understanding of the nature and mission of the Church. A christological emphasis on the level of the incarnation led the Latin Church to excessive institutional rigidity.[1] As a two-thousand-year-old institution, it no longer exudes happiness or joy, only respectability and weight. Theology and Gospel, which attempt to demonstrate the joy of the good news and the birth of a grand liberation, are affected by such an image. The institution has difficulty translating these characteristics, joy and hope, fruits of the Spirit. The Spirit is at the heart of all the great events of history: in creation, in the raising up of the people of Israel, in the calling of the prophets, in Jesus' conception, in his baptism, in the descent upon the apostles at Pentecost, in their decision to go among the Gentiles, thus giving concrete beginning to the Church, in the eucharist that transforms the bread and the wine into the body and blood of the Lord.

Theologically, the Church begins with the resurrection and Pentecost. It is an event of the Spirit, the Spirit who first raised Jesus from among the dead, changing his nature from carnal to spiritual (pneumatic), and who later descended upon the Twelve, making them apostles and founders of the ecclesial communities. The Spirit thus gives life to a specific type of organization.[2]

The Spirit and Its Charisms
Are Given to All the People of God

Ekklesia in common Greek means the gathering of citizens (free people), brought together by a herald to discuss in public forum the problems of the community. *Ekklesia* also means the event itself and the time of the gathering which does not necessarily imply continuity. In a theological sense, it

154

can be said that the Church is the encounter of the community of the faithful, an encounter prompted by Christ and the Spirit to celebrate, deepen faith, and to discuss the questions of the community in the light of the Gospel. Church, in this primitive sense, is more an *event* that may take place beneath an oak tree, in the house of some coordinator, or within a church building, rather than an *institution* with all of its goods, services, laws, doctrines, ministries, and historical continuity.

The cohesiveness and organized continuity of the faithful can better be expressed by the term People of God. Every people has its own history and activity, a consciousness of its values and idiosyncracies, a historical task around which everyone rallies, and an inherent power of organization. The Church, as People of God, has all of these characteristics and also possesses a religious, supernatural, and transcendent perspective. Everyone belongs to this people, previous to any internal differences. At the start, everyone in the People of God is equal, a citizen of the Kingdom. The mission of the People of God is not entrusted only to a few but is given to all; sacred power is, initially, held by everyone and only later is held by sacred ministers. All are sent out to proclaim the good news about the bright future of history and about the meaning of the world already won and anticipated by the resurrection that makes Jesus' utopic truth about the Kingdom real and concrete.

According to 1 Peter 2:5–10 the entire Church is a chosen nation, a royal palace (*basileion*), a priestly community (*hierateuma*), a holy nation, a people chosen by God to proclaim his saving act for all of humanity (cf. Rev 1:6; 5:10). According to this view the historical bearer of the cause of Jesus and the Spirit is the entire people. They are an organized people, but their organization is only justified if it benefits all of the members, and not if the means of organization expropriates Christ's sacred power which has been granted to and inherited by each individual. The distinction between the laity and the hierarchy, between the Church *discens* and the Church *docens* is only justified when the purpose of each is safeguarded. Therefore, one must say, as Vatican II did *not*, that collegiality involves not only the bishops and priests but also the laity. Like apostolicity, collegiality is a characteristic of the entire Church and not only certain of its members.

It is a fundamental concept that there is a basic equality in the Church: according to Matthew (23:8) we are all "brothers" (and sisters), we are all children, we are all immersed in the risen Christ and anointed by the Holy Spirit. This leads to the idea of democracy, with the difference that ecclesial power is understood as derived from and sharing in the power of the Spirit and the risen Christ, active in the community, and not simply derived from the people alone (as is commonly understood in other forms of democracy).

The presence of the Spirit is made visible by a "plurality of gifts" or "charisms" (1 Cor 12:5). In Pauline terminology, these are simply services which he enumerates at great length (1 Cor 12:8–10; Rom 12:6–7; Eph 4:11–12).[3] Some of these services-gifts attend to the collective needs of the community, such as the service of mercy (Rom 12:8) or that of exhortation (Rom 12:8), healing and miracles (1 Cor 12:9), while others meet structural needs such as teaching, leadership, discernment of spirits (1 Cor 12:10; Eph 4:11; Rom 12:8), all of which demand constant attention.

Thus, an alternative model for the organization of the ecclesial community is outlined, one that differs from the one emphasized in the Catholic epistles, especially by Ignatius of Antioch, wherein everything revolves around the bishop-priest-deacon triad. This accepted model makes the three to be privileged bearers of the Spirit, and the community is built around them, thereby establishing a division in which the members of the Church cease to be equal. This has been the concrete model adopted throughout history, not so much for theological reasons but because it could more easily be adopted to the authoritarian forms of power in the ancient and later feudal worlds. Yet, another model was proposed in the beginning, a more fraternal and circular model in which everyone shared equally. This older teaching has always remained in the back of the Church's memory; charismatic movements, powerful evangelical groups, and idealists have tried, over and over, to revive it. It has never ceased to nourish the Christian dream and continues to be taught in religious communities. Given the current growth in *comunidades eclesiales de base*, where the people express and achieve their desire for participation and where the hierarchy is rediscovering the paths of the people and so divests itself of its titles and ecclesiastical baggage, creating a common desire for community and equality— this model acquires an unexpected historical possibility.

What Is a Charism?

With one exception (1 Peter 4:10), Paul and the Pauline writings are the only ones that employ the word *charism*.[4] The word is rare in profane literature and is only used twice in the whole Old Testament (although there are variations). The term is derived from *charis* or *chairein*, words from the theological understanding of the Old and New Testaments meaning gratuity, benevolence, and God's gift that is granted to the individual. Paul introduced the word *charism* in the context of the organization of the community. It presupposes a profound mystical experience of the presence of Christ and the Spirit as living and active realities in the lives of individuals and in the communion of the faithful, living out the new ethos begun by the Gospel.

The reality of charism is brought out very well in the Old Testament.[5]

The Spirit's power and services are exercised in favor of the people's liberation through Samson in the book of Judges (13:25). Kings are anointed and invested with special powers for the people (1 Sam 11:6). The Spirit irrupts through the prophets. Joel (chap. 3) considered the descent of the Spirit upon the entire people as a characteristic of the end-times. Although the pneumatic reality is recognized in paganism, through oracles and inspired testimony, the activity of the Spirit never takes place as a part of the state, an established order, or the people as a whole. The reality of the Spirit is found in the arena of creativity, of the unconventional, in the irruption of something new, on the level of the individual.

Paul makes charism the structuring element of the community. His theology of justification rests on the belief that with the appearance of the Church, the end-times had begun. This is why the fullness of the Spirit had exploded in all its power. Charism is no longer extraordinary or unexpected but is the common rule for the structure of the community. For Paul charism means simply the concrete function that each person exercises within the community for the good of all (cf. 1 Cor 12:7; Rom 12:4; Eph 4:7).

Paul details this model by stating that the Church is a body with many members, all springing from the Spirit itself, each with its unique function. There is no noncharismatic member, no one is useless, everyone occupies a decisive place in the community: "each member serves the other members" (Rom 12:5). All enjoy equal dignity; there is no room for privileges that destroy the unity of the whole: "the eye cannot say to the hand 'I do not need you' nor can the head say to the feet 'I do not need you'" (1 Cor 12:21). The golden rule that preserves the health of the model, its fraternal circularity, was formulated by Paul: "all the members must be concerned for one another" (1 Cor 12:25).

This model of Christian life is very different from the one in which the hierarchy takes all sacred power and all the means of religious production, saying, in effect, "You will listen, obey, ask no questions, and do as we say." This is the complete domination of the head over the hands, the feet, and even the heart. The hierarchy considers itself to be the only fundamental charism, forgetting that the Church, the family of God, is built upon the foundation of the apostles as well as the prophets (Eph 2:20) and doctors (Eph 4:11; 1 Cor 12:28). The hierarchy is only one charismatic state in the Church, one that must not (as sometimes happens) step on the toes of other charisms that the Spirit raises in the community. Some charisms may be uncomfortable for someone in the hierarchy who prefers to expel those priests who do not preach according to his own teaching, prohibiting theologians to speak at the slightest suspicion, founding philosophical-theological institutes that simply repeat the doctrine of the councils due to a disdain for theological reflection that might accept the challenge of the signs of the times.

The Church is alive where the Spirit is not suffocated. Diverse charisms abound, creativity flourishes, and Jesus' message becomes, again, good news. People become true members of the Church, and not simply parishioners, allowing the religious realization of the diverse capabilities (charisms), placed at the service of the Gospel and all people.

The routine as well as the extraordinary is covered by the term *charism*. True charism blossoms where individuals place all that they are, all that they have, and all they can do at the service of God and neighbor. Their gifts come from the Spirit and become fruitful, like the talents in the gospel.

This way of organizing the ecclesial community preserves its integrity and avoids domination and the private appropriation of power only if love is the primary axis of the community. Paul understood this very well. After listing the most important charisms and services, he says that one must search for an even better way (1 Cor 12:31); he then begins his apology of love, with the necessary virtues for daily community life: patience and kindness, overcoming pride, envy, ambition, irritation and suspicion, seeking love alone and its interests (1 Cor 14:4–8; 14:1). This very real and simple love is the charism of charisms, service of all services, extended to everyone: "the greatest of these is love" (1 Cor 13:13).

What, then, is a charism? A charism is a manifestation of the Spirit's presence in the members of the community, causing everything that they are and do to be done and ordered for the good of all. Hans Küng defines charism in this way: "It signifies the call of God, addressed to an individual, to a particular ministry in the community, which brings with it the ability to fulfil that ministry."[6] Another scholar proposes this definition: "charism consists of the concrete calling received through the salvific event, exercised in the community, contributing to that community, continually building it up and serving all people in love."[7]

The Simultaneity of Charisms

Charisms, ordinary as well as extraordinary, come from God and the Spirit. They must, to continue to be charisms, always refer to the Spirit and not be linked to the desire for self-affirmation, directed not to one's own interests but to the common good. Charism is service. It is a function. The Spirit gives its gifts to each individual, as it wishes (1 Cor 12:11). Therefore, there is not only one type of charism, for example, those stemming from a particular sacrament (cf. Tim 1:6; "that is in you because of the imposition of my hands"). Charism is not imprisoned by the institutionalization of sacraments. Paul, speaking of charisms, does not mention the charisms linked to holy orders. He states: "Because in the Spirit you have been richly endowed . . . you lack no spiritual gift" (1 Cor 1:5–7); "you abound in all things" (2 Cor 8:7), and "God can multiply his favors among you so that you may always have enough of everything" (2 Cor 9:8).

This means that there is a simultaneity of charisms. Each one, according to its place, function, and capacity, serves the others. Any interference in the charism of another is an interference in the unity of the Church. This is true for those who speak in tongues, the wise, as well as for those who rule. Each one has his or her field, serving all others. Although there is this simultaneity of charisms, there is obviously a hierarchy among them, according to the needs of the Church. There are more necessary charisms. However, this does not mean that the more important charism has the right to prevent or repress other charisms, including the least of the charisms which also belong to the Church and emanate from the Spirit.

Each Person Has One or More Charisms

There are no passive members in the Church. Each person, within the body, exercises some function. Therefore, every Christian is charismatic. Paul says: "each one has his own gift from God, one this and another that" (1 Cor 7:7); "To each person the manifestation of the Spirit is given for the common good" (1 Cor 12:7). Peter confirms this in the same way: "As generous distributors of God's manifold grace, place your gifts at the service of one another, each in the measure he has received" (1 Pet 4:10). Acts states that the Spirit is "poured out on all mankind" (2:17).

Thus, charisms are not reserved for a certain group of persons, such as priests or bishops. No one should attempt to possess all charisms. "Are all apostles? Are all prophets? Are all teachers?" (1 Cor 12:29) Every Christian is invited to view his or her function, profession, abilities as gifts that have been received and that must be exercised in service to the entire community.

Charism as the Structure of the Community

If charism means the concrete way in which the Spirit and the risen Lord are present in the world, then charism belongs to the structure of the Church. Without it the Church is no longer a religious and theological reality. Charism was not just a privilege of the early days of the Church. It is the permanent condition of the Church as a community with diverse functions and services. Charism includes the hierarchical element, but not exclusively. Charism is more fundamental than the institution. Charism is the pneumatic force (*dynamis tou Theou*) that gives rise to institutions and keeps them alive. The principle of the structure of the Church is not the institution or the hierarchy but rather the charism that is at the root of all institutions and hierarchy. There is not one group of rulers and another group of those who are ruled; there is one group of faith. Those who rule as well as those who are ruled must all believe. Faith, or the charism of faith, is the *prius natura* (basic nature) and common factor giving rise to communication and fundamental fraternal equality among all members of the Church.

There is no Church without charism, that is, without the presence of the Spirit and risen Lord made manifest through its members and their functions. One scholar states: "The fundamental charismatic structure of the Church means that each individual has his or her place in the community, a place that is determined by the individual's charism; it also means that each one co-constitutes the Church. If the individual loses his or her place, or if that place is taken away, then the community is affected not only on a moral level but is also attacked at its core and even demoralized."[8]

If there is repression by one individual over another through the exercise of power, then a "human" spirit is at work instead of the Spirit of Christ. The freedom to which Christ called us (Gal 5:1ff) is stifled. Legalism, pharisaism, and decaying Judaism is the result. That is why Paul is so stern in his admonition "Do not stifle the Spirit" (1 Thes 5:19). The constant temptation in the Church is that of having power over others, of one charism prevailing over other charisms to the point of silencing them. The Church then runs the risk of no longer being a community of believers, those who hear the word of God, of the Spirit, of the risen Christ, but rather becoming a community that only hears dogmas, laws, rites, canonical prescriptions, edifying exhortations—and not the liberating word of the Spirit.

What would the Church be if there were no one who consoled, no one who gave encouragement, no one who spread hope and joy? It would be a Church of whiners and complainers. It is true that there must be order, discipline, and obedience; but this can also be found in an army. The Church is not an army, organized to learn to kill, but rather is organized to love God and all persons. The opposite is also true. What would the Church be if there were a multiplicity of charisms without any order among them? How would all the members constitute one body, if there were no one to see that the charisms were exercised for the common good?

All charisms, and not only some of them, are constitutive of the Church, such as order and unity, orthodox teaching, and presiding at the sacred liturgy. So, too, must the charisms of coresponsibility, constructive criticism, scientific and technical knowledge, and organization among others have their rightful place in the body of the Church. They cannot be merely tolerated or morally recognized. They must be seen as constitutive (of essence and nature) and not only as elements in the life of the Church. Christ and the Holy Spirit are Lord of the Church and they, through the services and charisms of the diverse members of the community, act and are proclaimed.

In terms of the exercise of leadership within the Church, it is not enough to appeal to a permanent charism that has been received through the sacrament of orders. It is crucial to look at the way in which it is exercised. There are ways in which it becomes domination, something Christ stigmatized as typical of the lords of this world (Matt 20:25). In the name of the Spirit and the liberty to which Christ has called us, this must be criticized and, in extreme cases, ignored because "it is better to obey God than men" (Acts 5:29; 4:19). Power structures in the Church do not necessarily violate its charismatic nature. Power can be a charism, as long as it serves everyone and is an instrument for building justice in the community.

True Charisms

A criterion is the norm for discerning whether a phenomenon comes from God's power or whether it can be explained simply by environmental circumstances.[9] Concerning charisms, if the phenomenon comes from God, and is always directed back to God by its receiver, then it is called a charism. What comes from God is difficult to determine. The best way to discern this is if the one who receives the charism refers to God as its giver. However, there is a further difficulty. The individual may attribute the "charism" entirely to God and yet be under false impressions. There may be self-interest and power deep within the subconscious that leads the person to be tricked into consciously attributing the gift to God. There must be another criterion, that of service to the community, a service that is disinterested and selfless.

The Spirit unifies the charismatic community (cf. 1 Cor 12:4; Eph 4:4; Rom 12:6). If, with his or her charism, someone divides the community, it disintegrates or creates an atmosphere of division and hatred within it, then the charism loses its nature and becomes a spiritualistic curiosity. Without the convergent and unifying reference, charisms become destructive to the community. They are like mushrooms that grow in fertile soil but destroy life with their poison. Paul condemns the disorderly desire for charisms (1 Cor 13:2). Charism is charism through its link with the Spirit of unity. The charism, as such, is out of the reach of human manipulation. It is always grace, free gift. The individual receives the charism and can only legitimately utilize the gift when it is recognized as received and sent by the Spirit.

Charism versus Human Talent

There is a very close relationship between charism and human talent. Talent is grace. One may be responsible or irresponsible for a talent that has been given (Matt 25:14ff). The talent put to good use humanizes if it is continually lived in a spirit of gratitude. It is a grace and achieves its true state when it is recognized as a gift for which the individual is responsible. Once the talent is separated from its origin, it lives on but forgetful of its divine and gracious source. It develops and is lived in a merely human way; it does not cease to have an origin in grace but is perverted because the source that nourishes it is forgotten.

Charism is this same talent (even when it is ordinary) but with the constant memory of its origin in God, that it is always received and not earned. Thus, talent and charism, natural gift and grace, are not opposed but are the same reality even if lived by the individual in different ways. One person lives it as a gift from God and calls it charism; the other lives it as if it were the product of his or her own effort and so calls it a natural gift. This latter interpretation does not change the structure of the talent but changes the structure of the individual who lives under such false consciousness.

Charism Builds Community

It is not enough that the charism comes from the Spirit, thus guaranteeing its vertical dimension. It comes from God for humanity; charism is meant to build up the community, its horizontal dimension. If there is some break in the crossing of these lines, then the charism disappears. Paul takes as an example an unexpected and extraordinary charism, speaking in tongues. The one who speaks in tongues is only truly charismatic if his or her speech is understandable to others.

The community at Corinth had to listen to Paul's admonition, one that has lasting value: "'All things are lawful,' but not all are advantageous; 'All things are lawful'—but not everything is constructive" (1 Cor 10:23). This is the basic, simple, and natural criterion of service beyond the ego, of personal disinterestedness in service to others. Not much theological subtlety, sophisticated argumentation, or recourse to authority is needed to know if a gift, service, or work comes from God. It is enough to look at its function and usefulness for the community. It must be advantageous and edifying, not just good will and purity of intention. There may be gifts that are truly gifts but which overlook the needs and demands of the community. In such a case, this gift-charism-service still awaits its kairos (its time).

The norm is this: "No one should seek his own interest but rather that of the other" (1 Cor 10:24). Contrary to this, the rigid hierarchical structure of the Church appears to seek the advantage of every other order (religious, financial, social, influential, public privilege) for itself. The spirit of the racetrack abounds, each one striving for the first place, with servility, diplomatic statements, lack of compromise, hiding the truth, and the rejection of every prophetic spirit. Grasping for power and climbing the social ladder are the accepted practices. In place of a Church of pastors that build up their community is a group of mediocre, spineless spirits, more concerned with their own image than the truth of the Gospel, than with love for all people and for the poor for whom Christ risked everything.

When charism is not preserved as charism, there is concupiscence, or the will for power and possession; this is the original sin (John 8:44) and leads to all sin (Rom 1:24). It destroys the community. Paul illustrates the antitheses between the works of the flesh and the works of the Spirit (cf. Gal 5:16–25).

It may happen that a community is invaded by "hatred, discord, arguments, dissension, and envy" (Gal 5:20). In this case, the imperative for order and discipline is clear, imperatives that are also charisms (as long as they preserve their true function). They do not limit the other charisms but keep them within their limits, within the community and in service to it.

The Charism of Unity

The basic problem in every community is internal cohesion and unity, particularly when disintegrating factors abound. There is a charism, one among many but of prime importance, which is that of being responsible for harmony among the many and diverse charisms. This charism is proper to those who occupy positions of leadership within the community. We commonly call it the hierarchy.

The New Testament does not offer an expression for what today is understood as the hierarchical function. The closest term, according to Ernst Käsemann, is charism.[10] To properly understand the charism of ordination in the community, one needs to abstract from historical models, be they profane (monarchical, feudal, democratic) or ecclesiastical (bishop, Pope, pastor)—especially the latter because it has been subject to much self-sanctification. The New Testament avoids profane titles as well as sacred ones. It totally secularizes all titles in order not to give any hint of domination (profane power) or aggrandizement and privilege (sacred power). It utilizes, to the scandal of those used to Byzantine titles, terms that mean merely mundane and service positions: *diakonia* and *oikonomia*, service and leadership in the home! In the New Testament, there are no ministries, only ministers. The ministers, responsible for running the community, have the "charism of direction, presidency, assistance, and leadership" (1 Cor 12:28; 1 Thes 5:12; Rom 12:8; 1 Cor 16:16).

The New Testament also speak of the *episkopoi* (bishops) and the *diakonoi* (deacons: Phil 1:1). Bishop and deacon, contrary to the present understanding, had nothing to do with the sacraments or liturgy. The bishop, in its simple and plain acceptance, was responsible for overseeing things so that everything functioned satisfactorily. The deacon was a servant or assistant, second in command. The priest came from another tradition, namely Judaism, where they were the group of the oldest and most venerated in the community who took on the function of general assistance and organization. As is clear, the dominant theme is not tied to the sacred but to the service of overseeing and assistance.

The specific function of the hierarchy (those who are in leadership roles) is not accumulation but integration, making way for unity and harmony among the various services so that any single one does not trip up, drown out, or downplay another. From this comes the immediate subordination of the members to those in the hierarchy. However, the hierarchy does not exist to subordinate but rather to nourish the spirit of fraternity and unity. This charism of unity implies all other charisms, such as dialogue, patience, listening, serenity, knowledge of the human heart with its desire for power and self-affirmation. This hierarchical function is carried out by the coordinator of a local ecclesial community, by the bishop in his diocese, and by the Pope in the universal Church.

Due to the charism of unity, there are those who preside at the celebrations of the community, those who are primarily responsible for orthodox doctrine, and for the order of charity. It is particularly necessary for these persons to discern the spirit of the community and to watch that all charisms retain their nature as charism, in service for the good of the community (cf. *Lumen Gentium*, 12; *Apostolicam Actuositatem*, 1339).

This model of organization may shape the living of the Gospel in small groups, building more and more of a network of communities that embrace Christians, religious, priests, and bishops. It provides the opportunity for the Church, born from the faith of the people through the Spirit of God, to make this organization, envisioned by Paul, real and viable. At the very least, it will foster a spirit which, in the strength of the Holy Spirit, will revitalize the traditional and hierarchical institutions of the Church. And, the history of salvation tells us that where the Spirit is active, we can count on the unexpected, the new that has not yet been seen.

NOTES

Chapter 1 / Models and Pastoral Practices of the Church

1. This work reflects the ecclesial experience of one who has spent more than ten years travelling throughout the world, especially in Latin America, serving various *comunidades eclesiales de base,* and reflecting theologically on the reality that is taking place in the Church throughout the world. In spite of this rather personal perspective, the following bibliographical references are offered to aid the reader in exploring the subject:

G. Arroyo, P.J. Krischke, and others, *The Church and Politics in Latin America* (Toronto, 1977); P. Bigo, *L'Eglise et la révolution du tiers monde* (Paris, 1974);

Clodovis Boff, *Comunidade eclesial, Comunidade política: Ensaios eclesiológicos* (Petrópolis, 1978); idem, "*A inflûencia política das comunidades eclesiais de base*" in *SEDOC* 11 (1979) 797–818;

L. Boff, *Igreja e vida religiosa no processo de libertação* (Petrópolis, 1975); idem, "Mission et universalité concrète de l'Eglise" in *Lumière et Vie* 137 (1978) 33–52; idem, *Eglise en génèse: Les communautés eclesiales de base réinventent l'Eglise* (Paris, 1978); idem, *O caminhar da Igreja com os oprimidos: Do vale de lágrimas rumo à terra prometida* (Rio de Janeiro, 1980); idem, *Teologia do cativeiro e da libertação* (Petrópolis, 1980), pp. 201–20;

CELAM, *Conflicto social y compromiso cristiano en América Latina* (Bogotá, 1976); CLAR, *Pueblo de Dios y comunidad liberadora: Perspectivas eclesiológicas desde las comunidades religiosas que caminan con el pueblo* (Bogotá, 1977);

R. Muñoz, *Nueva Conciencia de la Iglesia en América Latina* (São Paulo, 1976); idem, "Sobre el capítulo eclesiológico de las conclusiones de Puebla" in *Puebla* 3 (1979) 141–51; L. Proaño, *Pour une Eglise Libératrice* (Paris, 1973); various, "Igreja, povo que se liberta: Estudos sobre a eclesiologia das comunidades de base no Brasil" in *SEDOC* 11 (1979) 705–862; R. Vidales, *La Iglesia latino-americana y la política después de Medellín* (Quito, 1972).

Chapter 2 / Theological Tendencies and Pastoral Practices

1. The classic manuals of theology fall into this category: the Spanish with *Sacrae Theologiae Summa* (BAC, 1952); the German with Phle-Gummersbach, *Handbuch der Dogmatik*, 3 vols. (Innsbruck, 1952); the French with *Initiation*

théologique (Paris, 1952), a commentary on the *Summa Theologica*; and the Italian (Latin) with many manuals from the Gregorianum in Rome.

2. See M. Schmaus, *Katholische Dogmatik* (Munich, 1956) and *Der Glaube der Kirche*, 4 vols. (Munich, 1970).

3. One needs only cite the voluminous manual of theology begun during the Second Vatican Council, *Mysterium Salutis: Grundriss heilsgeschichtlicher Dogmatik*, ed. J. Feiner and M. Lohrer, 6 vols. in 8 (Einsiedeln, 1965–81).

4. See the vast work by Karl Rahner and his school, *Lexicon für Theologie und Kirche*, 11 vols. (Freiburg, 1957–67), and *Handbuch der Pastoraltheologie*, 5 vols. in 8 (Freiburg, 1964–72); and the postconciliar works of Flick and Alszeghy, professors at the Gregorianum in Rome, on anthropology, grace and revelation.

5. Notably, J. B. Metz, *Theology of the World* (New York, 1969); J. Moltmann, *Theology of Hope* (New York, 1976); and in French the many systematic studies of C. Duquoc on secularization.

6. See G. Gutiérrez, *Theology of Liberation* (Maryknoll, N.Y., 1973); L. Boff, *Teología do cativeiro e da libertação* (Petrópolis, 1980); and Clodovis Boff, *Teoría e prática: A teologia do político e suas mediações* (Petrópolis, 1977).

Chapter 3 / The Church and the Struggle for Justice
and the Rights of the Poor

1. *Folha de São Paulo*, 5/2/76.
2. *O São Paulo*, 2/6–22/74, p. 3.
3. Pedro Casaldáliga, *Antología retirante* (Rio de Janeiro, 1978), p. 168.
4. Cf. L. Boff, *Teología do cativeiro e da libertação* (Petrópolis, 1980).

Chapter 4 / The Violation of Human Rights in the Church

1. The remarks of Friar Bonaventura Kloppenburg (*El cristiano secularizado* [Petrópolis, 1970], pp. 168–69) are right to the point: "The council was very generous in its speech. But this way of speaking is new. Looking at the past history of the Church it is not hard to verify that *diakonia* often became domination and absolutism, that pastoral *munus* took on an authoritarian and imposing character, that the ecclesiastical magisterium became a uniform and intangible theological body, that discipline took the form of rigid and static legalism, that the continuity of the Church turned into an immobile and sacred tradition.... Today I read in *Lumen Gentium* 8 that 'the Church is at the same time holy and in constant need of purification'; I read in *Gaudium et Spes* 21 that the Church 'must ceaselessly renew itself under the guidance of the Holy Spirit'; but I also read in number 6 of the *Mirari vos* of Gregory XVI that 'it is of the utmost absurdity and highly injurious to say that a certain restoration or regeneration [of the Church] is necessary for it to return to its primitive security, giving it new life, as if to believe that the Church is susceptible to defect, ignorance, or any other human imperfection.' In practice we fell into an ecclesiastical monophysitism that identified human authority with divine authority,

making the virtue of obedience the true characteristic of the 'faithful,' which was the simplest designation for a Christian."

2. We will take some examples from the recent history of the Church; the more abundant examples from the past would even better illumine the question that is presented here.

3. *Herderkorrespondenz* 25 (1971) 592–97, esp. 593–95: "Das Thema Gerechtigkeit auf der römischen Bischofssynode"; J. Gremillion, *The Gospel of Peace and Justice* (Maryknoll, N.Y., 1976), pp. 513–30.

4. "Nuevas normas para la reducción de sacerdotes al estado laical" in *SEDOC* 4 (1971) 304–11.

5. Ibid., p. 309: "In this same document [*Sacerdotalis Coelibatus*] the Supreme Pontiff, mindful of the motives by which the Church judges it necessary to grant certain priests laicization by dispensing them from the obligation to observe celibacy, admonishes that they 'experience every means of persuasion with the aim of aiding the brother who vacillates to again find peace and trust, to follow the path of repentance, and to return to the fold; it is only when there is no other solution that the Church's unhappy minister is excluded from the exercise of priestly ministry' (87). The Pope adds that 'if this priest is unable to be saved for the priesthood and yet shows good and serious dispositions for a Christian life as a lay person, the Apostolic See, after having studied all the circumstances and in accord with the local ordinary or with the religious superior, allowing love to triumph over pain, will sometimes grant all the required dispensations.'"

6. The Sacred Congregation for the Doctrine of the Faith, "Declaration on the Question of the Admission of Women to the Ministerial Priesthood" in *L'Osservatore Romano*, 1/30/77.

7. For a synthesis of the theological arguments, see my "O sacerdócio da mulher" in *Convergência* (1973), pp. 663–97.

8. *Herderkorrespondenz* 25 (1971) 593.

9. "Derechos humanos y la tarea de la Iglesia" in CEI Supplement 15: *Direitos Humanos* (Rio de Janeiro, 1976), p. 28. See the article written by L. Bouyer, writing in the same issue of *L'Osservatore Romano* (1/30/77) in which the document prohibiting priesthood to women was published: "The religion of the Bible, Judaism, and even more so Christianity, has proclaimed the fundamental equality of men and women, but not in the priesthood." Either the right of equality is universal or one cannot speak of equality without cynicism.

10. J. Neumann, "Ketzerverfahren—eine Form der Wahrhietsfindung?" in *Theologische Quartalschrift* 154 (1974) 328–39; here p. 338.

11. Cf. "El Reglamiento para el Examen de la Doctrina" in *SEDOC* 3 (1971) 1075–76. Cf. also the interview with J. Hammer the secretary for the Sacred Congregation for the Doctrine of Faith in *Herderkorrespondenz* 28 (1974) 238–46; and the critical interviews with the canon lawyer J. Neumann in the same issue, pp. 287–97, and with Hans Küng in issue 27 (1973) 422–27.

12. Cf. the procedure against the Catholic biblical scholar H. Haag and his treatment of original sin: "Ein Verfahren der Glaubenskongregation" in *Theologische Quartalschrift* 153 (1973) 184–92, esp. p. 190.

13. Hans Küng, in *Herderkorrespondenz* 27 (1973) 426.

14. Ibid. The procedure against Ivan Illich became famous for its ideological violence to all rights. The interrogation began like this:

"My name is Illich."

"I know that."

"Monsignor, what is your name?"

"I am the judge."

"I thought I might know your name!"

"That is not important. My name is Casoira."

They wanted to obligate Illich under oath to maintain absolute secrecy as to what was to take place in the halls of the Sacred Congregation, something Illich did not accept. The interrogation mixed trivial questions about his institute with questions about some fifty people, questions of faith, disputed subjects in theology, and "subversive interpretations." These included questions such as "Is it true that you want women to go to confession without the separation of a curtain?": cf. L. Kaufmann, *Schicksal eines Propheten* (Munich, 1970).

15. J. Neumann in *Herderkorrespondenz* 28 (1974) 297.

16. Catholic doctrine is certainly not a rigid and lifeless corpse. It was created; it did not fall out of the sky ready-made; it continues to be shaped, growing and embracing the bottomless wealth of the deposit of faith. Every age, with its questions and anxieties, is important for revealing unsuspected dimensions of the Christian mystery. Theology, along with the entire Church and the supreme magisterium, is called to explore, to translate, and to live the good news of liberation brought by Jesus Christ. There are not only certainties and dogmas; there is also room for hypotheses, for probability, and for healthy pluralism. What is of value for Sacred Scripture has equal value for theology, as stated by the Biblical Commission in 1915: "Everything that Holy Scripture affirms, states explicitly, and insinuates must be taken as affirmed, stated, and insinuated by the Holy Spirit" (*Enchiridion biblicum*, 433). In other words, in the Bible "there is, alongside categorical affirmation, the proposition of a probability, a possibility, a simple conjecture, and even doubt": P. Benoit, *L'inspiration* (Initiation Biblique; Tournai, 1954), p. 37; P. Grelot, *La Bible: Parole de Dieu* (Paris-Tournai, 1965), p. 108. This is even more valuable for theology which cannot count on divine inspiration!

17. By system, we mean the definite relation of elements (persons and institutions) that are mutually connected and influenced, forming a more or less ordered body with its particular theories and practices. The Church is considered to be one system with many sub-systems (hierarchies, magisterium, proclamation, and the organization of its members). The system of the Church, in turn, is a sub-system of society, influenced by society and in turn capable of exerting influence on that society. The Church is understood only when this reality and its practices are studied together with the principal system, that is, global society.

18. Cf. B. Sauer, "Autoritäre Systeme in der Kirche heute" in *Autorität*, ed. J. Türk (Maguncia, 1973), pp. 114–25; R. Tilmann, "Die Autoritätskrise in den Kirchen" in *Autorität*, pp. 26–40.

19. Cf. the detailed analysis of the system of power in the Church by C. A. Medina and Pedro A. Ribeiro de Oliveira, *Autoridade e participação: Estudo sociológico da Igreja Católica* (Petrópolis, 1973). Also *Macht, Dienst, Herrschaft in Kirche und Gesellschaft*, ed. W. Weber (Freiburg, 1974).

20. Thomas Merton, quoting in *Faith and Violence* (Notre Dame, 1965, p. 58) from *The Prison Meditations of Father Delp*: "At some future date the honest historian will have some bitter things to say about the contribution of the Churches to the creation of the mass mind, of collectivism, dictatorships and so on."

21. E. Durkheim, *Les formes élémentaires de la vie religieuse* (Paris, 1937), p. 618 (E.T. *The Elementary Forms of the Religious Life*, 1954).

22. Although doctrinal texts such as *Lumen Gentium, Apostolicam Actuositatem,* and others state that the whole Church (lay and ordained) are responsible for the preservation and integrity of faith and revelation, in practice the hierarchy behaves as if it alone were solely responsible.

23. Freud demonstrated that when there is a conflict between the psyche and reality, the former has the tendency to substitute the latter with words, thereby avoiding real contact with it. "When someone fears contact with reality, words are placed like a veil between what is said and one's surroundings, as well as between what is verbalized and one's own body": N. Brown, *Vida contra muerte* (Petrópolis, 1973; English original: *Love Against Death*). The fear of life comes from the basic structure of life itself, which is dynamic, unforeseeable, and destructive of all pretension. Words, however, are stable, ready-made recipes, generate certainty, and are able to be manipulated.

24. For a brief historical overview of the ideological presuppositions of the institution of the Inquisition, of the Holy Office and the Sacred Congregation for the Doctrine of Faith, see J. Neumann, "Ketzerverfahren," cited in n. 10 above.

25. Clodovis Boff, "Teología e prática" in *Revista Eclesiástica Brasileira* 36 (1975) 789–810, here p. 798: "After Marx, theology could no longer put in parentheses the material conditions of life on the threat of 'mystifying' the reality of iniquitous conditions. The theological word concerning the social realm has no credibility except as a second word, that is, after having done justice to the abovementioned situations. This is precisely the function of socioanalytical study. Against both theoretical pragmatism and epistemological idealism, one must recognize that the practice of theology implies two separate and distinct areas: internal and external. The first is defined by the autonomy of theory, whose rules must be respected. The second corresponds to theology's dependence on the social conditions of production or the economy of social goods, over which the theologian is called to exercise a constant ideopolitical watch."

26. See the entire issue of *Concilium* 63 (1971) entitled *Democratization of the Church*, ed. A. Muller.

27. Cf. the summary of modern changes within the Church in *Autorität*, pp. 26–41, 216ff.; N. Greinacher, "A Community Free of Rule," in *Concilium* 63 (1971) 87–107.

28. R. Pesch, "The New Testament Foundations of a Democratic Form of Life in the Church" in *Concilium* 63 (1971) 58. The opening quote is from J. Blank, *Das Evangelium als Garantie der Freiheit* (Würzburg, 1970), pp. 67f.

29. A. Weiser, "Autorität im Alten und Neuen Testament" in *Autorität*, pp. 60–76; W. Thüsing, "Dienstfunktionen und Vollmacht kirchlicher Ämter nach dem Neuen Testament" in *Macht, Dienst, Herrschaft in Kirche und Gesellschaft*, pp. 61–74.

30. Cardinal Paolo Evaristo Arns, "Derechos humanos y la tarea de la Iglesia," p. 29 (cited in n. 9 above).

Chapter 5 / The Power of the Institutional Church:
Can It Be Converted?

1. The visit of the Pope to Brazil in July 1980 is a testimony to this experience. See the entire issue of *Revista Eclesiástica Brasileira* 39 (1980) entitled "Balance de la visita del Papa Juan Pablo II."

2. It is worth noting the courage and veracity of Cardinal Aloisio Lorscheider upon inaugurating the 1974 Synod in Rome: "Panorama de la Iglesia Universal a partir de 1971" in *CNBB Press Bulletin* 47 (1974), September 27, 1974.

3. G. Hasenhüttl, "Church and Institution" in *Concilium* 91 (1974) entitled *The Church as Institution*, ed. G. Baum and A. Greeley, pp. 11–21. See also the entire issue of *Concilium* 90 (1970) entitled *Power and the Word of God*, ed. F. Bockle and J.-M. Pohier.

4. Concerning the question of institutions, see M. Honecker, *Kirche als Gestalt und Ereignis* (Munich, 1963) where the various sociological aspects are studied; for the socioanthropological aspects, see A. Gehlen, *Der Mensch* (Bonn, 1953); idem, *Anthropologische Forschung* (Hamburg, 1961), pp. 69ff.; F. Jonas, *Institutionslehre A. Gehlens* (Tübingen, 1966), pp. 43ff.; M. Kehl, *Die Kirche als Institution* (Frankfurt, 1976); L. Dullaart, *Kirche und Ekklesiologie* (Maguncia, 1975).

5. For an overview, see J. Barnadas, "Christian Faith and the Colonial Situation in Latin America" in *Concilium* 90 (1973) 129–36; E. Dussel, *Hipótesis para una Historia de la Iglesia in América Latina* (Barcelona, 1967); E. Hoornaert, *Formação do catolicismo brasileiro 1550–1800* (Petrópolis, 1974); F. C. Turner, *Catholicism and Political Development in Latin America* (University of North Carolina, 1971); C. P. Ferreira de Camargo, *Igreja e desenvolvimento* (São Paulo, 1971); T. Bruneau, *O catolicismo brasileiro em época de transição* (São Paulo, 1974).

6. J. Comblin, *Théologie de la révolution: Théorie* (Paris, 1970), pp. 216–34.

7. For the historical-theological question of the first three generations of Christians, see: G. Hasenhüttl, *Charisma, Ordnungsprinzip der Kirche* (Freiburg, 1968); P. Dias, *Viefalt der Kirche in der Vielfalt der Jünger, Zeugen und Diener* (Freiburg, 1968); Hans Küng, *The Church* (New York, 1976); J. Daniélou and H. Morrou, *Christian Centuries: First Six Hundred Years* (New York, 1968).

8. Cf. D. Warwick, "The Centralization of Ecclesiastical Authority: An Organizational Perspective" in *Concilium* 91 (1974) 109–18.

9. R. Hernegger, *Macht ohne Auftrag? Die Entstehung der Staats- und Volkskirche* (Olten and Freiburg, 1963), p. 431.

10. J. Comblin, *Théologie de la révolution*, p. 244.

11. E. Iserloh, "Prophetisches Charisma und Leitungsauftrag des Amtes in Spannung und Begegnung als historisches Phänomen" in *Macht, Dienst, Herrschaft in Kirche und Gesellschaft*, ed. W. Weber (Freiburg, 1974), pp. 143–53.

12. Cf. A. Fliche, *La réforme grégorienne*, 2 vols. (Louvain, 1924–25); G. B. Ladner, "The Concepts of 'Ecclesia' and 'Christianitas' and Their Relation to the Idea of Papal 'plenitudo potestatis' from Gregory VII to Boniface VIII" in *Miscell. Hist. Pontif.* 18 (1954) 49–77.

13. R. Laurentin, "Peter as the Foundation Stone in the Present Uncertainty" in *Concilium* 83 (1973) entitled *Truth and Certainty*, ed. E. Schillebeeckx and B. van Iersel, p. 102.

14. St. John Bosco, *Meditazioni*, 2nd ed., vol. 1, pp. 89–90, cited by Laurentin, ibid., p. 103; other examples by Hans Küng, *Infallible? An Inquiry* (2nd ed. New York, 1970), passim.

15. P. Rudge, "The Sociology of Conflict and Ecclesiastical Life" in *Concilium* 91 (1974), pp. 100–108.

16. See the excellent critical study of C. A. de Medina and Pedro A. de Ribeiro de Oliveira, *Autoridade e participação* (Petrópolis, 1973); H. Dombois, *Hierarchie: Grund und Grenze einer umstrittenen Struktur* (Freiburg, 1971), esp. pp. 47–65; Otto Maduro, *Religión y lucha de clases* (Caracas, 1979), pp. 123–63 (E.T. *Religion and Social Conflicts* [Maryknoll, N.Y., 1982]).

17. There is a surprising parallel between the Church's form of government and that of the Communist Party in Russia as described by one expert:

"When the political stance of the institution is studied, the sole importance of the Pope and the bishops must be highlighted. They are above all the authors of the Church's politics. The priests are the actors. The supporting cast, and the laity are the extras. The position of the Pope in relation to other members of the hierarchy is similar to that of the General Secretary of the Communist Party in the Soviet Union. The Pope is, traditionally, the infallible guide of politics and, by dogma, the infallible interpreter of doctrine. The General Secretary of the Communist Party is in an equivalent position; he has his equivalent 'theological' authority as the principal interpreter of doctrine, that being the works of Marx and Lenin. Both are the heads of gigantic bureaucracies that include all the faithful—the Christian masses and the socialist proletariat—and these two leaders take on the right to speak in their name. They also have a similar freedom to determine the political course that the multinational conglomerates beneath their control will follow. This political line is invariably linked to the special interests of the center of power, that is, those of the Vatican on the one hand and those of the Soviet Union on the other. Involvement in the internal matters of local entities—national churches or local parties—is based on the principles of hierarchical recognition and international solidarity. The organization behind the exercise of their power is comprised of an elite group selected from professional and career personnel characterized by a clear national predominance: the Roman Curia that is largely Italian and the Politburo that is clearly Russian. Despite the executive or doctrinal importance of this elite group, the power to elect the number one man remains in the hands of an assembly whose national components are less homogeneous: the College of Cardinals and the Central Committee. Theoretically, the recruitment of members to this assembly does not discriminate against social groups in that equal opportunity for advancement is given to all. Nevertheless, the bourgeoisie enjoy the privileges while the proletariat do not. These latter must adhere uncritically to the established power structures, promising obedience to them. Their freedom of expression is limited for loftier reasons—the interests of the proletariat and the revolution or the interests of the greater Church. Formation of these elite assemblies takes place in specialized schools whose ideology is strictly controlled by the bureaucratic machine and whose professors are chosen for their orthodoxy, loyalty, and knowledge of doctrine. Both bureaucracies run specialized organizations, charged with purity of doctrine, propaganda, and international relations. Both bureaucracies depend on well prepared international assemblies in order to resolve theoretical problems, to reinforce the control held by the supreme leader, to face crises and division; this is the purpose of the councils and synods on the one hand and the conferences of communist parties on the other. Development of local level organizations is based on a policy of sending permanent personnel who specialize in proselytism and propaganda. Ideological teaching is marked by inflexibility, excluding all *démarche* and holding a unique interpretation of history: evolution through the reconciliation of humanity in the one case and progress through class struggle in the other. Ideological inflexibility creates an equal intolerance toward schismatics and lies at the root of police organizations, limits on freedom of expression, inquisitions, probes, and purges.

The fundamental difference between these two bureaucracies is the greater solidarity in the older system of the Church because the Pope has no equal in the national churches while the General Secretary of the Communist Party must understand himself alongside the general secretaries of fellow parties who, theoretically, possess the same importance. Thus, the doctrinal reasons for the hegemony of the Pope are more explicit. Between the two bureaucracies, it has been the power of the Pope that has better resisted those who contest that power when international tensions rise in favor of greater pluralism and freer theoretical development. Today, when policies affecting national churches are studied, one cites the words of the Sovereign Pontiff uttered thirty years ago. The same cannot be done when speaking of the General Secretary of the Communist Party in the Soviet Union" (M. Moreira Alves, *L'Eglise et la politique au Brésil* [Paris, 1972], pp. 75–78).

18. Cf. A. Görres, "Pathologie des katholischen Christentums" in *Handbuch der Pastoraltheologie*, II/1 (Freiburg, 1966), pp. 277–343; T. O'Day, "Pathology and Renewal of Religious Institutions" in *Concilium* 91 (1974) 119–27.

19. Cf. J. B. Metz, "La autoridad eclesiástica frente a la historia de la libertad" in *Ilustración y teoría teológica* (Salamanca, 1973), pp. 47–48.

20. G. Lewy, *The Catholic Church and Nazi Germany* (McGraw-Hill Paperback Edition, 1965), p. 330. Lewy (p. 328) also quotes Christopher Dawson who wrote that Catholicism "is by no means hostile to the authoritarian ideal of the State. Against the liberal doctrines of the divine right of majorities and the unrestrained freedom of opinion the Church has always maintained the principles of authority and hierarchy and a high conception of the prerogatives of the State." Dawson added that the ideals contained in the encyclicals of Leo XIII and Pius XI "have far more affinity with those of Fascism than those of either Liberalism or Socialism" (Dawson, *Religion and the Modern State* [New York, 1936], pp. 135–36).

21. Lewy, p. 326, here quoting Sidney Hook.

22. Lewy, p. 331, adds: "And when the Hitler government reacted with anger to the statement of *L'Osservatore Romano* in July 1933, that the conclusion of the Concordat between Germany and the Holy See did not entail the recognition of a specific political doctrine, the bishops were able to explain: 'The assertion of *L'Osservatore Romano* that the conclusion of the Concordat did not express assent to the National Socialist state does by no means signify a basic rejection of that state. Otherwise the Concordat would never have been concluded. It merely represents the intentional suspension of a evaluation, made necessary by the relations of the Holy See to all other states.'" The German bishops' statement is found in *Ver-*

handlungen der Vertreter der Fuldaer Plenar-Bischofskonferenz im Reichsinnen-ministerium vom 25. bis 30. Juni 1933, p. 27.

23. Cf. The encyclical *Firmissimam Constantiam* of March 28, 1937.

24. P. Congar, "Renewal of the Spirit and Reform of the Institution" in *Concilium* 73 (1972) entitled *Ongoing Reform in the Church*, ed. A. Muller and N. Grein-acher, pp. 39–49; here pp. 47–48.

25. R. Siebert, "Religion in the Perspective of Critical Sociology" in *Concilium* 91 (1974) 56–69, here p. 63.

26. Cardinal Aloisio Lorscheider, "Panorama da Igreja Universal" (cited in n. 2 above), respectively: II, 2, p. 4; III, 2, p. 6; III, 3, p. 7.

27. *Handbuch der Pastoraltheologie*, II/1:275–76.

28. P. A. Liégé, "A Igreja diante de seu pecado" in *A Igreja do futuro* (Petrópolis, 1973), p. 121. Cardinal Lorscheider, in his "Panorama" piece cited in note 26 above, states: "The idea of a hierarchical Church that places all rights and powers within its grip has, without a doubt, prejudiced the expansion of the Church" (III, 3, p. 7).

29. L. Boff, "Libertação de Jesus Cristo pelo caminho da oppresão" in *Grande Sinai* 28 (1974) 589–615, esp. 594–606.

30. J. Reese, "The Event of Jesus—Power in Flesh" in *Concilium* 90 (1973) 40–50; W. Foerster, "Exousia" in *Theological Dictionary of the New Testament*, vol. 2, ed. G. Kittel (Grand Rapids, 1964), pp. 562–75.

31. H. Eising and K. Löning, "Herrschaft Gottes und Befreiung des Menschen" in *Macht, Dienst, Herrschaft*, p. 58.

32. Cf. K. Kertelge, *Gemeinde und Amt in Neuen Testament* (Munich, 1972), pp. 158–68.

33. W. Thüsing, "Dienstfunktion und Vollmacht kirchlicher Ämter nach dem Neuen Testament" in *Macht, Dienst, Herrschaft*, pp. 62–65.

34. L. Proaño, *Pour une Eglise libératrice* (Paris, 1973), esp. pp. 133–59; B. Dumas, *Los dos rostros alienados de la Iglesia una* (Buenos Aires, 1971), pp. 125–72; A. Gregory, *Comunidades eclesiais de base* (Petrópolis, 1973).

35. Andrew Greeley, "The Advantages and Drawbacks of a Centre of Communi-cations in the Church: Sociological Point of View" in *Concilium* 64 (1971) entitled *Papal Ministry in the Church*, ed. H. Küng, pp. 101–14.

36. Cf. "Igreja e mutações sócio-culturais" in *A Igreja do futuro*, pp. 15–34.

37. See the expressive poetry of Lothar Zenetti, a German. Here is a rough trans-lation of an appropriate text: "Ask one hundred Catholics what is most important in the Church and they will say the Mass. Ask one hundred Catholics what is the most important thing in the Mass and they will say the changing of bread and wine into the body and blood of the Lord! But, then try and tell one hundred Catholics that the most important thing in the Church must be change, and they will become angry and say 'No! Everything must remain as it is!'"

Chapter 6 / Roman Catholicism: Structure, Health, Pathologies

1. Cf. the principal bibliography on the subject: H. Wagner, *An den Ursprüngen des frühkatholischen Problems: Die Ortbestimmung des Katholizismus im älteren*

Luthertum (Frankfurt, 1973), esp. pp. 295–317; idem, "Zum Problem des Frühkatholizismus" in *Zeitschrift für katholische Theologie* 94 (1972) 433–44; K. H. Neufeld, "Frühkatholizismus—Idee und Begriff" in *ZKT* 94 (1972) 1–28; A. Erhard, *Urkirche und Frühkatholizismus* (Bonn, 1935); A. Loisy, *The Gospel and the Church* (New York, 1912); P. Batiffol, *L'Eglise naissante et le catholicisme* (Paris, 1909); H. De Lubac, *Catholicisme: Les aspects sociaux du dogme* (Paris, 1952), pp. 241–60 (E.T. *Catholicism*, 1950); M. De Certeau and J. H. Domenach, *Le christianisme éclaté* (Paris, 1974); R. Hernegger, *Macht ohne Auftrag: Die Entstehung der Staats- und Volkskirche* (Olten-Freiburg, 1963); P. Stockmeier, *Glaube und Religion in der frühen Kirche* (Freiburg, 1973).

2. E. Troeltsch, *Die Soziallehre der christlichen Kirchen und Gruppen (Gesammelte Schriften*, vol. 1; Tübingen, 1911), pp. 83–178 (E.T. *The Social Teaching of the Christian Churches*, 1931).

3. WA 511, p. 478; cf. W. Höhne, *Luthers Anschauungen über die Kontinuität der Kirche* (Berlin-Hamburg, 1963).

4. Cf. the summary of this thesis in Wagner's "Zum Problem des Frühkatholizismus," pp. 434–35.

5. A. Harnack, *Das Wesen des Christentums* (Leipzig, 1920), p. 129 (E.T. *What Is Christianity?* 1901).

6. E. Käsemann, "Kritische Analyse" in *Das Neue Testament als Kanon: Documentation und kritische Analyse zur gegenwärtigen Diskussion*, ed. E. Käsemann (Göttingen, 1970), p. 372, note 77.

7. A. Harnack, *Entstehung und Entwicklung der Kirchenfassung und des Kirchenrechts in den zwei ersten Jahrhunderten nebst einer Kritik der Abhandlung R. Sohms: "Wesen und Ursprung des Katholizismus" und Untersuchungen über "Evangelium," "Wort Gottes" und das trinitarische Bekenntnis* (Leipzig, 1910); idem, *Die Mission und Ausbreitung des Christentums in den ersten drei Jahrhunderten* (Leipzig, 1906; E.T. *The Mission and Expansion of Christianity in the First Three Centuries*, 1908); idem, *Lehrbuch der Dogmengeschichte*, vol. 1 (Freiburg-Leipzig, 1934; E.T. *History of Dogma*, vol. 1, 1900).

8. A. Harnack, *Entstehung und Entwicklung*, p. 182, n. 1.

9. A. Harnack, *Lehrbuch der Dogmengeschichte*, 1:20.

10. A. Harnack, *Entstehung und Entwicklung*, pp. 184–85.

11. R. Sohm, *Wesen und Ursprung des Katholizismus* (Darmstadt, 1967), a photocopy of the second edition of 1912; *Kirchenrecht 1: Die geschichtlichen Grundlagen* (Leipzig, 1892); *Katholisches Kirchenrecht* (Leipzig, 1923); *Das altkatholische Kirchenrecht und das Dekret Gratians* (Leipzig, 1918).

12. On the modern discussion beginning with Sohm, see L. Boff, *Die Kirche als Sakrament im Horizont der Welterfahrung* (Paderborn, 1972), pp. 392–99.

13. R. Sohm, *Das altkatholische Kirchenrecht*, p. 537.

14. R. Sohm, *Wesen und Ursprung des Katholizismus*, p. 56.

15. Ibid., p. 68.

16. Ibid., p. 8.

17. Ibid.

18. R. Sohm, *Kirchenrecht*, 1:23.

19. R. Sohm, *Wesen und Ursprung*, p. 13.

20. R. Sohm, *Das altkatholische Kirchenrecht*, pp. 67ff.

21. E. Troeltsch, *Die Soziallehre der christlichen Kirchen und Gruppen*, pp. 83–178; Neufeld, "Frühkatholizismus," pp. 16–20; Honecker, *Kirche als Gestalt und Ereignis* (Munich, 1963), pp. 31–55.

22. E. Troeltsch, "Die Alte Kirche" in *Aufsätze zur Geistesgeschichte und Religionssoziologie (Gesammelte Schriften*, vol. 4; Tübingen, 1925), p. 66.

23. E. Troeltsch, *Soziallehre*, p. 87.

24. Cf. I. Lonning, *Kanon im Kanon* (Oslo-Munich, 1972); I. Frank, *Der Sinn der Kanonbildung* (Freiburg, 1971), esp. pp. 203–11; N. Appel, *Kanon und Kirche* (Paderborn, 1964), pp. 333ff.; E. Käsemann, ed., *Das Neue Testament als Kanon*.

25. E. Käsemann, "Is the Gospel Objective?" in *Essays on New Testament Themes* (London, 1964), pp. 48–62, here p. 57; see also his "The Canon of the New Testament and the Unity of the Church" in *Essays on New Testament Themes*, pp. 95–107.

26. W. Marxsen, *Der Frühkatholizismus im Neuen Testament* (Biblische Studien 21; Neukirchen, 1958).

27. Ibid., p. 67; cf. W. Marxsen, *Das neue Testament als Buch der Kirche* (Gütersloh, 1964), pp. 131–32 (E.T. *The New Testament as the Church's Book*, 1972).

28. J. A. Möhler, *Tübinger Theologische Quartalschrift* 5 (1823) 497.

29. Cf. J. Ratzinger, *Das neue Volk Gottes: Entwürfe zur Ekklesiologie* (Düsseldorf, 1970), pp. 75–87; N. Appel, *Kanon und Kirche*, pp. 351–80.

30. E. Peterson, "Die Kirche" in *Theologische Traktate* (Munich, 1951), pp. 411–29, here p. 417.

31. J. Ratzinger, "Zeichen unter den Völken" in *Wahrheit und Zeugnis* (Düsseldorf, 1964), p. 458.

32. E. Peterson, "Die Kirche," p. 421.

33. H. Schlier, *Das bleibende Katholische: Ein Versuch über ein Prinzip des Katholischen* (Münster, 1970).

34. Ibid., p. 34.

35. R. Schnackenburg, "Kirche" in *Lexicon für Theologie und Kirche*, 6:167–88; idem, "Die nachösterliche Gemeinde und Jesus" in *Die Aktion Jesu und die Re-Aktion der Kirche* (Würzburg, 1972), pp. 122–26; idem, *Die Kirche im Neuen Testament* (Freiburg, 1961).

36. J. Blank, "Der historische Jesus und die Kirche" in *Wort und Wahrheit* 26 (1971) 291–307.

37. A. Vögtle, "Jesus und die Kirche" in *Begegnung der Christen* (Stuttgart-Freiburg, 1960), pp. 54–81.

38. E. Peterson, "Die Kirche."

39. J. Ratzinger, "O destino de Jesus e a Igreja" in *A Igreja en nosos dias* (São Paulo, 1969), pp. 9–29.

40. H. Küng, *The Church* (New York: Image Books, 1976), pp. 69–144.

41. L. Boff, "O Jesus histórico e a Igreja" in *Perspectiva teológica* 5 (1973) 157–71.

42. *Lumen Gentium* 8. In all of the drafts of the Dogmatic Constitution on the Church presented to the Second Vatican Council, the pure and simple identity between the Church of Christ and the Roman Catholic Church was affirmed. In the schema of 1963, number 8 reads: "Haec igitur ecclesia, vera omnium Mater et

Magistra, in hoc mundo ut societas constituta et ordinata, est Ecclesia catholica a Romano Pontifice et Episcopis in eius communion directa." In 1964, the *est* was changed to *subsistit* and the following explanation was given: "Loco 'est' . . . dicitur 'subsistit in' ut expressio melius concordet cum affirmatione de elementis ecclesialibus quae alibi adsunt" (Vatican Polyglot Press, 1964); cf. F. Ricken, "Ecclesia . . . universale salutis sacramentum: Theologische Erwägungen zur Lehre der Dogmatischen Konstitution 'De Ecclesia' über die Kirchenzugehörigkeit" in *Scholastik* 40 (1965) 352–88.

43. E. Käsemann, "The Canon of the New Testament and the Unity of the Church" in *Essays on New Testament Themes*, pp. 95–107.

44. Hans Küng, "Der Frühkatholizismus im Neuen Testament als kontroverstheologisches Problem" in *Das Neue Testament als Kanon*, pp. 175–204, esp. pp. 198ff.

45. Cf. L. Boff, "O qué significa propriamente sacramento?" in *Revista Eclesiástica Brasileira* 34 (1974) 860–95.

46. Cf. J. M. Scheeben, *Die Mysterien des Christentums* (Freiburg, 1941), p. 459; E.T. *The Mysteries of Christianity* (1946).

47. Cf. P. E. Persson, *Evangelisch und Römisch-Katholisch* (Göttingen, 1961). This treats the subject on a very lucid ecumenical level, especially pp. 28–60.

48. K. Beyschlag, *Clemens Romanus und der Frühkatholizismus* (Tübingen, 1966), p. 308.

49. P. Stockmeier, *Glaube und Religion in der frühen Kirche* (Freiburg, 1973); cf. the critical commentary by J. Blank, "Überformung des Glaubens durch Religion" in *Herderkorrespondenz* 37 (1973) 590–94.

50. Cicero in *De harusp. resp.* 19 could say: "Despite how good we think we are, we do not surpass the Spaniards in number, nor the Gallics in strength, nor the Punics in skill, nor the Greeks in art, nor the Italians and Latins in love; but we Romans surpass everyone in religiosity and because of this unique wisdom we understand that everything must fall under the rule and guidance of the gods."

51. P. Stockmeier, *Glaube und Religion*, pp. 24–30, 120.

52. Ignatius, *Magn.* 10, 3.

53. Tacitus, *Annals* XV, 44, characterizes Christianity as "*exitiabilis superstitio*"; Suetonius, *Nero* XVI, 2, calls it "*genus hominum superstitionis novae ac maleficae*"; Pliny, *Ep. ad Traianum* 96, 8, "*superstitio prava, immodica*"; Minucius Felix, *Octavius* IX, 2, terms it "*vana et demens superstitio*" (CSEL 2, 13).

54. *Octavius* XX, 1 (CSEL, 2, 28).

55. P. Stockmeier, *Glaube und Religion*, p. 102.

56. *Praescr. haeret.* 14 (CChr 1, 198).

57. *Sermon* 82, 1; PL 54, 422–23.

58. Cf. E. Stemplinger, *Antiker Volksglaube* (Stuttgart, 1948); R. Hernegger, *Macht ohne Auftrag*, pp. 287–356.

59. *De cor.* III, 4 (CChr 2, 1043).

60. *Retract.* I, 13.

61. *Ep.* XI, 76; PL 77, 1215.

62. *Ep.* 55, 19, 35 (CSEL 34, 2, 210); cf. *Ep.* 54, 1, 1.

63. *In Psalm.* 147, 19; PL 37, 1929.

64. John Henry Newman, *Le développement du dogme chrétien*, p. 266 (English original: *Essay on the Development of Christian Doctrine*).

65. *Sermon* 36, 4.

66. A. Görres, "Pathologie des katholischen Christentums" in *Handbuch der Pastoraltheologie*, II/1:277-343; B. Welte, "Wesen und Unwesen der Religion" in *Auf der Spur des Ewigen* (Freiburg, 1965), pp. 279-96.

67. M. De Certeau and J. H. Demenach, *Le christianisme éclaté*, p. 47.

68. P. Ribeiro de Oliveira, "Religiosidade popular na América Latina" in *Revista Eclesiástica Brasileira* 32 (1972) 354-64, esp. p. 355.

69. Cf. J. Comblin, "Para una tipología do catolicismo no Brasil" in *Revista Eclesiástica Brasileira* 28 (1968) 46-73: "The difference between the Catholicism of the clergy and popular Catholicism is only this: the clergy imagine that their Catholicism is pure and the only authentic truth while the other has no problems with orthodoxy or authenticity. In reality there are different systems for translating Christianity into the concrete conditions of human life. The popular forms deserve as much respect as the official forms. The conversion to Christianity does not take place through the imposition of an official Christianity defined a priori by the clergy but rather through renewed contact with the Gospel that each individual affirms with his or her own structures. We must not destroy popular Catholicism but allow the popular Christians themselves to improve it with its own dynamic. However, this attitude presupposes that we at least recognize the existence and coherence of popular Catholics."

Chapter 7 / In Favor of Syncretism:
The Catholicity of Catholicism

1. Among the principal titles on this subject, see: E. Hoornaert, *Formação do catolicismo brasileiro 1550-1850* (Petrópolis, 1974), esp. "Catolicismo y sincretismo," pp. 22-30, and "Verdadero y falso sincretismo," pp. 137-40; Kamastra, *Synkretismus* (Leiden, 1970); J. D. Y. Peel, "Syncretism and Religious Change" in *Comparative Studies in Society and History* 10 (1967-68) 121-41; G. Thils, *Syncrétisme ou catholicité* (Louvain, 1967); W. A. Visser 't Hooft, *Cristianismo e outras religiões* (Rio de Janeiro, 1968); idem, *L'Eglise face au syncrétisme* (Geneva, 1963); M. Breeveld, "Uma revisão do conceito de sincretismo religioso e perspectivas de pesquisa" in *Revista Eclesiástica Brasileira* 35 (1975) 415-23; R. Hernegger, *Macht ohne Auftrag: Die Entstehung der Staats- und Volkskirche* (Olten-Freiburg, 1963); P. Stockmeier, *Glaube und Religion in der frühen Kirche* (Freiburg, 1973); F. J. Dölger, "Mysterienwesen und Urchristentum" in *Theologische Revue* 15 (1916) 385-93 and 433-38; K. Latte, *Die Religion der Römer und der Syncretismus der Kaiserzeit* (Tübingen, 1927); J. C. Maraldo, "Syncretism" in *Sacramentum Mundi*, 6:201-3; R. Pettazoni, "Sincretismo e conversione nella storia della religione" in *Bulletin de comité international des sciences historiques* (Paris, 1933; E. P. de la Boullaye, "Sincretismo" in *Enciclopedia Cattolica* XI (Rome, 1953), pp. 662-82; other sources are cited individually throughout the text.

Syncretism means "to do as the Cretans" who, although they were a divided people, united to combat a common enemy (Plutarch, *De fraterno amore*). During the Reformation, the term was used by Erasmus to mean the uniting of the Protestant reformers with the humanists. Writing to Melanchthon, he said, "You see with how much hatred some conspire against the fine arts; it is right that we too syncretize (like the Cretans) *aequum est nos quoque 'synkretizein'*" (Melanchthon, *Corpus Reformatorum* 1, 78). In the seventeenth century the word was derived from *synkerannymi*, a Greek word meaning to mix, to meld, to harmonize (doctrines, philosophies, etc.).

2. W. A. Visser 't Hooft, *L'Eglise face au syncrétisme*, p. 12.

3. Cf. L. Boff, "Catolicismo popular: ¿qué es catolicismo?" in *Revista Eclesiástica Brasileira* 36 (1976) 19–52.

4. A. von Harnack, F. J. Dölger, A. Möhler, F. Heiler, and most recently P. Stockmeier in *Glaube und Religion in der frühen Kirche*.

5. Cf. G. Thils, *Propos et problèmes de la théologie des religions non chrétiennes* (Tournai, 1956), esp. the bibliography.

6. Cf. Justin, *IIApol.* 8, 10, 13; PG 6, 380, 457, 460.

7. *Ad Lucil. Epist.* XII, 10; XVI, 6.

8. Reference in n. 6 above. See also Clement of Alexandria, *Protrept.* 6, 7; 8. 173; Augustine, *De doctrina christ.* II, 18, 25, 40; PL 49, 54, 63.

9. A more detailed explanation is found in L. Boff, *Die Kirche als Sakrament* (Paderborn, 1972), pp. 63ff., 87ff.

10. Augustine, *Retractions* 1, 13.

11. Origen, *Contra Celsum*, V, 44; VII, 63.

12. Cf. B. Kloppenburg, "Ensaio de uma nova posição pastoral perante a Umbanda" in *Revista Eclesiástica Brasileira* 28 (1968) 404–17; on pages 406–7 he comments on the principal texts of Vatican II on the value of non-Christian religions.

13. *En. in Psalm.* 70, 2, 1; PL 38, 891.

14. L. Boff, *Die Kirche als Sakrament*, pp. 476–93.

15. We recommend Clodovis Boff's study "A religião contra a fé?" in *Vozes* 63 (1969) 100–116.

16. L. Boff, *Liberating Grace* (Maryknoll, N.Y., 1978), pp. 56–62.

17. C. Boff, "A religião contra a fé?," p. 103.

18. Ibid., p. 106.

19. H. Küng, *The Church* (New York: Image Books, 1976), pp. 388–90.

20. Cf. *Lumen Gentium*, 13; *Gaudium et Spes*, 42; *Ad Gentes*, 9, 18, 22; *Nostra Aetate*, 2.

21. Cf. J. B. Libânio, "Critérios de autenticidade do catolicismo" in *Revista Eclesiástica Brasileira* 36 (1976) 53–81.

22. Cf. M. R. M. Koch-Weser, *Die Yoruba-Religion in Brasilien* (Bonn, 1976), mimeograph, pp. 275ff. and 368ff.

23. Just as the Holy Trinity was revealed in the life and work of Jesus; cf. F. J. Schierse in *Mysterium Salutis*, vol. 2 (Einsiedeln, 1967), pp. 85–129.

24. L. Boff, "Catolicismo popular," pp. 40–46.

25. Cf. C. J. Hefele, *Conziliengeschichte*, I: 770; R. Hernegger, *Macht ohne Auftrag*, pp. 345–56.

26. R. Hernegger, *Macht ohne Auftrag*, p. 345.

27. Cited by F. J. Dölger, *Antike und Christentum*, vol. 3 (1932), p. 84.
28. *Contra Faustum* 20, 21; *Ep.* 201, 3, 18.
29. *Ep.* 55, 19, 35; cf. *Ep.* 54, 1, 1.
30. B. Kloppenburg, "Ensaio," pp. 404–5.
31. C. Boff, "Religião contra a fé?," pp. 112–14.

Chapter 8 / Characteristics of the Church in a Class Society

1. Yves Congar, "Theologiegeschichtliche Hinweise zur Problematik der Kenn-zeichen" in *Mysterium Salutis*, IV/1 (Einsiedeln, 1972), pp. 359–62.
2. The basic work continues to be G. Thils, *Les notes de l'Eglise dans l'apologé-tique catholique depuis la Réforme* (Gembloux, 1937).
3. Cf. F. Grivec, "De via empirica notarum Ecclesiae" in *Antonianum* 36 (1961) 395–400.
4. Hans Küng's *The Church* is valuable for taking advantage of historical and exegetical research to renew the vision of the Church, but it is very inadequate in terms of the relationship of Church to the world. The Church is studied as an entity unto itself, prescinding from its conception within economic, political, and social history of society with its particular means of production.
5. For this section we are indebted to Clodovis Boff, "Igreja e política" in *Com-unidade eclesial—comunidade política* (Petrópolis, 1978), pp. 64–94; P. Bourdieu, *A economía das trocas simbólicas* (São Paulo, 1974); and principally Otto Maduro, *Campo religioso y conflictos sociales* (Louvain, 1978; E.T. *Religion and Social Conflicts* [Maryknoll, N.Y., 1982]).
6. Cf. P. Bourdieu, "Gênese e estrutura de campo religioso" in *A economía*, pp. 27–78; Maduro, *Campo religioso*, pp. 47, 111, passim.
7. O. Maduro, pp. 51–54; cf. A. Touraine, *Production de la société* (Paris, 1973), pp. 145ff.
8. E. Hoornaert, "Comunidades de base: dez años de experiência" in *Revista Eclesiástica Brasileira* 38 (1978) 474–502.
9. Cf. A. Faivre, "Naissance d'une hiérarchie: les premières étapes du cursus clé-rical" in *Theol. Hist.* 40 (Paris, 1977); see also *Macht, Dienst, Herrschaft in Kirche und Gesellschaft* (Freiburg, 1973); and *Autorität* (Maguncia, 1973).
10. Cf. Maduro, *Campo religioso*, pp. 104–22.
11. J. Guitton, *Diálogos con Pablo VI* (Madrid, 1967), p. 392.
12. To analyze this phenomenon and to justify its theological-dogmatic possi-bility was the object of my book *Eclesiogênese: Las comunidades de base reinven-tan la Iglesia* (Petrópolis, 1977).
13. Cf. CLAR, *Pueblo de Dios y comunidad liberadora: Perspectivas eclesioló-gicas desde las comunidades religiosas que caminan con el pueblo*, Document 33 (Bogotá, 1977)
14. J. Sobrino, *Resurrección de una Iglesia popular* (San Salvador, 1978), p. 17.
15. This is the central thesis of P. Richard's *Mort des Chrétientés et naissance de l'Eglise: Analyse historique et interpretation théologique de l'Eglise en Amérique Latine*, mimeograph (Paris, 1978).

16. Cf. my study *Minima sacramentalia* (Petrópolis, 1976), wherein I attempt to give the theological foundation for the sacramental teaching in the grassroots.

17. Cf. L. Boff, "Missão universal e libertação concreta" in *A fé na periferia do mundo* (Petrópolis, 1978), pp. 76–94.

18. J. Dupont, *Le nom d'Apôtre a-t-il été donné aux Douze par Jésus?* (Louvain, 1957); Yves Congar, "Die apostolische Kirche" in *Mysterium Salutis*, IV/3:535–94; F. Klostermann, *Das christliche Apostolat* (Innsbruck, 1962), pp. 119–28.

19. Saint Augustine saw a mark of the true Church in persecution in the cause of justice (*Ep.* 93, 8; 185, 9).

Chapter 11 / *Ecclesia Docens* versus *Ecclesia Discens*

1. J. Salaverri, "La potestad de Magisterio Eclesiástico y asentimiento que le es debido" in *Estudios Eclesiásticos* 29 (1955) 155–95, here p. 174; idem, "De ecclesia Christi" in *Sacrae Theologiae Summa*, vol. 1 (1952), pp. 117–41.

2. Cf. L. Boff, *Eglise in genèse* (Paris, 1978), pp. 64–88; H. Küng, *The Church* (New York: Image Books, 1976), pp. 103–14.

3. Cf. H. Dombois, *Hierarchie, Grund und Grenze einer umstrittenen Struktur* (Freiburg, 1971), pp. 11–22.

4. Cf. M. Weber, *Wirtschaft und Gesellschaft*, vol. 1 (Berlin, 1964), pp. 124ff., 688ff.; P. Bourdieu, "Genèse et structure du champ religieux" in *Revue Française de Sociologie* 12 (1971) 295–334; Otto Maduro, *Religión y lucha de clases* (Caracas, 1979), pp. 125–62 (E.T. *Religion and Social Conflicts* [Maryknoll, N.Y., 1982]).

5. P. Bourdieu, *A economia das trocas simbólicas* (São Paulo, 1974), p. 38.

6. E. Durkheim, *The Division of Labor in Society* (New York, 1933), pp. 49–70.

7. Cf. Yves Congar, *L'ecclésiologie du haut Moyen-Age* (Paris, 1968), pp. 92–98.

8. Cf. M. Schmaus, *Der Glaube der Kirche*, vol. 2 (Munich, 1970), p. 102.

9. Paulo Freire, *Pedagogy of the Oppressed* (New York, 1970); idem, *Education for Critical Consciousness* (New York, 1973).

10. P. Freire, *Education for Critical Consciousness*, p. 5.

Chapter 12 / An Alternative View: The Church as Sacrament of the Holy Spirit

1. Cf. Yves Congar, "Dogme christologique et Ecclésiologie" in *Sainte Église* (Paris, 1964), pp. 69–104; A. Bandera, "Analogía de la Iglesia con el misterio de la Encarnación" in *Teología espiritual* 8 (1964) 44–91; A. Ancel, "Estructura teándrica de la Iglesia: Historia y significado eclesiológico del número 8 de Lumen Gentium" in *Estudios Eclesiásticos* 42 (1967) 39–72.

2. Cf. Herrade Mehl-Koennlein, *L'homme selon l'apôtre Paul* (Neuchatel, 1951), pp. 31–37; C. Spicq, *Dieu et l'homme selon le Nouveau Testament* (Paris, 1961), pp. 158–61.

3. Cf. L. Boff, *O Evangelho do Cristo Cósmico* (Petrópolis, 1970).

4. Cf. E. Peterson, "Die Kirche" in *Theologische Traktate* (Munich, 1951), pp. 411–29; J. Ratzinger, "Zeichen unter den Völken" in *Wahreit und Zeugnis* (Düsseldorf, 1964), pp. 456–66; idem, "Kirche" in *Lexicon für Theologie und Kirche*, 6:173–83; idem, "Menschheit und Staatenbau in der Sicht der frühen Kirche" in *Studium Generale* 14 (1961) 664–82; idem, "Das Geschick Jesu und der Kirche" in *Entwürfe zur Ekklesiologie* (Düsseldorf, 1970); idem, *Introduction to Christianity* (London, 1969); and L. Boff, *Die Kirche als Sakrament im Horizont der Welterfahrung* (Paderborn, 1972).

5. The principal literature consulted in preparing this section: L. Hermann, *Kyrios und Pneuma* (Munich, 1961); T. Maertens, *Der Geist des Herrn erfüllt den Erdkreis* (Düsseldorf, 1959); E. Mühlen, *Der Geist als Person* (Münster, 1963); idem, *Una mystica Persona* (Munich, 1964); idem, "Die Kirche als die geschichtliche Erscheinung des übergeschichtlichen Geistes Christi" in *Theologie und Glaube* 55 (1965) 270–89; Käsemann, Schmidt, and Prenter, "Geist" in *Religion in Geschichte und Gegenwart*, 2:1272–86; Yves Congar, "L'Esprit dans l'Église" in *Lumière et Vie* 10 (1953) 51–74; E. Brady, *Le Saint-Esprit en nous et dans l'Église d'après le Nouveau Testament* (Albi, 1950); H. D. Wendland, "Das Wirken des Heiligen Geistes in den Gläubigen bei Paulus" in *Theologische Literaturzeitung* 77 (1952) 457–70; H. Stirnimann, "Die Kirche und der Geist Christi" in *Divus Thomas* 31 (1953) 5–17; K. Rahner, *The Dynamic Element in the Church* (New York, 1964); H. Volk, "Das Wirken des Heiligen Geistes in den Gläuben" in *Catholica* 3 (1952) 13–35.

6. Cf. E. Schweizer, "Pneuma" in *Theological Dictionary of the New Testament*, vol. 6, ed. G. Friedrich (Grand Rapids, 1968), pp. 404f.

7. G. Tyrrell, *Das Christentum am Scheideweg* (Munich, 1959), p. 177 (English original: *Christianity at the Cross-Roads*, 1909).

8. Cf. K. Prümm, "Die katholische Auselgung von 2 Kor 3, 17 in den letzen vier Jahrzehnten nach ihren Hauptrichtungen" in *Biblica* 31 (1950) 315–45, 459–82; 32 (1951) 1–24.

9. Cf. Hermann, Mühlen, Käsemann, and the other authors cited in n. 5 above.

10. See E. Schweizer, "Pneuma," pp. 417f.

11. Cf. A. Deissmann, *Die neutestamentliche Formel "in Christo Jesu"* (Marburg, 1892), pp. 84–90.

12. Ibid., pp. 89–90.

13. Thomas Aquinas, *Contra err. Graec.*, c. 9.

14. M. Scheeben, *Dogmatik*, 3: 276, n. 1612; H. Mühlen, *Una mystica Persona*, pp. 242f.; idem, "Die Kirche als die geschichtliche Erscheinung," p. 278.

15. C. Feuerer, *Unsere Kirche im Kommen* (Freiburg, 1939).

16. Cf. U. Valeske, *Votum Ecclesiae* (Munich, 1962), p. 163; A. Vikenhauser, *Die Kirche als der mystiche Leib Christi nach dem Apostel Paulus* (Münster, 1937), pp. 119f.

17. J. Alfaro, "Cristo, Sacramento de Dios Padre—La Iglesia Sacramento de Cristo Glorificado" in *Gregorianum* 48 (1967) 5–27; E. Schillebeeckx, *Christ the Sacrament of the Encounter with God* (London, 1963), pp. 47–89.

18. L. Cerfaux, "Le symbolisme attaché au miracle des langues" in *Ephemerides theologicae lovaniensis* 13 (1936) 258; J. G. Davies, "Pentecost and Glossolalia"

in *Theological Studies* 3 (1952) 228; S. Weinstock, "Zum Pfingstwunder Acts 2:9-11" in *Journal of Roman Studies* 39 (1948) 43-46; L. Boff, "Simbolismo no milagre de Pentecostes" in *Vozes* 64 (1970) 325-26.

19. Irenaeus, *Adv. Haer.* III, 38, 1.

20. Cf. E. Schweizer, "Pneuma," p. 409 with the bibliography cited there.

21. J. Jeremias, *Unbekannte Jesusworte* (Gütersloh, 1953), pp. 101-4 (E.T. *Unknown Sayings of Jesus*, 1957).

22. Cf. the important book by G. Hasenhüttl, *Charisma: Ordnungsprinzip der Kirche* (Freiburg, 1969).

**Chapter 13 / An Alternative Structure:
Charism as the Organizing Principle**

1. Cf. Yves Congar, "Pneumatologie ou Christomonisme dans la tradition latine" in *Ecclesia a Spiritu Sancto* (Gembloux, 1970), pp. 41-63.

2. See the principal bibliography: G. Hasenhüttl, *Charisma* (see n. 22 in chap. 12 above); J. Ratzinger, "Das geistliche Amt und die Einheit der Kirche" in *Das neue Volk Gottes* (Düsseldorf, 1969), pp. 105-20; W. Kasper, "Kollegiale Strukturen in der Kirche" in *Glaube und Geschichte* (Maguncia, 1970), pp. 355-70; idem, "Espírito, Cristo, Igreja" in *A experiência do Espírito Santo* (Petrópolis), pp. 72-90; J. Goitia, *La fuerza del Espíritu: Pneuma-Dynamis* (Bilbao, 1974); J. Moltmann, *The Church in the Power of the Spirit* (New York, 1977); Yves Congar, *I Believe in the Holy Spirit*, vol. 2 (New York, 1982); H. W. Robinson, *Christian Experience of the Holy Spirit* (London, 1962), pp. 123-39; H. Mühlen, *Una mystica Persona* (Paderborn, 1968); H. Küng, "The Charismatic Structure of the Church" in *Concilium* I (1965) 31-46; S. Voigt, "Vida religiosa como carisma" in *Grande Sinai* 26 (1972) 323-37.

3. For a detailed analysis of each of the charisms enumerated by Paul, see Hasenhüttl, *Charisma*, pp. 129-232.

4. Cf. K. Wennemer, "Die charismatische Begabung der Kirche nach dem Paulus" in *Scholastik* 34 (1959) 503-25.

5. Cf. G. Haya-Prats, *L'Esprit, force de l'Église* (Paris, 1975); Hasenhüttl, *Charisma*, pp. 108-12.

6. H. Küng, *The Church* (New York: Image Books, 1976), p. 247.

7. G. Hasenhüttl, *Charisma*, p. 238.

8. Ibid., p. 235.

9. Ibid., pp. 113-29.

10. E. Käsemann, "Ministry and Community in the New Testament" in *Essays on New Testament Themes* (London, 1964), pp. 63-94; cf. also W. Kasper, *Glaube und Geschichte*, pp. 362-65.